D1068888

DISNEY
The Mouse Betrayed

Greed,
corruption,
and children
at risk

Peter Schweizer
Rochelle Schweizer

Since 1947
REGNERY
PUBLISHING, INC.
An Eagle Publishing Company • Washington DC

Library of Congress Cataloging-in-Publication Data

Schweizer, Peter, 1964–
        Disney: The Mouse Betrayed / Peter Schweizer, Rochelle Schweizer
            p.   cm.
        Includes bibliographical references and index.
        ISBN 0-89526-387-4 (alk. paper)
        1. Walt Disney Company—Corrupt practices.

I. Schweizer, Rochelle, 1961–
        . II. Title
        PN1999.W27S38   1998
        384'.8'0979494—dc21   98-29875
                                                          CIP

Published in the United States by
Regnery Publishing, Inc.
One Massachusetts Avenue, NW
Washington, DC 20001

Distributed to the trade by
National Book Network
4720-A Boston Way
Lanham, MD 20706

Printed on acid-free paper.
Manufactured in the United States of America

10 9 8 7 6 5 4 3 2

Books are available in quantity for promotional or premium use. Write to Director of Special Sales, Regnery Publishing, Inc., One Massachusetts Avenue, NW, Washington, DC 20001, for information on discounts and terms or call (202) 216-0600.

BOOK DESIGN BY MARJA WALKER
SET IN KEPLER

To Evelyn

TABLE OF CONTENTS

PART V   DISNEY'S OTHER FACES

WARNING

In order to accurately portray the Disney Company we have had to include material that is unsuitable for children and that some adult readers may find offensive.

—The authors

PART I
New Frontiers

CHAPTER ONE

The New Disney

I t was Sunday afternoon, September 22, 1984, and Michael Eisner had just walked into the corporate offices at the Disney Studio lot. Earlier that morning, the former president of Paramount had been elected Chairman and CEO of the Walt Disney Company. The vote had not been an easy one.

Weeks earlier the company's directors had rejected Eisner, thinking he might not be up to the job. But board member Stanley Gold convinced Eisner to lobby for it. So Eisner got on the telephone and visited board members personally, and he successfully changed their minds.

Michael Eisner would be the first outsider to ever run the Disney company. After Walt's death, his brother Roy ran the company. When he passed on, Card Walker, a forty-year veteran of the company, called the shots. By 1983 Ron Miller, Walt's son-in-law, was elected CEO. The company continued expanding in those years, building EPCOT in Orlando, and starting a new label for films called Touchstone Pictures. They even launched a new cable television channel, "The Disney Channel." But despite these efforts, the company was in financial trouble. Revenue had stagnated at the parks and dropped at the box office. The board was looking for someone to reverse the company's fortunes.

Eisner had never worked for Disney before and really had no connection to the company. Eisner said publicly, "I grew up on Disney." But in reality, he never saw *Cinderella*, *Alice in Wonderland*, *Peter Pan*, *Dumbo*, *Bambi*, or *Fantasia* when he was young. Brought up on

Disney Chairman Michael Eisner was known at Paramount for movies that were glossy urban fairy tales. He had only one inviolable rule: no sappy family pictures.

Park Avenue in an old-money family, he quietly admitted to friends that he saw the Disney classics later on in life, when his own kids were growing up.

While Michael Eisner was not a Mouse insider, he was an enormously successful Hollywood executive as president of Paramount. By the end of 1982, Eisner could take credit for bringing to the screen six of the fifty highest grossing films of all time (*Saturday Night Fever, Grease, Heaven Can Wait, Raiders of the Lost Ark, An Officer and a Gentleman,* and *Airplane!*). There had, of course, been some embarrassments along the way. He had insisted on producing *White Dog*, a movie about a racist canine that attacked only blacks. (It was considered so bad, it was shown only on pay cable.) But the failures were few and the successes many. His record had to be attractive to any entertainment company.

Michael Eisner and Disney provided an interesting contrast in cultures. Eisner was known for movies that were glossy urban fairy tales. He had operated at Paramount with one inviolable rule: no sappy family pictures. As he told associates, "No snow, no rural." He was the consummate Hollywood insider.

The Disney company, on the other hand, was anything but. Company executives referred to Hollywood as "over the hill," a far-off distant place. Walt had set up his studio in Burbank, in the San Fernando Valley, purposely to get away from the glitter of Hollywood. And even though by the early 1980s many other major studios were located in the San Fernando Valley, the mindset remained. While Hollywood movie execs were driving convertible Porsches, the Disney company sprang for company cars for its top 50 execs and offered Ford LTD sedans.

And indeed when Michael Eisner walked into the executive suite that September, the company was in a time warp. In contrast to the Hollywood power lunch, the Disney commissary advertised chili dogs for 35 cents. Tom Hanks, who had eaten there when he worked on *Splash*, compared it to "a Greyhound bus station in the '50s." Eisner himself was quietly jesting to his friends that Disney was "dusty." "They are still making Don Knotts movies," is what he told friends.

Changes were, of course, needed. Many of the company's most important resources weren't even being used. Disney had not tapped into the treasure trove of Disney classics and released them on videocassette. The company wasn't even advertising for its theme parks. And the film studio had passed on some wonderful family films, including *ET: The Extraterrestrial.* So Michael Eisner set out to transform the company.

In the first six months of his tenure, 1,000 Disney employees were shown the door. At the same time, the new Head Mouse brought in sixty new executives, most coming from Paramount. Jeffrey Katzenberg came over to head up the studio, Richard Frank to take over television. And David Hoberman was tapped to run the new film division, Touchstone Pictures. The Industry press began calling the Mouse "Paramount in the Valley." The new Disney was born.

Michael Eisner also set about to boost the company's profitability by more successfully exploiting the

> **"Before, you knew when you bought something 'Disney,' it was safe. Not anymore."**
>
> —KEN WALES, former vice president of the Disney Channel

Disney resources he inherited. Before Eisner became CEO, admission to the Magic Kingdom had been relatively cheap, reflecting Walt's desire that "every child in America" be able to afford a visit. It was a hope that welled up from Walt's own childhood experiences. Walking home from school as a young boy in Missouri, Walt used to pass Fairmont Park, an amusement center. He never went inside because he didn't have the money to pay for admission. Instead, he stood outside, listening to the music and watching other people having fun. The boyhood experience gave him a lifelong belief that entertainment needed to remain affordable.

But in 1984 such sensibilities were pushed aside. Admission fees to the theme parks were jacked up 45 percent. And they have risen consistently ever since. From 1989 to 1997 the cost of a one-day adult pass to Disneyland rose 53 percent. Michael Eisner discovered that the theme parks were enormously lucrative—the profit margins were 23 percent. The flow of cash surged. Bill Burns, director of Walt

Disney World's Magic Kingdom in Orlando, joked only a few years later, "We don't count money, we weigh it."

As theme park ticket prices rose, the company also began distributing Disney classics on videocassette. The new Disney soon discovered that *Pinnochio, Fantasia, Snow White, Peter Pan,* and others were enormous cash cows. The Mouse could count on netting hundreds of millions of dollars worldwide on thirty-year-old films that kids (and adults) around the world still loved.

Nothing was beyond the purview of boosting profits. Disney even cancelled the use of Jiminy Cricket to serve as "spokescricket" for Poison Prevention Month. "We've used Jiminy for 18 years with Disney's written permission," said Fred Mayer, president of the Poison Prevention Campaign, sadly. "Disney demands cash on the barrelhead to use their characters now, even from public service nonprofits."

But the balance sheet was not the only thing that was changing at Disney. Spencer Craig had joined Disney World in 1971, starting out as a retail clerk supervisor. By the early 1980s he was heading up training for EPCOT at Disney University. He also served from time to time as duty manager for the Magic Kingdom, with responsibility for running the park on any given night. He says Eisner brought profitability to Disney. But he says other things were changing at Disney beyond the balance sheet. "I remember when the first evidence of change came," he told us. "We always took real pride in handing out our business cards. We had a gold Mickey on the front, and on the back of it was our motto: 'We create the finest in family entertainment.' One of the first things that happened under Michael Eisner in 1984 was they removed that saying."

Craig says Disney was being reborn as something different. And the new management had little interest in what the company had stood for over the years. "It reached a point where you didn't want to wear your twenty-year ring or pin because you didn't want to go into a meeting and let them know you are a dinosaur. There was a concerted effort to minimize Walt's legacy in the company. You'd hear things like 'Walt's not here now.' And 'who cares if he rolls over in his grave.'" Craig left the company in 1995.

Others began noticing the change as well. When Michael Eisner first became a candidate for Head Mouse, the Disney board centered around Philip Hawley, CEO of Carter Hawley Hale. Hawley had served as a Disney director for eleven years and had been appointed by the board to head the search for a new CEO. Hawley voted to bring Eisner on as the new Chairman and CEO. But looking back on all the changes he brought, Hawley says the board got more than it bargained for. "I thought back in '84 we needed a change in management," he told us recently. "But what we ended up getting was a change in company mission. Does the company stand for what it used to? I don't think so."

Starting with the steady cash from videocassette sales and higher park prices, Michael Eisner has shrewdly built Disney into a global media empire, with holdings in broadcasting, publishing, movie studios, theme parks, resorts, professional sports, and music. What Walt Disney began in 1923 with $40, a handful of sharpened pencils, and a dream, is today a worldwide media empire and the third most recognized brand name on the planet, just behind Coca-Cola and McDonalds.

But he has changed Disney, and not only in size.

● ● ●

SHORTLY AFTER WE MOVED to Florida in 1994, our family did what millions of other Americans do every year—we went to Disney World. And because the Magic Kingdom was now so close, we even became annual season pass holders, which allowed us unfettered access to the park throughout the year.

Buying the passes was an almost necessary indulgence: Since childhood Disney has cast its magic spell on both of us. The kaleidoscope of Disney movies, cartoons, toys, and theme parks had been part of our lives since we could barely walk. And we had hoped to share that Magic with our children.

We were not unique in our plans. Millions of others feel the same way about the Disney of their youth. The company that bears the name Walt Disney has an enormous pull on our national imagination.

It's hard to say precisely when, for us, the sugar confection began to blow off Disney. Perhaps it was living in Florida. The Sunshine State is *the* tourist state, and Disney World is the epicenter of that state industry. While living here, we met plenty of people who had interacted with the Mouse, not just as tourists, but as neighbors and employees. Around the same time, we also started reading about the controversies over how Disney was branching out into new areas, releasing films like *Priest* and *KIDS*. This led us to think that perhaps we needed to revisit the Magic Kingdom of our youth with an eye for detail.

Armed with our annual passes, we decided to poke around Disney World. We talked with current and former employees who worked at both the theme parks and the movie studios. We listened to stories and read confidential company documents. We tracked down former employees. It was a long and demanding process, which also became disheartening. Along the way, we decided we had to write this book, even though the subject strayed far from Peter's ordinary beat of national defense and security policy.

Some disappointment in what we found at Disney could only be expected. Any close encounter with a global business empire is likely to wipe away some childhood myths. But what we discovered went beyond naive illusions colliding with the realities of a real-world media conglomerate. What we uncovered was downright disturbing—even shocking.

We found that today there is a schism through the heart of Disney. The same company that produces television programming for kids also quietly owns part of a pay-per-view service that releases exclusive skin flicks starring porn industry veterans Marilyn Chambers and Becky LeBeau. The same company that promotes the innocence of its animated features also infuses those movies, in the words of Disney animators, with "sex and gender politics." The same company that produces children's music for *The Lion King* and *Beauty and the Beast* releases songs for adolescents about sex with the Virgin Mary, murder, and rape, while actively promoting the drug culture. The same company that released the animated film *Hercules*, about the mythical strong man, distributed *The House of Yes*, a movie that boldly attempts to make incest look sexy.

But what we uncovered goes beyond what products the new Disney releases to the public. Even more surprising, we discovered that the way Disney conducts itself in dealing with the outside world is not so magical. The same company that continuously peddles its "child friendly" image won't cooperate with police efforts to deal with the very real pedophile problem at Disney World. The company that touts its commitment to the safety of its guests covers up serious crimes and has created safety concerns about the operation of the park with new policies designed to boost short-term profits. The same company that publicly parades its commitment to the welfare of children around the world doesn't show much interest in cracking down on the practices of licensees who produce Disney products with child labor. And the same company that proudly proclaims its creative abilities and commitment to high ethical standards seems all too willing to blatantly steal the ideas of others.

> **"There was a concerted effort to minimize Walt's legacy in the company. You'd hear things like 'Walt's not here now.'"**

Along the way, we discovered that there are people in the Magic Kingdom Disney would rather not have us know about. People like Christopher Bradley, an Emmy award–winning Disney animator who worked on Winnie the Pooh, who also happens to be a pedophile who keeps child pornography. We learned Bradley was part of a serious pedophile problem at Disney World, though it is a problem the company seems uninterested in solving.

We also discovered that Disney World had its other mysteries. Disney World security stifling homocide investigations on their property. Sex crimes that went unreported. Disney employees that were caught peeping on guests in changing rooms and were never fired. We also learned about a group of firefighters at Disney World who claim they were subjected to serious sexual attacks by their coworkers that the company took little interest in halting.

During the course of our research we ran across people like Ken

Wales. A director and producer, Wales used to work as vice president of the Disney Channel. But his bond to Disney was even more personal. As a student at the University of Southern California, Wales received a scholarship from Walt that got him through film school. He went on to direct numerous feature films and then the acclaimed television program *Christy* for CBS. He saw the evolution of Disney up close and told us he barely recognizes the company that has been a part of his life for so long. "Before, you knew when you bought something 'Disney', it was safe," he told us. "Not anymore."

We also spoke with current employees at Disney World. People like Murray Cohen, Ben Keen, Deborah Clark, Sheila Randolph, Todd Eversen, Frank Kubicki, and Michael Overcash. Much to our surprise, they agreed to speak on the record. Why would they offer their candid views to us and risk the wrath of the Mouse? Because they said their concerns about safety and conditions at the park were so great they felt they could be silent no longer. Working popular rides such as Splash Mountain, Space Mountain, Jungle Cruise, and Dumbo, they said they had experienced serious safety problems caused by current company policy. Deborah Clark, a fifteen-year Disney World veteran, told us she used to think the company didn't care about employee safety, only about guest safety. "But they aren't even really concerned about that anymore."

To bolster these claims, we received internal Disney documents from another source. These documents demonstrate that in some recent years Disney World boasted an employee injury-accident rate twice the industry average nationwide. We also gained access to private internal survey results conducted by the company, which indicate that a majority of those employees surveyed believe safety is being compromised.

Those surveys also demonstrated extreme morale problems within a company that markets itself as a model for managing people. The 1997 Cast Excellence Analysis Tool asked employees at Walt Disney World eighty-four questions. The response of service employees who work on the rides were startling:

"The heritage and traditions of Walt Disney World continue to be valued by our company." 65 percent *disagreed*.

"Walt Disney World does not compromise on quality." Fully 71 percent *disagreed*.

"We effectively resolve guest complaints where I work." 67 percent *disagreed*.

As the evidence began to accumulate, we considered our motives. Were we being fair to Disney? Doesn't any major conglomerate have its flaws? No doubt they all have some skeletons in their closet. In the case of Disney, however, we found that many of the problems were not mistakes soon corrected, but were systemic to the company.

Then we considered our perspective. Had we as adults simply cast a more critical and mature eye on a company that has always operated this way? Sadly we discovered there was much more to it than that. It wasn't so much that we had changed, but that Disney had.

Disney is supposed to be different. "Disney is judged by a higher standard," Michael Eisner told company shareholders in 1992, "and we should be." The Disney chairman claims his company is a squeaky clean alternative to Hollywood, with higher ethical standards. In an April 3, 1998, speech before the American Society of Newspaper Editors, the Disney chairman made some strong statements in which he argued for a higher standard in entertainment. "How many times have you seen entertainment executives justify the release of vile programs and repugnant lyrics by sanctimoniously proclaiming 'freedom of speech'?" he asked the audience. Eisner then went on to call for an ethical standard in Hollywood that was based on good judgment and common sense. "We are dealing with the human core here. We know what is embarrassing, what makes us so anxious as to be unpleasant, what forces us to lose our poise and cover our face. Edit we must... not to stifle conflict or conviction, but to eliminate debasement. I guess what I am talking about is good taste and good judgment." And the Disney chairman told the crowd that entertainment executives have a commitment that goes beyond generating a profit. "There is a boundary—and, generally, we can all recognize where that line is— where fantasy and adventure and escape turn to irresponsible depiction and inappropriate behavior. Short-term profits—maybe even long-term profits—do not excuse clearly unethical decisions."

It sounds like a reasonable yardstick. But how does the new Disney measure up to the Eisner standard? You be the judge.

This book is not about the Disney you publicly hear about. Nor is it intended to serve as a complete history of the company. It does not describe Disney's recent creative triumphs nor its laudable philanthropic work. Instead, this is a look at the Magic Kingdom few people have ever seen or heard. Much of the information contained in this book is disturbing, and some readers may find it offensive.

The keen reader will notice that this book is not a collection of stories based on off-the-record interviews. Indeed, because of the explosive and shocking nature of much of the materials found here, we have relied almost exclusively on interviews that were conducted on the record, including some from current employees. We have also included a lot of squeaks from the Mouse itself, in the form of internal company documents. Where crimes and criminal activity are discussed, we rely on attributed statements from law enforcement officials and official records.

CHAPTER TWO

Mickey Rocks:
Sex, Drugs, and Satan

*"You need to be more cautious
here than any other entertainment
company in Hollywood."*

—Disney Studios Chairman Joe Roth, who oversees music

When Ricky Vodka arrived at Disney's commissary, he was hungover and in a nasty mood. The lead guitarist for the hard-charging, punk-rock band Humble Gods was visiting Disney's Hollywood Records, located in the old Disney "imagineering" division. "In this building," says one Hollywood Records executive, "they built the first Disneyland—the teacups, the whole thing." But these days it houses a division dedicated to heavy-metal and punk-rock bands that sing about suicide, Satan, and sex with the Virgin Mary.

Hollywood Records has signed Humble Gods to a contract, the band's first with a major record label. Amidst streets named for Disney characters and walls decorated with posters of Mickey and Minnie Mouse, trash/punk bands seem totally out of place—at least they used to. At the new Disney, they seem to fit right in. "To put it bluntly," says Hollywood Records in its promotional material, "Humble Gods are not for the faint of heart. As a barometer of each gig, success is measured in terms of sweat, hurtling bodies, and collisions-per-song."

Guitarist Doug Carrion concurs. "We're a pretty confrontational band. It's not some lovey-dovey fun thing."

This isn't merely promotional hype. Ricky Vodka counts among his friends the late serial murderer John Gacy, who killed at least thirty-three boys and young men, and buried most of them under his home near Chicago. Ricky found that intriguing and one day decided to write the mass murderer, who was on death row. They began an active

correspondence in late 1991, and, over the course of several dozen letters and phone calls, the two became friends. In May 1994, seven days
prior to Gacy's execution by lethal injection, they finally met at
Stateville Prison in Joliet, Illinois.

"What Gacy did was horrible," says Vodka rather matter-of-factly.
"But I wanted to meet him so I could form my own opinion about
what a serial killer is actually like. I expected to meet a monster, and
instead I met a chubby man who was capable of being very charming
and funny; kind of like your dad's buddy who tells corny, dirty jokes."

Humble Gods drummer Lou Gaez has his own stories to tell. One
of them involved a federal offense. In the fall of 1996, while boarding
a plane to a performance, Gaez found himself "kind of pissed off" by
the way a stewardess handled the bag that contained his camcorder.
So he claimed it might be a bomb and had to be forcibly removed from
the plane by airport security.

The group formed in the summer of 1994 and was named by member Brad X after he read a poem about the apocalypse. Doug Carrion
(whose mom played a bit part in the science fiction film *Soylent
Green*) is the band's visionary. "It seems like one of us gets injured at
every gig," Doug laughs. "I've always liked bands that fly by the seat of
their pants, where, at any moment, the stage could collapse, and gui-
tars could snap, and everything could blow up."

Sometimes it goes beyond injury. Bassist Jason Thirsk took his own
life during the recording of *No Heroes*, Humble Gods' first album for
Hollywood Records. Punk reviewers note that Humble Gods' songs
are "fierce, fast and cutting. They're filled with all the usual punk
angst and distaste for authority." One Humble God's song, "Lied and
Cheated," goes like this:

Tie you to the railroad tracks.
Have Lizzy Borden give you forty whacks.
Push you off the plank, feed you to the sharks—
Bathe you in gasoline with lots of sparks.

Humble Gods was not exactly a household word when Disney signed them. In fact both the band and much of the industry were surprised when Disney offered a contract. Clearly it's more than the band ever expected. "This bad seed of an idea has grown out of control," laughs Doug. "We're signed to a label, for godsakes [sic]."

The *No Heroes* CD also features dark lyrics and lashes out at just about everything and everyone. Songs include "Paralyzed" and "F——- Up."

PARALYZED

Paralyzed
You gotta be a mean motherf——-,
When you're taking the hill
gotta be a fierce motherf——-.
Be willing to kill
you gotta be ready motherf——-.
In this game called life
keep it real motherf——-.
They'll take you for a ride.
Paralyzed, Paralyzed, Paralyzed

F——- UP

F——- up
Drunk
Outta tune again...
Nobody sins, nobody wins.
No one's my friend, and no one knows it
better than me.
Everyone's high,
everyone lies,
everyone dies,
and no one knows it better than me.
Ricky Vodka when will you learn
your world spins as your head turns?
If I left it all up to you
we'd be a wrecking crew.

Bored boys with nothing to do.
F——- up
Drunk
Outta tune again

Disney obviously believed the cocktail of violence and aggression would sell to the youth of America. Disney's marketing of the group plays up the band's violent image. "So let the sweat drip where it will; let the fists fly where they will," the company declares in recent promotional material.

Walt Disney Records has been producing children's music for years and is the biggest company in the kids' music business, with more than fifty platinum albums. Walt saw the company as an opportunity to sell songs from Disney movies to children, songs of innocent fun.

Disney Chairman Michael Eisner formed Hollywood Records in 1989, believing an adult music company would add a new revenue stream to Disney's diverse collection of entertainment companies. Hollywood Records performers are consistently on the outer limits of mainstream pop music. Humble Gods isn't an exception; it's typical. *The Great Malenko,* by Insane Clown Posse, a Disney group from Detroit, was filled with lyrics like these:

He gets buck naked,
and then he walks through the streets
winkin' at freaks
with a two-liter stuck in his butt cheeks.

That CD stirred such controversy that Disney pulled it from shelves just six hours after its June 1997 release—and shortly after the Southern Baptist Convention announced its boycott of Disney. But those who might have hoped this motion suggested Disney was cleaning up its act were quickly disappointed. Far more offensive Disney material stayed in release or was released afterward. What explains Disney's bizarre choices at Hollywood Records? Not corporate ignorance. Michael Eisner has been heavily involved in the company and knows precisely what the company is producing. He regularly reviews the music and even now attends the weekly staff meetings. In 1995 Eisner had the record company moved onto the Disney Studio Lot so he could be more deeply involved in running the company. Disney attorneys review all of their contracts and albums, and Joe Roth, Chairman of Disney Studios, has taken an active role in managing Hollywood Records' affairs by listening to each album prior to its release. Disney clearly knows what Hollywood Records is producing. In fact, groups like Insane Clown Posse and Humble Gods fit in well with their roster of acts.

Joe Roth claims that *The Great Malenko* was pulled because he found it "foul and offensive." He says that he doesn't want "music that's about abusing women or encouraging violence." But some bands on the current Hollywood Records roster make Insane Clown Posse seem relatively benign.

Rap music was the industry rage, and Disney's Hollywood Records executives thought a band of convicts was a great concept.

With the exception of the rock band Queen, the company has never been interested in recruiting established talent. It's too costly. "Michael [Eisner] doesn't believe in it, and I don't believe in it," says Roth. "When you do that, it appears desperate." Since the real money is in developing up-and-coming performers, Hollywood Records has, instead, sifted its way through almost every conceivable musical outpost in search for the next great hit. And when the talent hasn't been there, the morbid, vicious, and obscene have been used to gain publicity.

When the label was launched in 1989, Michael Eisner looked for a music industry professional who could run the company. He personally picked a music industry attorney named Peter Paterno to head the new company. Paterno was an industry veteran who had represented groups like Guns 'N Roses, Metallica, and Delicious Vinyl. The Disney chairman knew what he was getting. Paterno was good friends with then Eisner pal David Geffen.

His clients were certainly evidence of what Eisner could expect from Paterno. Delicious Vinyl was a pioneer in rap music that helped to launch the careers of rappers Tone Loc, Def Jef, Mellow Man Ace, and Young MC. But Paterno was also deeply involved in the heavy metal music scene. He represented Metallica, which offered a bold message of violence in its songs. An early album was titled *Kill 'Em All,* and included songs like "Am I Evil?"

Am I Evil? Yes I am.
Am I Evil? I am man, yes I am.
On with the action now, I'll strip your pride.
I'll spread your blood around, I'll see you ride.
Your face is scarred with steel, wounds deep and neat.
Like a double dozen before ya, smells so sweet.

The band became notorious in heavy metal circles in the early 1980s by selling promotional T-shirts that read "Metal Up Your A—."

But for Michael Eisner, Peter Paterno was the perfect man to lead Mickey's new label. "It is our good fortune to be able to enlist the services of Mr. Paterno," he said, "a proven leader in the music industry and a man whose judgment we respect very highly." Eisner promised that Paterno "will work closely with me" in developing the company.

As a young company, Hollywood Records was desperate for attention. Once at the helm of Disney's new record label, Paterno backed some of the most controversial bands in music. He started out by signing up an obscure rapper named Prince Akeem, who sang about how black poverty arose from a white conspiracy. That same year the company released "Belly of the Beast," a single from a band called The Lifers Group, comprised of felons from New Jersey's Rahway Prison. One of the Lifers, Maxwell Melvins, was a friend of David Funenklein, then an executive working for Paterno.

Rap music was the industry rage, and Hollywood Records executives thought a band of convicts was a great concept. But barbed wire and cell block lockdowns presented unusual logistical problems for production. To record the music, a studio was set up at Rahway Prison. When someone came up with the idea of shooting a video to promote a single from the album, it was filmed in the exercise yard at the penitentiary and featured prisoners rapping about the crimes for which they were imprisoned. Later an album was cut, entitled *Lifers Group, World Tour—Rahway Prison. That's It.*

Another early Hollywood Records group, Sacred Reich, fit right in with the company's search for outrageous and tasteless promotional schemes. In one early song, the band sings:

Racist, piece of s—-
Bullet
is the only way you'll learn.
A bullet in your f——- head.

Sacred Reich is involved in the drug legalization movement and contributed a song called "Sweet Leaf" to a promotional CD called *Hempilation,* produced by the magazine *High Times.* So when Hollywood Records released its own album by the group, a drug tie-in seemed natural. Someone at the company (no one seems willing to take the credit) had the bright idea of sending thousands of plastic marijuana bongs to radio stations as an enticement to play the Sacred Reich album. The bongs were shipped, but sales didn't improve. Several months later the label staged a London press event featuring a dozen topless women riding bicycles. And at one point, Paterno even proposed that one of his rockers appear at an A-list Beverly Hills restaurant leading his girlfriend on a leash. (That idea was eventually nixed.) Throughout all of this, Michael Eisner and Disney executives never disavowed these marketing antics and Peter Paterno remained at the helm of Hollywood Records. He left only after his contract expired.

Ironically if the point of debasing the Disney name was to pull in profits, it wasn't working. Hollywood Records had lost more than $100 million by 1994. In the five years Paterno headed the company, it never produced a hit. The biggest contract Hollywood Records ever signed was with the rock band Queen, a proven hit-maker. And while the group had a track record of successful albums dating back to the

1970s, there was one slight problem: Lead singer Freddie Mercury was dying of AIDS. Hollywood Records forked over $12 million anyway, only months before Mercury died. By 1994 the company was known in music circles as "The Titanic captained by the Three Stooges."

The problems continued after Paterno left. Mark Hudson was a top staff producer who joined Hollywood Records in July 1994. A former member of the Hudson Brothers band, he had gone on to work as a songwriter and producer for performers like Alice Cooper and Aerosmith. Disney brought him on board to sharpen production, identify new acts, and shape its albums into something that would sell.

But from the start, his association with the company caused problems. Female employees repeatedly complained of sexual harassment; they alleged that he made lewd comments and pressured them into dates. As complaints piled up, Disney executives did nothing, except to ask that he visit a counselor. Two of the women who complained about his behavior were transferred to other jobs.

Disney's attempts to conceal the problem failed when singer Danielle Brisebois went public with exactly what Hudson had done to her when she was only seventeen years old. "I played him a song of mine," she told *Seconds* magazine. "While I'm playing him my tape, I look up and he's masturbating." Brisebois says she told him to stop, but Hudson responded with an anatomical reference. She fled the studio in disgust.

Stung by the public embarrassment, Disney let Hudson go in March of 1995. That same month, Bob Pfeifer became the label's new president, replacing Peter Paterno. Pfeifer, however, was hardly new blood. He had served as vice president of the company under Paterno. Nevertheless, he tried to start anew, by clearing out the company's artist roster and retaining only Queen and one other band. The staff was cut from eighty-five to fifty.

Eisner and Roth both committed to playing a larger role in the management of the company. Hollywood Records was relocated to the Disney Studio Lot so both men could more easily be involved in the company. Both began attending weekly staff meetings. Rap music acts were on the way out; on the way in were bands that sang about Satan, suicide, drugs, and rape.

• • •

"IF IT'S TOO HOT IN HELL," offers singer Glen Danzig, "then don't sign up."

Danzig always wears black. A massive tattoo on his left arm features various skeletal creatures, a vampire bat, and the slogan "Wolf's Blood." "Most kids are really frustrated," he said in a recent interview. "They're living under things I didn't have to live under when I was a kid, like AIDS and guns in school. We had guns and knives in school, but not nine millimeters. It wasn't like today. Why do you see so many people end their lives so young? Life looks bleak now."

Listening to Danzig's music probably won't pull them out of the doldrums. Bleakness, despondency, and darkness are what the group sings about. *The New Rolling Stone Encyclopedia of Rock and Roll* describes Danzig as "everything about heavy metal parents fear: Satanic, profane, antiauthoritarian, and no doubt proud of its cult status." In 1996 Disney signed the band to a lucrative seven-figure deal. One of Hollywood Record's largest deals ever, it had to be approved by Disney Studios Chairman Joe Roth. It was a stunning move, since Danzig's records don't sell very well and no other music company came even close to making such an offer.

Danzig's work is heavily tied to satanic themes. A 1990 album *Lucifuge* featured songs like "Long Way Back From Hell," "Tired of Being Alive," and "Her Black Wings." Glen Danzig describes the song "Invocation" as a tune "about a demon f——- somebody." Other albums like *How the Gods Kill* and *Demonsweatlive* are built on the same dark imagery. Those early albums were released on small, independent labels—limiting their audience. The Disney deal gave the contract with Danzig the marketing force to reach a larger audience.

Danzig's cult status has been honed by the group's outrageousness. The group once submitted a video to MTV entitled "It's Coming Down," filled with scenes of sadomasochism, masturbation, urination, and genital mutilation. MTV refused to air the piece. Even the Playboy Channel took a pass.

Glen Danzig has a problem with religion in general and Christianity in particular. "The Catholics and Baptists have perverted the teachings of Christ," he claims. "Worshipping their version of Christ [w]ould be considered by some to be as bad as worshipping Satan." He accuses the Catholic Church of practicing "genocide" and says modern-day America is "a repressive society bordering on a fascist society."

Glen Danzig has turned satanic themes into a cottage industry of sorts. In January 1994 he launched a new venture aimed at "pumping a touch of Satan into the world of comics." Thus far he has produced two serials. *Verotika* is a bimonthly erotic horror anthology, and *Satanika* is a bimonthly comic about a half-human, half-demon woman on a mission of vengeance against her demon father.

On October 30, 1996, Disney released Danzig's *Blackacidevil*. The release date was picked to coincide with the celebration of "Devil's Night," the night before Halloween. The album artwork features a hooded man changing into a satanic skull, hanging menacingly over a cross. "On *Blackacidevil*, I wanted to do something that nobody else was doing," says Glen Danzig. Undoubtedly, he succeeded.

POWER OF DARKNESS

Rape the garden of infernal delights,
rack our body on the left and right.
Like, you're floating on a river of pain,
thirsty knife and the hungry brain.
Rip your body on the left and right,
take your body to another plane.
Rape the garden of infernal delights,
wrap the snake in between your legs.

As far as Hollywood Records is concerned, this is really nothing to worry about. Danzig, they say, is harmless and simply misunderstood, much as Elvis was in the 1950s. "It's only Rock 'n Roll," says Sue Sawyer of Hollywood Records. "For forty years people have been scandalized by it." In fact, Disney's relationship with Danzig goes beyond music. In 1998 he costarred in the movie *Prophecy II*, produced by Disney's Miramax.

Suicide plays as prominent a role as Satan at Disney's "adult" label. Brijette West fronts for the band NY Loose, which the English rock publication *New Music Express* described as smelling like "sex, sleaze, alcohol and leather." Hollywood Records signed NY Loose in 1995.

If you're looking for an upbeat tempo and warm lyrics with perspective, you've got the wrong band. "For some reason," says West, "I zero in on sadness. I zero in on despair. It's not so much that I'm attached to it, it's more like somehow it's attached itself to me. So it definitely comes out in my lyrics."

NY Loose's CD *Year of the Rat,* released by Hollywood Records, is a patchwork of songs about suicide, curling up on the floor in despair, and profound brokenness, including songs like "Broken," "Trash the Given Chance," "Rip Me Up," and "Pretty Suicide." The latter was inspired by a photo in *Life* magazine. Where others saw tragedy, NY Loose saw beauty. "A girl committed suicide by jumping off the Empire State Building and landed on the roof of a car," said West in an interview. "And she landed in the most angelic, graceful final pose. No blood or splatter—just this beautiful state of relaxation. It seemed like the ultimate example of the collision between violence and tragedy and beauty. It's ironic," she says with a smile, "because it was probably the best photo that this girl had ever taken."

She was such a pretty suicide;
oh, what a beautiful mess.
She was such a pretty suicide;
right now she looks her best.

Suicide looms so large in Disney's new music that Pfeifer even signed a band with the name in it. Like Humble Gods, Danzig, and NY Loose, The Suicide Machines' first major label deal was with Disney. Guitarist and vocalist Dan Suicide Machine (formerly Lukacinsky), who fronts for the Detroit-area band, explains that the band chose the name "as a reflection of the peculiar fatalism" that afflicts teens in modern-day America.

Fatalism also colors the work of Human Waste Project, another recent Hollywood Records acquisition. The band gets its name, according to bassist Jeff Schartoff, from the group's view of life. "Human Waste Project is an observation," he says, "the result of a black hole in the mind that has to do with the separation of the physical plane to nowhere, the part of the human condition that's lost— the end of the line."

Hollywood Records released the band's first album, *E-Lux*, on September 30, 1997. Amidst the shrieking, unearthly whines of the tortured guitar and the angry, ominous grumble of the bass, you hear songs like "Disease," which is supposed to be about relationships.

Well
I bet you thought
you knew everything about me
but you don't.
You don't you don't know everything;
no.
So just f—- off,
whore.

In another track, Human Waste Project croons about sex with "Virgin Mary."

His Virgin Mary
away she has come
he's blinded always by her innocence.

He quivers as her mouth glides eagerly across the flesh;
His eyes close,
he turns away—but she still just shines, shines, shines—
too bright for him to look at.
Shine, shine, shine away my Mary. Shine, shine, shine.

In darkness his whore she lies in wait—she's ever ready to devour him.
Quivers as her mouth glides eagerly across the flesh;
His eyes close,
he turns away—but she still just shines, shines, shines—
too bright for him to look at.
Shine, shine, shine away my Mary. Shine, shine, shine.

Suicide is the third leading cause of death among young people aged fifteen to twenty-four. But if that doesn't seem to Disney like a good reason not to glorify suicide to the same kids who grew up on Goofy, Donald, and the Little Mermaid, then it probably should come as no surprise that Hollywood Records also cheerleads for an even greater scourge of teen life today: Drugs. Besides shipping promotional bongs, the company's bands sing about drugs. On their album *Spanaway*, Disney's group Seaweed sings a snappy song called "Free Drug Zone" (as opposed to Drug Free Zone). Humble Gods sing a song called "Mary's in Bondage Pants," about a girl who pops "black beauties." And another Hollywood Records act, Super 8, sings a song entitled "Pills":

The feeling I get in my brain
is ecstasy within my mind.
No limitation to my dreaming.
I'm the moon and the sky;
I can wade beneath the ocean floor,
ignore your knock upon my door.
Reality is too demanding;
it asks too much of me.

The promotional material for Hollywood Records' band Flipp gleefully describes the drummer "Kilo" (whose name refers to the metric unit used to measure drugs like cocaine or marijuana) as the "band burnout." With "a never-ending stash of kind herb, Kilo is Flipp's supplier." Kilo is perhaps the first Disney drug-dealer role model for our youth.

The Hollywood Records promotional literature for the band Into Another includes an interview with vocalist Richie Birkenhead discussing his wild reputation. "A few months ago," he brags, "I heard a rumor that I was on stage and had done so much cocaine that my nose exploded into a bloody mess and I had to have plastic surgery. That was a pretty good one."

In April 1997 Bob Pfeifer resigned as company president. Eisner took the occasion to praise Pfeifer's artistic management: "Bob and his team have been successful in creating a nurturing artist-oriented environment at Hollywood Records," said Michael Eisner at the time. "He leaves a far stronger business than the one he was named to lead." But the company was still not profitable.

With Paterno and Pfeifer gone and the bottom line still sagging, Eisner and Disney had every excuse to change the direction of Hollywood Records. To the contrary, following Pfeifer's departure, Disney began courting Tom Whalley to take the helm at Hollywood Records. Whalley is the president of Interscope Records, an enormously profitable company and the industry leader in producing "gangsta rap." Under Whalley, Interscope has produced albums by Tha Dogg Pound, Snoop Doggy Dogg, and Dr. Dre, which offer plenty of songs about violence and death. About the same time Disney was courting Whalley, the *Wall Street Journal* reported that the FBI was nosing around Interscope and its label Death Row Records, asking questions about guns, drugs, and money laudering. Death Row's Marion "Suge" Knight, hired by Whalley, was in jail at the time, having been caught on hotel surveillance video beating up a guy, in violation of his probation agreement. Nevertheless Eisner offered Whalley a multimillion dollar signing bonus to join the Mouse, but in the end he elected to stay at Interscope.

In another attempt to boost its position in the adult music business, Disney bought a small record label in July 1997. Mammoth Records is based out of Carrboro, North Carolina, and cost the Mouse $25 million.

Like Hollywood Records, Mammoth promotes the drug culture along with its bands. One act it has signed is called Children of the

Bong. The Mammoth website describes the founding of another band, Vowel Movement, this way: "Holly and Johnette formed the band on New Year's Eve in 1993 when neither of them had a date. They drank, smoked pot. Did each others Tarot cards, then the I-Ching, drank some more, Johnette picked up her bass, Holly got on her drums, Johnette started mumbling... and Vowel Movement was born."

Mammoth's website quotes Scott Hill, vocalist and guitarist of Fu Manchu: "I did an interview with this guy the other day who was saying how did I feel about being called stoner rock. Then he said he was smoking out on a huge bong while listening to it... so I guess that's what it is."

"Inhale!" Mammoth exclaims at the bottom of the promotional piece.

> **When Disney's Hollywood Records released an album by Sacred Reich, a drug tie-in seemed natural. So they sent thousands of marijuana bongs to radio stations as an enticement to play the album.**

Just months after Disney bought Mammoth, Mammoth signed a joint venture agreement with a couple of producers (Michael Simpson and John King) known as the Dust Brothers to identify and develop new talent. While the Dust Brothers have produced such mainstream acts as Hanson, they have spent most of their professional life working with shock groups like Marilyn Manson and Butthole Surfers. For Manson, they produced part of the new album *Antichrist Superstar*.

Mammoth President Jay Faires praises the Dust Brothers for "their creative foresight and artistic passion." As far as Disney is concerned, Faires believes the sky is the limit. "I think I can rock on this thing and blow it through the... roof. I am psyched to be working with Joe [Roth] and Michael [Eisner.]"

CHAPTER THREE

Minnie Makes Room for Marilyn Chambers

Award-winning science fiction writer Harlan Ellison likes to tell the story of his stint at Disney. Sometime around 1970 he was hired by the company to work as a writer for Disney Studios. On his first day he arrived at the Mouse ready to start on a project, but since he didn't know for which picture he'd be writing, he spent the first few hours bantering with some colleagues. Late in the morning they moved on to the studio commissary for lunch and gathered around the Writers' Table. Ellison began joking that they consider producing a "Disney porno flick" and proceeded to loudly act out the parts, imitating the voices of several Disney animated characters. While everyone had a good laugh, little did Ellison know that Roy Disney and other studio heads were sitting at a nearby table. When he returned to his office there was a pink slip on his desk. He had worked for the company for a total of four hours, including lunch.

In June 1989 Disney became a full partner in Viewer's Choice, today a leader in pay-per-view "soft-core" pornography.

Harlan Ellison was let go because he violated an important company rule: You don't besmirch the Disney name by linking it to something as disreputable as the "adult entertainment industry." And today Disney still prides itself on its wholesome image and continues to advertise the fact that it will not push the boundaries of propriety. When the new Virgin Megastore opened recently at Downtown Disney, a retail shopping center in Orlando, Disney officials made sure no adult videos would be sold. Disney has a strict rule for all of its film companies, including Miramax, Hollywood Pictures, and Touchstone Pictures: No movies beyond an R rating.

One of the ventures Disney undertook in the late 1980s, however, proves that Ellison's real mistake was that he was a man ahead of his time. Like the company's foray into punk rock and the rap music business, the new Disney has seen fit to broaden its business activities into distributing skin flicks. Disney's link to the porno industry is no longer an idle joke. It is a fact, and it confirms that the new Disney will do just about anything to make a buck.

Disney got involved in the cable television business in the early 1980s, before Michael Esiner became chairman. The Disney Channel offers family-friendly cartoons, movies, concerts, and TV shows. But Michael Eisner and company execs felt there was a real potential for growth in the new pay-per-view market, where cable subscribers pay to watch individual movies and events. So in June 1989 Walt Disney Pictures and Television became a full partner with several cable companies in a new venture called Viewer's Choice, a pioneer in pay-per-view television. Disney was a pioneer in the business as the first motion picture studio to participate as a full-fledged partner. "This is a major step in the development of the pay-per-view industry as well as in the development of successful long-term relationships between cable operators and program suppliers," said James Heyworth, Viewer's Choice president and CEO at the time. "It broadens the support and increases the number of companies committed to making the pay-per-view system work." He called the Disney/Viewer's Choice partnership a "natural evolution of conversations" the two companies had originally had about a licensing agreement to air Disney films.

Disney made it very clear from the outset that it wanted to play an active role in Viewer's Choice. No other company had a larger stake in the company than Disney. (Viewer's Choice would not disclose how much of the company Disney owns, but it did say that no other company owns a larger stake than Disney.) And Hal Richardson, then vice president of pay-per-view television for Disney, said that the Mouse didn't want to simply provide films to show on the service, it wanted to have a "participatory role in the business." That meant input into the development of the company and a voice in decision-making. Mickey was not going to be a silent Mouse.

At that time Viewer's Choice served 250 cable systems with

1,000,000 basic subscribers. The service ran typical action films and comedies from big Hollywood studios like Paramount Pictures, Universal Pictures, Warner Brothers, and Disney. Profits were relatively good. (Since this is a privately held company, exact figures are not available.)

Still, the partners thought they could do better. As the pay-per-view and cable television market began to develop, it became clear that one of the most profitable segments of the market was in so-called "soft-core" pornography. It seemed a perfect fit for the service. Not only did pay-per-view television save the consumer a possibly embarrassing outing to the adult video store, but Heyworth also figured that the company could run short-length, soft-core features and charge higher prices than for the traditional G, PG, PG-13, and R feature-length films. Instead of running a two-hour, feature-length film and charging $3, the company could show a one-hour, soft-porn program and charge $5.

The economics made sense, and on February 1, 1993, Viewer's Choice launched a service called Hot Choice. Mickey was now in the soft-porn business. Viewer's Choice gave the new service an urban, contemporary theme song and a jazzy slogan to help promote it as the place for adult entertainment. Although it began by running sophomoric adult movies like *Honey* and *Bikini Party*, the core of their programming soon became original programs marketed as part of a "sexy series."

To develop original programming, Viewer's Choice partners, including Disney, lured porn star Becky LeBeau away from the Playboy Channel by offering her a lucrative, seven-figure deal and a share of the profits. LeBeau, who appeared in features like *B-Movie Bimbos*, had previously developed a television series for Playboy called *Soft Bodies*, an all-nude modeling program with explicit footage of women, some as young as eighteen. Viewer's Choice then decided to buy the rights to *Soft Bodies*. This series has become the most widely watched television program of its kind in the world. "Make a date with a couple of sweethearts" is the tease for *Soft Bodies' Sweethearts*. "Join Becky LeBeau and her sexy girlfriends for some pulsating Jacuzzi madness, then some heartwarming fun in the sun.

These all-natural centerfolds are guaranteed to please." For *Becky LeBeau's Party Girls*, Viewer's Choice says, "Join five wild and willing nude models as they invite you to their bouncy bash of arousing fun and very sexy surprises. You've never received party favors like this before!"

LeBeau, who describes herself as the "Queen of Pay-Per-View," is clearly very pleased with the opportunity Viewer's Choice has given her. "*Soft Bodies* specials do extremely well every time they are offered on pay-per-view, and the series has developed an extremely loyal and consistent following," she says proudly. LeBeau produces three shows annually for Hot Choice, and they air regularly throughout the year.

Around the same time, Viewer's Choice aggressively pursued another porn industry veteran—Marilyn Chambers—to produce a regular stable of programs. Chambers made her first movie appearance in the 1972 hard-core film *Behind the Green Door*, and is regarded as one of the founding stars of the adult movie industry. In 1992 the Adult Video Association gave her the "Lifetime Achievement Award" for her "groundbreaking work and significance in the industry." For Viewer's Choice that must have been the seal of approval, because the following year they signed her to an exclusive multiproject deal.

Chambers has appeared on Viewer's Choice more than any other actor or "performer." Her movies offered on Hot Choice include an "erotic comedy" called *Marilyn Chambers' Desire*, the story of an erotic film director who has "gone out of control." Marilyn plays the female porn star who wants the leading man fired. Meanwhile, the producer wants to cast his "sexy but talentless nieces, and the cast and crew can't keep their hands off each other."

Breakfast in Bed is another "erotic comedy." This time Chambers plays "a sultry, sexy movie star whose career is on the downswing." When her manager steals all of her money, she turns a bed and breakfast into "the hottest, most erotic retreat in town, and her guests aren't the only ones finding passion." In *Marilyn Chambers' Party Incorporated* she goes into the business of throwing "exotic and erotic parties with all the trimmings," and in *Garden of Erotic Delights* she promises to "take you into her private garden where chance encounters and spontaneous seduction are among the erotic delights that blossom."

LeBeau and Chambers aren't the only providers of porno material for Viewer's Choice. A series called *The New Video Vixens* (Volumes 1 through 7) appears almost monthly on the service part owned by Mickey. "More Vixens, more sexy skits, and more flesh," promises Viewer's Choice. The program is sort of like "Where's Waldo?" without clothes: "Where will they show up next? Topless dancers appear in the most unlikeliest of places." Viewer's Choice fills you in on all the pertinent details, like the fact that *Video Vixens 2* features Venus De Light, six-time winner of Miss Nude Universe.

Other "sexy series" programming includes *Wild Pairs*: "When two supermodels team up to play erotic games, you come up a winner every time." If it's foreign travel you want, try *Erotic Heat: Hot Salsa*: "Temperatures rise while girls vacationing at a villa south of the border discover that nights are more than hot and spicy." And let's not forget *Hot Date*: "Go out on the hottest date of your life with four of the most erotic and beautiful girls of the year." And for the leather crowd, Viewer's Choice offers *Hot Date VII: Beautiful Kinky Nudes*: "Go out on the hottest, most erotic date of your life! You're bound to enjoy the leather, the masks, the fetish delights of a date with beautiful nudes."

> **In one month Viewer's Choice featured only one Disney film: *101 Dalmatians*. It also offered *Erotic Nights*, *Forbidden Games II*, and *Sexual Roulette*, among others.**

Can't you just feel the Disney magic?

Viewer's Choice also has an exclusive contract with a production company for a series called *American Stripper on Tour*. A film crew visits strip joints around the country in cities like Miami and Las Vegas and shoots lots of footage. "You've hit the jackpot," Hot Choice's promotional materials blab about the Vegas program, "when five dazzling dancers steam up the strip with all-nude performances."

But there is more. *Erotic Confessions* is a regular program about a hostess named Jacqueline Stowe who "receives erotic letters from strangers who reveal their most lurid sexual experiences." Some recent episodes:

"A man goes on a wild ride when he offers a sensuous stranger a lift."

"Coworkers locked-in overnight unleash hidden passions and desires."

"Detectives reenact the erotic possibilities surrounding a jewelry heist."

"Uptight Angela unwinds when she encounters a hunk motorcycle rebel."

"While his wife is away, a bored husband has a chance meeting with an erotic dancer."

"Two neglected housewives find the recipe for romance at a restaurant."

"A mailroom clerk at an erotic magazine is assigned a special project by his sexy superior."

No word yet if an episode about Snow White lusting for the Seven Dwarfs is in the works.

If it's character development you want, Disney-owned Hot Choice suggests *Confessions of a Lap Dancer*. What is the film about? "Erica Pancey is a stripper who turns tricks on the side." Hot Choice also offers *In Bed with Amy Lynn Baxter*, whose problem is "Too much time on her hands and a roving mind full of daydream delights." For the nautically inclined there is *Seduction at Sea with Amy Lynn Baxter*: "When Amy Lynn invites a sexy male photographer and his six luscious models aboard her luxurious yacht, you know sex and seduction are on her sea-faring mind! Co-stars the 1997 Playgirl Man of the Year, Jonathan Prandi."

When Disney bought into Viewer's Choice in 1989 it was billed as another venue for Disney films. But very few Disney films actually appear on the pay-per-view service. In October 1997 Viewer's Choice featured only one Disney film: *101 Dalmatians*. In the same month it seemed as if the service offered 101 erotic programs with films such as *Erotic Nights, Forbidden Games II, Sexual Roulette, Marilyn Chambers' Garden of Erotic Delights*, and *Super Natural* ("a young beauty finds eternal erotic pleasure when seduced by a harem of gorgeous vampires") as well as specials like *American Stripper On Tour: Las Vegas*, *Hot Date II* ("Party one on one with the girl of your dreams!"), *In Search of a Ten: The Clubs* (an exclusive look inside the country's hottest strip clubs), and *The New Video Vixens 7*.

Every time someone watches these programs, each partner in the company gets a cut, including the new Disney. And that cut is big. Disney is now a partner in the biggest player in the soft-core pornography market, serving more than 1,000 affiliated cable systems, with more than 59 million pay-per-view channel subscribers in nearly 18 million addressable homes nationwide. It has been so masterful in developing the soft-porn pay-per-view business that Jim English, Viewer's Choice executive in charge of adult programming, was hired away by the Playboy Channel to take over as president.

But despite all of this success, Disney seems shy about sharing the news of its good fortune. If you look in any Disney Annual Report, you won't find any mention of Hot Choice, Becky LeBeau, or Marilyn Chambers. The company won't talk about its role as a partner in this company or the size of its profits. But at Viewer's Choice, Disney has not expressed any concern about its involvement in the soft-porn business. According to Rebecca Kramer, a spokeswoman at Viewer's Choice, none of the partners in the venture has expressed objections to any of the programming. "Everyone seems pleased," she told us.

PART II

Disney's Secret World

CHAPTER FOUR

"Safety Comes Last"

Talk about pressure. Spencer Craig had been with Disney for about ten years when they tapped him for one of the company's most challenging jobs: duty manager of the Magic Kingdom. Responsible for tens of thousands of guests and employees, the duty manager runs the park. He is the sole person in control. And when presented with a crisis, he makes decisions.

"That night I was responsible for *everything* that happened in the park," he told us. "You talk about a pressure situation. Every location, every employee, every guest. You were constantly looking for lost kids. During a parade one time a kid got away and went over the fence and ultimately drowned in the moat. We were missing a $35,000 trained dog that was supposed to be in the parade. There was a big chunk that had fallen out of Space Mountain. Small World was being closed down. You have all of these things to hassle with. But at the same time you are making decisions about life and death. I got a call that a lady was giving birth in the middle of the antique store. She was all excited. She was going to name her kid 'Mickey.' Here's all these guests around with their cameras getting ready to film the birth on video. Let me tell you, you can't allow that sort of thing to happen on Disney property."

> **"They make more money continuing to operate in a dangerous situation and getting sued than they would shutting down and fixing the problem."**

The new Disney may have branched out into questionable ventures involving pay-per-view soft porn and punk rockers, but it still has Disney World. Walt Disney World encompasses forty-three square miles, an area twice the size of Manhattan Island. While it includes the well-known parks—Magic Kingdom, EPCOT Center, and Disney-

MGM—there are also water parks, a botanical and zoological park, a nightlife entertainment area, and several golf courses. Disney World is a metropolis.

Both Disneyland and Disney World grew out of Walt Disney's fervent desire to create theme parks that were clean, safe, and enjoyable. Attention was paid to the most obscure details. Ever notice that there are no newspapers available for sale in the park? Walt didn't want people exposed to any of the world's harsh realities while in the Magic Kingdom. Every care was taken to make the parks a truly mythical place, shielded from the cares of everyday living.

One of the key elements in that effort was the heavy emphasis on safety. In one internal memo Walt wrote about his plans for a park where "emphasis [would be] on comfort and safety, with concern for the users." Even today, the Disney Standard Operating Procedure (S.O.P.) is based on a formula originally developed by Walt Disney himself. "The four basic elements of operation at the Magic Kingdom park are safety, show, courtesy and capacity. SAFETY is the most important element. SAFETY is engineered INTO EVERY factor of the Operations Division and was given prime consideration in the development of the Standard Operating Procedures for each area."

The company's reputation for safety is something Disney continues to cultivate when it markets itself to families around the world. But current Disney employees say that reputation is no longer deserved. And internal company documents and surveys support

WALT DISNEY WORLD AMUSEMENT PARKS Injury, Illness, and Lost Workdays 1990 and 1991				
	1990		1991	
	Industry Average	WDW Rate	Industry Average	WDW Rate
Illness/Injury Rate (per 100 workers)	9.5	18.4	8.8	17.4
Lost Work Day Rate	74.8	212.7	73.0	231.5

their on-the-record views that the Mouse's commitment to safety is not what it used to be.

Disney's safety records are closely guarded and have never appeared outside its well-protected walls. They have never been published before. We, however, obtained a copy of a 1994 internal company report titled "Walt Disney World Comprehensive Health and Safety Process." After reviewing it, you can understand why the Mouse is not interested in having this information become public. The facts are staggering: According to the company's own records in recent years, its injury and illness rates are twice the industry average.

WALT DISNEY WORLD HOTELS Injury, Illness, and Lost Workdays 1990 and 1991				
	1990		1991	
	Industry Average	WDW Rate	Industry Average	WDW Rate
Illness/Injury Rate (per 100 workers)	10.6	18.9	10.4	19.3
Lost Work Day Rate	97.4	281.5	101.1	316.6

The 1994 report notes that in the six months from July 1993 to January 1994 there were 8,397 incidents involving the health and safety of Disney employees. Forty-four percent required first aid and 46 percent required further medical attention. Perhaps the most startling part of the report is the finding concerning the ratio of on-the-job employee injuries. Under the question: "How do we compare?" the report notes that while the national average for on-the-job injuries is 1 for every 10 employees, Disney's rate is 1 for every 4. We were unable to obtain such hard data for *customer* injuries, but, as numerous Disney employees and other experts made clear to us, in the theme park business employee injuries and customer injuries usually go together: the same conditions and abuses that lead to employee injuries lead to customer injuries, as numerous stories straight from the mouths of Disney employees clearly show.

These numbers for employee injuries may be surprising to those of us who work outside the walls of the Magic Kingdom. We are accustomed to thinking of Disney parks as clean, safe, and well run. Yet the data do not surprise current Disney World employees. In a series of exclusive, on-the-record interviews, these workers stepped forward, to speak up about their safety concerns. Several of these employees headed up safety committees the company established at the park and others are involved in training new employees. They are deeply concerned by what they have seen.

Their comments echo what appears in the 1994 report. These current employees say recent years have been marked by cutbacks and an emphasis on a strict, bottom-line approach to running the park. To maximize profits, shortcuts have been taken and dangerous risks accepted, even in the area of safety. And it is those dangerous risks that they said led them to go on the record.

Sheila Randolph is an eight-year employee at the Magic Kingdom who works the Dumbo ride and has worked at It's a Small World. She helps to train new employees and supervises new hires. Sheila caught the Disney magic at a young age and moved to Orlando to work for the Mouse. While she enjoys her coworkers, she is concerned about safety, and what she sees as the company taking shortcuts. "They teach you safety, show, courtesy, and capacity," she told us matter-of-factly. "But safety comes last when the almighty dollar talks."

Ben Keen, tall and slender with dark hair, has worked for the past three years at the Splash Mountain roller coaster. Keen says he sees safety problems arise regularly, but says the company doesn't seem all that concerned about safety problems on Splash Mountain or other rides. In observing how safety complaints are handled and the attractions are operated, he says Disney has made a cold calculation. "They make more money continuing to operate in a dangerous situation and getting sued than they would shutting down and fixing the problem," he told us.

Other employees agree that the company is playing a numbers game, willing to risk the welfare of guests and employees by not making safety improvements. Michael Overcash has worked at a variety of rides in the Magic Kingdom, including Peter Pan and Space Mountain. Overcash says there is a lot he likes about Disney, but not how it handles safety. Indeed, he says he was surprised how the company operated after watching his supervisors at work. "They decide 'What is the possibility that we can get sued? What is the amount that lawsuit would cost us, and what would it cost us to prevent that?' If the prevention costs more than the lawsuit, they figure you might as well deal with the lawsuit."

Murray Cohen is a seven-year Disney World employee who works Space Mountain, Splash Mountain, and Big Thunder Mountain. He has also served as the cochair of the Magic Kingdom Safety Committee, established by the company. He told us bluntly, "The company will operate in an unsafe manner if they think they can get away with it and if it saves them money."

Deborah Clark is a fifteen-year EPCOT employee who says she sees preventable injuries occur all the time. And supervisors don't show much interest in fixing the problem. "I've worked at the attractions for fifteen years," she told us. "I used to work at Spaceship Earth. There were so many different injuries to customers all the time, but not enough [in number] or tragic enough that they would do the improvements we suggested. Customers would step off into the moving platform. A lot of them would immediately lose their balance and fall. But it didn't matter. One day I was working at the front-load position and this man stepped off onto the revolving platform, fell immediately, and rolled under the vehicle. His arm was trapped under the door. He was trapped under the car, and the ride stopped just six inches from shearing off his arm." Clark says she used to think that even if the company didn't care about employee safety, at least it cared about guest safety. "But they aren't even really concerned about that anymore."

What has changed at Disney? Employees say part of the problem stems from new policies implemented in recent years. For example, several years ago, the company established something called Operational Hourly Ride Capacity (OHRC) for each attraction to determine how many guests should be getting on each ride per hour. "Management sent people out to New York, Chicago, and other cities and talked to people who visited Disney World and asked them about their visit," says Randolph, who participated in the first OHRC tests in Fantasyland. "The biggest problem the guests had was they had to wait in line so long. On an average day they were able to go on only seven rides, because they had to wait so long."

Park attendance at Magic Kingdom used to be capped. "We would close the park at approximately 50,000," says Spencer Craig, who served as duty manager of the park in the early 1980s. But today company officials run well beyond that. Rather than cap attendance, Disney management came up with OHRC. Fantasyland was the test site. "They started with the Dumbo ride," Randolph says. "[They] took the fact that we have sixteen Dumbos, the fact that we put slightly more than two people in a Dumbo on average, and they figure the ride runs one and a half minutes, and they figure it takes us one and a half minutes to load the guests and check all the Dumbos. So they calculated in a hour that we should get five hundred fifty through. If you don't, they want to know why." Sheila says she has watched the implementation of OHRC and "There is definitely a higher number of injuries and a greater risk."

The problem is the emphasis on numbers doesn't factor in many important considerations. "They don't factor in the people in wheelchairs or little kids crying and slowing you down," she told us. "They don't take into account when it rains and slows people down and makes the ground slick. So OHRC is unrealistic and it creates enormous pressure."

Michael Overcash served on the OHRC Committee in Tomorrowland and saw the same emphasis on numbers leading to a dangerous rush. Three hundred an hour was once considered satisfactory for the Astro Orbiter. Then the quota was jacked up to four hundred, a 25 percent increase. "You have to figure out a way to slam it out faster, get more people on."

Before OHRC the focus at Disney World was on service and safety. But the company also figures that every guest waiting in line is one less patron buying food and trinkets on Main Street. "Now it's all about getting people through," says Murray Cohen. "We jokingly call guests 'revenue units' because that's how management sees them."

Frank Kubicki is an eight-year employee who works at the Jungle Cruise and assists in training new employees. He also served as a cochair of the Magic Kingdom Safety Committee established by the company. "People have to run around and do things that are relatively unsafe to meet the OHRC goals," he told us. Kubicki believes OHRC is evidence that the company is more concerned with the immediate bottom line than in catering to guest needs and safety. "Every hour OHRC is reported up the chain of command to see how it is going. If you compare it to the accidents that have happened and could happen to you and to guests, you wonder 'Why do this?'. And of course it's about money."

OHRC creates an environment where, in the end, numbers become more important than safety. At Splash Mountain, for example, the OHRC is two thousand guests per hour. To make that number, says Keen, boats are sent out before everyone has a seat, just to keep the boats moving. The employees have adopted a "two-feet, two-cheek rule. If their body is over the boat—whether they are sitting down or not, we send them on the way. People are continually falling."

> **"When there is an accident, it's usually guest claims that gets called first, then 911. They want someone there before the ambulance to kiss butt."**

Murray Cohen says that when he held boats and waited for people to sit down at Splash Mountain, his manager sternly asked him, "What's the hold up?"

According to Keen, the emphasis on pushing people through creates a bind for employees at the new Disney. "Management will sit there and watch you dispatch boats when people are standing, and they don't care because OHRC is being met. But when a guest gets hurt, you are responsible for that."

Disney actually encourages competition between attractions to see who can get more people through in any given hour. According to Sheila Randolph, "Every year around Christmas, Small World challenges Pirates to an OHRC competition. The loaders are just shoving people into the boat. People get so into it that they send the boats with people standing up. You get in such a hurry you can't pay attention."

Sometimes the demands of the hourly rate count create inherent dangers in the operation of rides. At the Jungle Cruise, management decided to add a fourth boat to meet the quota. Kubicki says it has already produced safety problems. "Obviously when you have four boats at the dock you can shuttle more people but you have a much greater chance of collisions because there is less space. It wasn't designed for four boats. There are a lot more accidents happening."

Keeping the rides going during dangerous weather conditions is another practice at the new Disney. Central Florida experiences frequent electrical storms, and the park used to stop operating its rides during these powerful storms that produced severe lightning. According to Spencer Craig, "We would shut down the large outdoor rides [in the 1980s] during bad electrical storms. That was the procedure, no questions asked." But apparently no longer. Even after complaints by both workers and guests, Disney World rarely shuts down its rides.

Sometimes this can lead to serious injuries. "I've seen vicious lightning storms, and supervisors refuse to shut down the rides, to keep the crowds moving," says Cohen. "There was a lightning storm but the supervisor wouldn't shut down Big Thunder Mountain. One of the customers even came up and said we were idiots for keeping the ride running. I had a friend working out front of Big Thunder Mountain. He was a greeter. Lightning struck and went through the underground piping and my buddy got hit. He had to go to the hospital." According to Cohen, several years earlier another friend was left in harm's way when supervisors kept the 20,000 Leagues Under the Sea attraction running during an electrical storm. The employee was in the cab of the sub when lightning struck.

Cohen says he doesn't know of any guests that have been hit, at least not yet. "One time Big Thunder Mountain got hit by lightning, and the whole ride just froze. At the time there were a couple of trains out on the tracks. It was pouring down rain, and there was thunder and lightning. And the guests were just stuck out there. They were in danger. We had to go out and get them. We just couldn't leave them out there."

The Disney Skyway is another danger spot during storms. "At the transfer station," where the Skyway shifts direction, "there are [lightning] strikes constantly," says Randolph who has worked the Skyway. The ride "runs during electrical storms and during lightning. They [management] wanted to keep the rides going." This practice even frightens some guests, who are given what Randolph calls false reassurances. "Sometimes the guests don't want to get into the cabin, but we are supposed to tell them 'It's okay.'"

The safety problems caused by OHRC are compounded by another practice at the new Disney: employee cutbacks. Not only are more guests being pushed through the turnstiles at a faster rate, there are also now fewer employees to help them onto the rides. Many rides, for example, that used to have three employees assisting guests now have only two. "It used to be dropping a position at an attraction was not something that happened," says Ben Keen. "But now it's common practice because the budgets have been cut so much. You are already running at a minimal staff."

Murray Cohen says he has personally observed managers cutting a position, usually one that helps guests on the ride. He says he raised the issue as cochairman of the Magic Kingdom Safety Committee, but management wasn't interested. "At Splash Mountain, they do not hesitate when they think it's financially necessary to drop one of the loading positions," he told us. "The person doing loads has two positions."

Longtime Disney employees see a trend. After twenty-five years on the job, Spencer Craig left the company in 1995. Cutbacks are part of Michael Eisner's strict bottom-line approach that places a premium on cost-cutting and boosting short-term profits. But Craig sees a danger in such downsizing. "Cutbacks create real safety concerns," he told us. "As the cutbacks come, an inherent danger comes. Fewer people are available to do a given job, and more incidents occur."

Disney has also cut back on training. So not only are there fewer employees running a given ride, they are also less well prepared to deal with safety problems that might arise. New hires at Space Mountain, for example, used to receive forty hours of training for the job. "When I came on six years ago, Space Mountain trained everyone in Basic Ride Systems Operations," says Todd Eversen, a Disney Operations Host who has spent six years with the company. "That training included the entire mechanical process of how the ride worked. The technical information included each of the separate ride systems and lots of hands-on training. But the company doesn't train that way anymore. Three years ago, they cut it back." Today Space Mountain employees receive only twenty-four hours of training, even though the mechanics and operation of the ride remains essentially the same. Frank Kubicki, who has served as cochair of the Magic Kingdom Safety Committee, agrees the lack of training creates safety problems. "New hires are not well-trained," he told us. "They don't know how to operate the safety features on the rides."

Orlando attorney John Overchuck claims he gets cases all the time from guests injured at the park. "Disney has been downsizing, and we are seeing more and more people injured because there are no longer the number of employees out there as there used to be." He recently handled a case at a Disney Water Park. "My client was at the top of the water slide and there was no one there to help her to get on. They usually had someone there. But they didn't want to spend the five dollars and fifty cents an hour on this particular day to pay someone to stay there. She tried to do it by herself, and ended up striking her head pretty severely. Disney settled out of court."

He adds that he hears more frequently about slip-and-fall accidents than he used to. "You get off a lot of rides by exiting onto a moving sidewalk," he says. "Disney's procedure is to have someone where the moving sidewalk stops. But now lots of times there is no one there, because of downsizing. Older people especially fall more frequently."

"Safety is definitely a concern," says Murray Cohen, having seen the cutbacks affect the big roller coasters over the past six years. "Everyone out there is worried about it. Fewer people are available to do a given job. Any time you lose a position there's an extra burden on someone else. And there is constant pressure to put more people on the ride—to meet your quota. You're supposed to get a certain number of people on the ride every hour, and, if you fall short, you're slacking. They are always looking to cut back on people. At a place like Space Mountain, the cutbacks affect customer safety."

And cutbacks at a big roller coaster like Space Mountain mean that the safety lap bars often don't get checked. "At Space Mountain we have an eight-person rotation," says Michael Overcash. "We have a position called mountain three, which is a multipurpose position. They're the roamer, the gofer, the guy that handles anything special that comes up. They handle wheelchairs. If we don't have enough people, we drop that position and go to a two-position rotation. If a wheelchair comes—and they frequently do—or something else needs to be taken care of, it falls on one of the load operators to take care of it. Then the pit person has to run two positions. They need to check lap bars and load people in, but you can't do a safe job of it alone."

Even on less intense rides like Dumbo, things get overlooked. In April 1992 three-year-old Dorian Weiss had her hand crushed by four hundred pounds of pressure from a gate that snapped shut on her. Disney had only recently decided to increase the number of elephants on the Dumbo ride from ten to sixteen without adding a position (they have since). Sheila Randolph, who works the Dumbo ride, says these sorts of injuries happen all the time. "They don't tell us the names, but kids get hurt very easily at Dumbo. It's amazing."

Disney is also laying off skilled technical workers who maintain the attractions. Just last year, Disneyland laid off supervisors and about fifty workers in the facilities division. Skilled workers—plumbers, iron workers, and electricians—were placed on a night shift to work four ten-hour days instead of the usual five-day-a-week schedule. The workers claim there are already warning signs that safety is being sacrificed. "All indications we're getting from the park is that shutdowns are at an all-time high and several rides are down at once," said Mike Potts, head of the Building and Construction Trades Council at the time.

Although Disney executives dismissed the criticism as union carping, the evidence was quick in coming. Only weeks later, on August 6, 1997, two boys sprinted to Space Mountain in Disneyland just after the park opened, hoping to be the first in line. Instead, they found the escalator leading to their favorite roller coaster on fire. Disneyland firefighters put out the blaze in about ten minutes. The blaze was, apparently, maintenance related. Fortunately, no one was injured. But had it happened during the day's peak hours, it might have been disastrous.

Safety inspectors at Disneyland regularly turn up violations. Between 1992 and 1995, Occupational Safety and Health Administration (OSHA) inspections of Disneyland turned up complaints close to 20 percent of the time. For example, the park was hit for a $3,750 fine for a trolley accident that resulted in worker cutting part of his finger. It was cited another time for an accident involving a gas truck in which a worker injured a leg.

In Orlando, Disney World employees also say that the safety equipment doesn't always function the way it is supposed to. Michael Overcash was three weeks out of training in 1995 when he had his first dangerous situation arise on the Peter Pan ride. "I had a guest that was late getting into the car and I saw that he wasn't going to get all the way in before hitting the wall," he told us. "So I hit the e-stat— the power pack," which is supposed to stop the ride, "and it didn't work. He got lodged between the railing and the boat. It moved about three more feet before the ride stopped."

Sheila Randolph says she has had the same experience. "The power packs don't work very well," she told us of Dumbo and Small World. "You hit the button to stop the ride, but it just keeps going."

Deborah Clark says the systems she has worked at Spaceship Earth don't function much better. "I remember one guy that got pinned between a car and the wall," she told us. "We had punched the shutoff button but it didn't stop." The man, she says, ended up at the hospital with serious injuries.

Because Disney is a unionized company, several of these workers are active in the Service Employees International Union. Are they simply disgruntled? If we relied on their statements alone, that might

PROCESS

QUESTIONS	% UNFAVOR-ABLE	% FAVORABLE	AVERAGE
28. I receive the training I need to do my job well. (20)	43	58 ★	
29. Communication is effective and timely where I work. (21)	79	21	
30. I have the information I need to do my job well. (22)	57	43	
31. The flexibility of my work schedule meets my personal needs. (NQ)	64	35	
32. To perform my role, I have sufficient knowledge of the range of products and services WDW offers its Guests (23)	75	25	
33. My work group has the computer equipment (e.g. current technology, timely installation, help desk support) we need to do our job well (NQ)	50	50	
34. I am able to get the supplies, tools, and resources I need to do my job. (NQ)	55	44	
35. I am able to get the supplies, tools, and resources I need to do my job (25)	40	60 ★	
36. There is cooperation within my work group. (26)	70	31	
37. There is cooperation between my work group and other groups we work with at WDW. (27)	67	33	
38. My work group receives high quality products and services from other work groups on whom we depend. (28)	64	34	
39. We provide high quality products or services to other work groups who depend upon us. (29)	63	38	
40. The methods and procedures used where I work enable us to produce quality work in a timely manner. (30)	45	55 ★	
41. Where I work, we put safety first to provide secure, safe experiences for Cast Members. (31)	67	33	
42. Where I work, we take steps to prevent problems from recurring. (32)	★ 85	15	
43. Our area has the right number of Cast Members to deliver excellent service. (33)	69	31	
44. The increased use of part time Cast Members does not affect the quality of services we provide. (34)	77	23	

1997 Cast Excellence Analysis Tool
2

WORK LOCATION/DEPARTMENT CULTURE

QUESTIONS	% UNFAVOR-ABLE	% FAVORABLE	AVERAGE
21. The heritage and traditions of WDW continue to be valued within my work location/department. (NQ)	70	30	
22. My work location/department does not compromise on quality. (NQ)	★ 85	15	
23. Within my work location/department, long term success isnot compromised by short term decisions. (NQ)	79	21	
24. Within my work location/department, decisions are made at the level where the most adequate and accurate information is available. (NQ)	78	21	
25. My work location/department has an open work environment where infromation is shared freely. (NQ)	71	29	
26. There is an atmosphere of trust within my work location/department. (NQ)	92	7	
27. Within my work location/department,hourly and salaried Cast Members are appreciated and respected equally. (NQ)	76	23	

Results from Walt Disney World's 1997 survey of employees who work the rides at the theme parks offer some startling results. Figures from these annual surveys have never been published before.

be a reasonable conclusion. But Disney's own safety data supports what they say. And internal surveys conducted by the company itself shows that these safety concerns are not simply union carping but are shared by the majority of Disney World workers in maintenance and safety-related positions.

Every year the Walt Disney Company commissions an annual survey of its employees and asks dozens of questions about everything related to their job: working conditions, coworkers, corporate philosophy, supervisors, and safety. In essence the survey is an annual check-up on how employees themselves believe the company is doing its job, including handling guests. As you can imagine, these Cast Excellence Analysis Tool Surveys are highly prized and secretive documents. Even senior Disney managers and executives have a difficult time catching a glimpse of the results. Spencer Craig served Disney in several positions, including as the head of training for EPCOT at Disney University. He says managers are allowed to look at the results, but not keep their own copies. "It isn't something they want you keeping in your desk."

The survey results have never been published, perhaps because of the truly shocking findings in recent surveys. Employees who work the rides at Disney World do give the company good marks for making "friendly, individualized service a priority." Seventy-eight percent agree that the company does a fine job in that area. They also give the company high marks in its efforts to "understand guest expectations" (86 percent). But when questions arise about safety, the responses are grim. Question 3 on the 1997 survey asks: "Regarding 'Safety' WDW [Walt Disney World] puts safety first to provide secure, safe experiences for Guests." Fully 57 percent *disagree* with that statement. And Question 41 asks: "Where I work, we put safety first to provide secure, safe experiences for Cast Members [employees]." Seventy-six percent *disagree* with that statement. Employee concerns about safety seem to be broadly held in the company.

When an accident does happen at Disney World, the primary concern seems to be protecting the interests of the company rather than the health of the injured guest. Several employees told us they have strict instructions on what to do in the event of an accident. "The first call you make, if there is an accident, is to a supervisor and guests claims," says Overcash. Guest claims is a department of the company that deals with, among other things, customers who have been injured or the victim of a crime at Disney World.

You mean they don't call for an ambulance? No, insists Ben Keen. "When there is an accident, it's usually guest claims that gets called first, then 911. They want someone there before the ambulance to kiss butt."

Deborah Clark remembers vividly how those instructions actually work in practice. She recalls a man who got scared at Spaceship Earth a few years ago. He was apparently claustrophobic, she says, and he jumped off the ride when it began its climb into a dark tunnel. "He got off on the wrong side and landed in a motor. His leg got ground up. In the meantime, the ride is moving along and a manager was over there in seconds blocking the line before anybody saw anything. They pulled customers aside, and they shut the ride down to get customers away from seeing it. It was hushed up. My supervisor was there smoothing things over before anybody made sure the ambulance was there."

> **"The fact of the matter is if they would have complied with basic regulations, it could have avoided this death."**
> —Dean Tryer, OSHA spokesman

Overcash says that during the last couple of years there have been two heart attacks at Space Mountain, and the procedure was the same. "This guy stood up from the ride, walked two feet and fell to the ground. He had a heart attack after the ride. I was in the tower, and we have these cameras. I happened to see him fall, and I immediately said 'dispatch inhibit' which means 'stop the trains.' They don't want anybody else in the building to see this guy. I contacted my supervisor, and only then did I contact the ambulance."

In mid-1995, when Overcash was working Small World, he saw up close how the company worked. "This little girl had lost a finger—it was cut off because it was squeezed between the boat and the railing," he told us. "Guest claims got there before the ambulance. They were trying to get papers signed, to get all the legal things smoothed over even before the girl headed off for medical attention."

Employees say they are downright reluctant to call 911, even when there appears to be serious enough reason to. "If you call 911 and it's not valid that you called, you are reprimanded," says Clark. "They will say, 'You didn't need to call 911 for that.' They like to cover things up."

At other times, Disney won't even make a minimal investment for something that could save lives. Jungle Cruise employee Frank Kubicki says there have been several instances over the years of people complaining about chest pains and even heart attacks while on the boat ride, but the company doesn't want to take even necessary precautions to save lives. "Jungle Cruise is a ten-minute boat ride," he told us. "We don't have radios in the boat. If someone has a heart attack, you fire the starter pistol four times in the air and supposedly someone will hear it and call 911, and they will meet you at the dock. But it's a poor solution because it's so noisy at the park. Also, to save money Disney has gone to a cheaper blank for the gun which doesn't make a lot of noise. But that's our communication system. When the guns get wet—as they frequently do—they make a 'piff' sound. When you fire your gun for help you get 'piff-piff-piff-piff' and hope somebody hears you. You obviously return to the dock as soon as you can, but when someone is having a heart attack, those few minutes can make all the difference."

Disney's safety record has also come into question in recent years on the set of its movies. Again, the pattern seems to be the same: cut corners. In 1995 stuntwoman Janet Wilder was killed on the set of the film *Gone Fishin'*. Wilder died in her husband's arms in December after a stunt went wrong and a fast-moving boat plowed into her. The Collier County Florida Attorney's office investigated the case and concluded that negligence and inexperience on the part of the stunt coordinator contributed to the accident. But Deputy County Attorney Mike Provost elected not to press criminal charges only because he could not prove reckless disregard. "The culpable negligence statute requires a recklesness or indifference to what might happen almost to the extent that it's an intentional act," he said.

On February 25, 1998, stuntman Matthew Gordy was electrocuted on the set of the Disney film *Dinosaur*. During the preparations for filming, a camera boom swung about 50 feet into the air and touched a 115,000 volt power line. Gordy died at a nearby hospital, and David Riggio suffered burns to his hands and feet. The California Division of Occupational Safety and Health (Cal/OSHA) investigated the deaths and cited Disney for four violations. Cal/OSHA said Disney failed to properly train the film crew members handling a camera boom, and didn't post warning signs for the electrical dangers on the set. They also violated a state requirement that film equipment be kept at least ten feet from power lines. "The fact of the matter is if they would have complied with basic regulations, it could have avoided this death," says Dean Fryer, a spokesman for Cal/OSHA.

CHAPTER FIVE

Mickey Mouse Justice

One of Disney World's best customers is Saudi Princess Maha El-Sadari, sister-in-law to King Fahd. She can drop $1.2 million a day during a stay. In September 1995 she checked into the Swan Hotel at Disney World in Orlando and rented ninety rooms—two entire hotel floors—for her massive entourage. Because of concerns for her safety, Disney Security helped guard the facility and arranged for seventy off-duty Orange County Sheriff's Deputies to provide additional protection.

But one day after the princess and her entourage returned from the Magic Kingdom, a maid to the princess discovered that more than $100,000 in cash was missing from the royal trunk. The princess informed Disney's Security, but didn't file a report with the Florida police. Instead, she opted to beat one of her entourage whom she suspected of being the thief. When that didn't extract a confession, she picked up a high-heeled shoe and attempted to gouge the man's eye out, but was stopped by another maid who intervened to protect him. The princess then turned on her. When she was done, the maid had multiple contusions on her head, torso, and neck, and was left in a locked room.

Law enforcement finds out only about the crimes Disney wishes. The 911 system is run by Disney.

Two Orange County Sheriff's Officers, providing off-duty security, actually witnessed the beating, but felt constrained from intervening on Disney property. The company doesn't even allow Sheriff's Officers to carry weapons on Disney property without the Mouse's permission. Deputies say they were told that the tenth and eleventh floors of the Swan, which were occupied by the Saudi princess and her entourage, were to be treated as Saudi soil. Some even had the impression that she had diplomatic immunity and could break any law she wished.

After two days of confinement, the maid was still in severe pain from the beating. She later told investigators that she believed that if she returned to Saudi Arabia, she would likely be executed. Through the assistance of another servant, she was able to elicit help from a sympathetic Sheriff's deputy, who helped her escape and get medical treatment.

The maid eventually obtained a sizable cash settlement from the Saudis in exchange for dropping assault charges against the princess. Meanwhile, two Orange County Sheriff's sergeants were disciplined for their failing to properly deal with the assaults after they occurred. And the princess? She returned to Disney World in the summer of 1997 and once again received royal treatment from the Mouse.

The Disney property in central Florida crosses county lines and encompasses two municipalities. It extends beyond the theme park itself and includes resort hotels and recreational areas. Disney's intended effect is for guests to always feel that they are within a controlled, safe environment, sealed off from the rest of the country and its problems. Most of the time it achieves this goal. Visitors really do feel as though they have been transported to a magical kingdom. But guests are often so pumped up on feel-good hype that they literally don't see what's going on around them: acts of serious crime. And if you happen to be a victim of one of these crimes or are accused of committing one, Disney follows its own code of conduct and ethics.

What happens in and around the park becomes much clearer when you take a look at the Walt Disney World security manual, excerpts of which we obtained. The top edge of each page warns "not [to] be duplicated nor disclosed to others without the consent of the Walt Disney Company." And when you read the contents, you can understand why. Section 1, "Investigations and Standard Operating Procedures," describes the types of crimes mentioned by the Internal Investigations Section. Some of the first offenses mentioned are "sex crimes." According to the manual, Disney personnel are to investigate offenses such as "sexual battery, sexual assault, sexual harassment, child

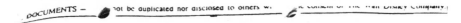

WALT DISNEY WORLD
INVESTIGATIONS STANDARD OPERATING PROCEDURES
SECTION 1
INTRODUCTION

- Economic Crimes - accepted name for what was once called "White Collar Crimes"; includes fraudulent checks, worthless checks, forged/ counterfeit travelers cheques, counterfeit cashier's checks, counterfeit/altered ticket media, stolen admission media, quick change artists, uttering of forged instruments, fraudulent claims, fraud, fraudulent insurance claims (user/provider), telephone fraud and telephone order fraud, mail order fraud, lost/stolen and counterfeit credit cards, computer and electronic systems fraud.

- Burglary - to include burglary to lodgings, vehicles, warehouse, retail shops, offices and vending machines.

- Grand Larceny Auto.

- Intoxicants/Possession/Use of Controlled Substance - possession, sale, use or receiving drugs or alcohol on WALT DISNEY WORLD property; alcohol sale to persons under the influence of alcohol or controlled substance.

- Disturbance/Assault/Battery - physical assaults, verbal and/or physical battery on guests, Cast Members, or participants.

- Malicious Threats - willful threat of harm, in person or telephonically, nuisance telephone calls; harassing telephone calls, bomb threats.

- Sexually Oriented - sexual battery, sexual assault, sexual harassment, child molestation, voyeurism, exhibitionism, public masturbation, indecent exposure, lewd and lascivious acts, prostitution, and obscene telephone calls.

- Counterfeit - the identification and verification of counterfeit currency and counterfeit media; the surveillance of subjects; and notification to appropriate law enforcement agency.

The Disney security manual, which as the top line indicates is not to be duplicated or disclosed to others, describes the sorts of crimes that security investigators handle at the theme parks.

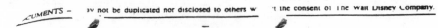

WALT DISNEY WORLD
INVESTIGATIONS STANDARD OPERATING PROCEDURES
SECTION 1
INTRODUCTION

Within the Internal Investigations section are Investigators possessing acquired skills, talent and capabilities which enable the unit to conduct investigations
involving sex crimes, comparative handwriting analysis,
forensic diagrams, identification composites, questioned documents, arson investigation, moulage cast-
ings, photograph, latent prints, tool markings,
electronic detection/surveillance, alcohol/tobacco
inspection, counter terrorist tactics and hostage
negotiations.

.4 TYPES OF INVESTIGATIONS

Investigations are divided into several different
categories as follows:

- Larceny - thefts from WALT DISNEY WORLD and
participants of monies, property or services; thefts from guests and Cast Members
of monies or property. This includes thefts
of the following nature: cash bag, manager's fund, register (overring, underring,
voids), merchandise, WALT DISNEY WORLD
assets, costuming, lost and found property,
and construction related thefts.

- Misappropriation, Destruction, Defacing -
misuse or unauthorized use of Company passes, I.D., discounts, copyright, logo, or
property; the impersonation or misrepresen-
tation of Company officials; malicious
damage to WALT DISNEY WORLD, guest, or Cast
Member property; and industrial sabotage.

- Violation of Company Policy - violation of
cash handling procedures, leaving work area
without permission, possession or exhibition
of a firearm, safety violations, out of
bounds guests, unlawful entry, disturbances,
soliciting, trespass after warning, chain
letters, gambling, loitering and prowling,
false alarms, false reports, falsification
of Company documents, misuse of confidential
information, falsification of application,
misconduct/moral turpitude.

molestation, voyeurism, exhibitionism, public masturbation, indecent exposure, lewd and lascivious acts, prostitution, and obscene telephone calls." Beyond sex crimes, other offenses listed in the manual include everything from larceny, theft, and unlawful entry to gambling.

To understand law and order Disney style, you need to know something about the structure of Disney World. All Disney property falls within something called the Reedy Creek Improvement District. There are only two cities within this municipality, Lake Buena Vista and Bay Lake, with a combined population of approximately forty-two residents. These residents live in Disney housing and work for the company. The city councils of these municipalities execute only one vote of consequence each year: turning over control of roads, utilities, inspections, licensing, and law enforcement functions to the Reedy Creek Improvement District.

Reedy Creek was set up in 1967 by the Florida Legislature at the request of the Walt Disney Company. The official Disney company line is that Reedy Creek is an independent, governing organization. But when you figure out how Reedy Creek is actually run, you realize this is sheer fantasy. In the words of Richard Fogelsong, a professor at nearby Rollins College and a veteran Disney watcher, "It's legal magic."

Charles Ray Maxwell is the city manager of Lake Buena Vista. But he is also the director of planning and finance for the Reedy Creek Improvement District. Plus, he's an employee of the Walt Disney World Company. Disney exerts control by directing the hiring, firing, promotion, and salaries of all Reedy Creek employees. That control is evident in a May 26, 1989, internal Disney memo obtained by the authors. The memo is from Steve Heise, of Disney's Compensation Department, to Disney Senior Vice President Phil Smith. It concerns Tom Moses, the top administrative officer for Reedy Creek. In the memo, Heise discusses both Moses's salary and employment status. The memo makes reference to the late Disney Company President Frank Wells and Dick Nunis, chairman of Walt Disney Attractions. It makes clear that Nunis will need to get approval from Wells on both the scope of the position and Tom Moses's compensation before any employment commitment can be made. In other words, Reedy Creek's top administrative officer's job and pay are determined by Disney executives.

If you want a job with Reedy Creek you are interviewed by Disney's "Casting Office." (Disney does not have employees at the park, only "Cast Members.") And if you are hired to work at Reedy Creek, you will be on the Disney health plan, have access to Disney benefits, and receive a company pin that identifies your years of service.

So why does Disney bother to create this fiction known as Reedy Creek? Because it gives Disney the power of a government, special authority like no other company in the United States. "They have immunity from state and local land use law," Fogelsong told us. "They can build a nuclear plant, distribute alcohol. They have powers that local communities don't have. They're like the Vatican with Mouse ears. Do they abuse this power? In my opinion, yes."

Reedy Creek contracts with Disney to provide security for Disney World. According to FBI veteran Perry Doran, until recently head of Disney World Security, the company today has eight hundred Security "hosts and hostesses" at Disney World, up from five hundred only a few years ago. While most of these are "blues"—uniformed Security officials who are present throughout the park—there is also a separate investigative division that includes thirty-eight investigators. "We have a rather large number of hosts/hostesses within the Security division, and their placement across Walt Disney World is both within the parks and the resorts," says Doran. They are trained to be "extremely proactive, extremely guest relations oriented."

While that may be Disney's public face, you discover something altogether different when you investigate their operations and the cases that occur on their property. Disney Security is not the police, but it does have powers that other security forces only dream of. And to protect its image, the company is quite willing to use its force at the public's expense. "I don't think there is any corporation like Disney," says former Florida Assistant State Attorney Eric Faddis, now an Orlando attorney. "There is no other corporation that has ever had the perceived power that Disney has."

To really grasp Disney's power, you need to listen to local law enforcement officers. Before any officer is allowed on Disney property, he must surrender his firearm. (If you own a business, try that the next time a law enforcement officer comes in and see how far you get.) Trooper Terry Hoops of the Florida Highway Patrol (FHP) remembers when Disney Security demanded he surrender his weapon. "I was instructed to meet a limousine at the airport with Oriental dignitaries in it, and I was instructed to escort them to Disney World, where they would remain for maybe thirty minutes. As they walked through the property, my instructions were to remain with them from the time I picked them up until the time they were released to travel to Tampa. Another trooper was also there to escort them from Orlando to Tampa.

"We met at Walt Disney World. The news media was there. There were pictures taken and so forth. Then once they entered through the turnstiles into the Magic Kingdom itself we did the same. We probably went fifty feet before we were approached by several gentlemen in suits that identified themselves as Walt Disney Security. I was satisfied that's who they were, and they instructed us that they did not allow firearms inside the park. And he instructed me to either release the firearm to him or secure it in my vehicle. I told him I was not going to do either one of those. Then he said, 'you need to wait outside the turnstiles until these dignitaries come back out.'" Because of the public attention and the presence of the media, Hoops says, "I didn't press the issue." Obviously the Mouse feels entirely comfortable telling law enforcement officials what they can and cannot do in Disney World.

> "They don't like law enforcement out there because they want it to be the Magic Kingdom. That's a fine image to portray. But it's a corporate mentality, not a concern for public safety."

Orange County Sheriff's Office Detective Matt Irwin says the same thing happened to him when he visited a Disney hotel for an official investigation. "We needed to go over to the Dolphin [hotel] on business and we had to hide our guns because the Dolphin wouldn't let us in with them," he told us. "Instead of making an issue out of it we just hid our guns and denied that we had any." Of course this is all about image—bad things just don't happen in the Magic Kingdom. No guns are allowed, even for law enforcement. "They don't like law enforcement out there because they want it to be the Magic Kingdom," says Irwin. "That's a fine image to portray. But it's a corporate mentality, not a concern for public safety."

Actions taken by Disney's Security also demonstrate that public safety is not its number one concern. Just ask Captain Robert Flemming of the FHP. Flemming is a district commander with approximately 110 men under his authority. One of his duties is to keep the roads of central Florida safe by dealing with drunk drivers. His unit conducts concentrated patrols near bars to identify intoxicated patrons getting into their cars to drive off. A local paramedic is ordered to administer a blood alcohol test to those identified, and, if they fail, they are charged on the spot.

During the course of the last ten years Disney has, with the opening of several bars, become active in the nightclub business. So it is only natural that some of these patrols would occur at Disney. But according to Flemming, Disney just isn't cooperating. While the FHP has run these patrols near Disney bars such as Pleasure Island, Reedy Creek paramedics refuse to draw blood for blood alcohol tests, thus leaving the patrols ineffective. This unwillingness to cooperate actually violates the law. A Florida statute makes it a misdemeanor if a paramedic or an emergency technician certified in Florida refuses a request by the FHP to draw blood.

But Disney does more than fail to cooperate with the law. On January 9, 1996, a car swerved down Bonnie Creek Road at Disney World and smashed into a light pole. The injured driver shook off the initial shock and then drove on. A Disney Security guard at a nearby EPCOT Center Security outpost witnessed the accident and called for an ambulance: "vehicle versus lightpole, female in her forties, facial injuries, alcohol related."

The intoxicated driver then steered her car into the intersection of Backstage Lane and Lake Buena Vista Drive, where it came to a complete stop. Disney Security Officer Jonathan Hall saw the vehicle and called the FHP. He said that an accident involving alcohol had occurred. But when a Disney Security supervisor learned that the drunk driver was a Disney manager, a cover-up was launched. Someone from Disney contacted the FHP and had the responding trooper called off. The FHP dispatch card reads: "authority to cancel call: Per Disney." Disney Security apparently took the manager home and never told the FHP the full story.

When asked about the incident, Disney explains that the whole thing was an innocent mistake. "This was a serious error in judgment—motivated by a sincere desire to help a fellow employee who needed treatment for minor injuries and a safe ride home." But the FHP says what the Disney manager really needed was a blood alcohol test. The Highway Patrol also believes Disney committed a crime by obstructing its investigation of a drunk driving accident. "That's a criminal offense, that's a crime scene," says Lieutenant Chuck Williams of the FHP, who is familiar with the case. "We view that as a crime scene, because DUI [Driving Under the Influence] is a crime."

In April 1998 Disney World announced that it would allow limited FHP patrols on its property, but it's unclear how much real access to the property the deputies will have.

Disney does have some law enforcement presence in the Magic Kingdom. There is an office which had six Sheriff's Officers up until April 1998, when the number increased to nineteen. Sergeant Barbara Lewis, who is highly thought of by her colleagues, is assigned to run the office. "Disney pays the Sheriff's Office a set amount of money, including the salaries of the deputies assigned here," she told us. "But we come under the complete control of the sheriff. We don't work for Disney."

Lewis says her chief job is to combat crimes in progress and to investigate serious offenses. Yet it's virtually impossible for deputies to investigate crimes without Disney's involvement. Lewis told us relations with Disney Security are "pretty good." But she cautions, "You have to remember, Disney Security is not a police agency. They are a private agency that works for the company's private interests." Usually a sergeant and only a couple of deputies are on duty at the same time.

And they find out about only those crimes Disney chooses to tell them about. The 911 system, which handles all emergency calls, is run by Disney and Reedy Creek. "If they are hiding something," she says with a laugh, "there wouldn't be any way for me to know about it."

Although every year thousands of guests report criminal activity, Disney simply writes a report that is rarely forwarded to law enforcement. According to Ann Davis of the Reedy Creek Improvement District, the district operates the 911 system and reports crimes to Disney. Then one of its eight hundred investigative or Security people start "substantiating and corroborating the evidence." Only if they see fit does the report get forwarded to the Sheriff's Office.

What Disney *is* hiding, along with drunk driving incidents and sex crimes, are cases of domestic battery and possible assaults that never get fully investigated. In November 1996, for example, Disney Security was called to a domestic battery scene at the Caribbean Beach Resort. According to Disney records, Security found a woman who claimed her attacker slapped her and tried to strangle her several times. She had red abrasions on her neck. Domestic violence is one of those crimes that, if a police officer sees signs of injury, somebody is going to jail even if the victim is reluctant to press charges. But Disney Security never even called the police. It was left to the victim to place a call nine hours later, but by that time the suspect had fled.

Disney officials will also tamper with a crime scene. "You can ask any deputy around here that Disney has had dead bodies moved from the property before calling the Sheriff's Office," says Detective Irwin. "You get a call to 'go to Sand Lake Hospital in reference to a death that occurred at Disney World.' That's the phrase you hear—no one dies on Disney property. Of course moving the body is a no-no. It destroys most of the evidence you need for an investigation."

Commander Brad Margeson of the Sheriff's Office recalls one instance when a homicide investigation was hampered. "There was an apparent suicide out on the Disney property, and by the time investigators arrived, Disney people had already begun to clean up from the crime scene, which is of course taboo. We wanted the area sealed off and nothing touched."

Disney's only reason for housing the Sheriff's Office on its property is to deal with the one group of crimes it does take seriously: economic crimes. "The biggest things we deal with are counterfeiting and petty theft," says Lewis.

Disney, in fact, is vigilant about economic crimes. "They have deputies out there every night to deal with shoplifters," says Detective Irwin. "Disney Security brings in statements from people who have been accused of shoplifting, and they just write it up and they take them to jail. They get strip searched, fumigated, the whole bit. That's a big deal. That is something Disney is obviously willing to participate in. But when it comes to something like more serious crimes, they aren't that interested."

You can only imagine what a problem shoplifting is with hundreds of thousands of guests moving through the turnstiles every week. According to sources in Disney Security, there are approximately eight shoplifting arrests a day at Walt Disney World. The company practices "zero tolerance." Even in cases in which an individual may have taken a 98-cent pen, Disney security calls the Sheriff's Office and has the suspected thief handcuffed and taken to jail.

But sometimes innocent tourists get trapped in this web. Before law enforcement is called to take them away, they may be held for up to four hours in a small room on Disney property with no access to a bathroom, telephone, or water.

Vicki Prusnofsky is a metropolitan New York social worker who made numerous trips to Disney World with her daughter and husband, a psychiatrist. One time, while the other two went to ride the little race cars at the Grand Prix attraction, Mrs. Prusnofsky—accessorized in Mickey and Minnie earrings and a Disney hat and sweatshirt—went to a shop to buy film. She said she didn't bother to take her receipt when exiting the shop.

"I finally went outside and sat on a bench and started loading the camera," she said. "These two obnoxious Security women came after me flashing their badges and saying that I stole the film." She asked to go back into the store. The cashier could vouch for her story, she said. But the Security women refused.

Instead, she was taken to a Security office where she was asked to present receipts for the Disney pins and clothing she'd purchased on previous trips. "I just started crying," she said. She was then turned over to Orange County Sheriff's Deputies, handcuffed, booked, fingerprinted, strip searched, and thrown into a cell with "whores and thieves," who, according to Mrs. Prusnofsky, harassed and flirted with her for hours.

Seventeen-year-old Terri Dorsett of Yadkinville, North Carolina, received similar treatment when she visited Disney World with her high school band in 1995. Following a performance, Terri and a few classmates visited a Disney store and were arrested for shoplifting. They were taken to the Security office, fingerprinted, and prevented from calling anybody. But Terri was innocent. One of the other girls admitted to dropping a $1.98 Mickey Mouse pen into Terri's shopping bag without her knowledge. Still the Mouse persisted in pressing shoplifting charges.

Thomas Dorsett, Terri's father, met with prosecutors and seemingly sympathetic Disney officials. He thought the company would drop her case, but it never did. Dorsett ended up hiring an attorney and spending $15,000 to fight the criminal charges. The case went to trial, and Terri was acquitted. Tom Dorsett expressed his frustration. "It's scary what can happen to a child," he said. "The prosecutor's office, they are scared of Disney. Disney rules that area with an iron fist. It's a joke. Mickey Mouse is not the guy we thought he was."

Even Disney "Cast Members" can get the shakedown. Michael Gibbons is a former Orange County prosecutor who now practices law in Orlando. He used to prosecute Disney employees and says that employees caught stealing can expect swift justice. "When they caught someone stealing money out of the till, any economic crime, they wanted the book thrown at them," he recalls. "But more serious crimes they seem unwilling to do much about. If it costs them money, they want justice. Otherwise, forget about it."

One seventeen-year-old employee who worked in the ice cream shop at Disneyland found out the hard way how things can work at the Mouse. Detained by security because she forgot to check her uniform in after leaving work, the young woman was questioned for two hours. Disneyland security refused even to let her call her mother, Marilyn Dortch. "There is no Constitution in Disneyland," one Security official told her. "We have our own laws."

And in a sense Disney does have their its own laws. David Sklansky, a law professor at UCLA, says, "One of the major problems is that we don't really know what Disney Security agents are doing—how often they stop, interrogate, search, or detain people. They're not subject to the same regulatory control as the civil police."

According to Kevin Beary, sheriff of Orange County, Florida, Disney has a distinct advantage by running its own internal investigations. "When they get information and they get a suspect to talk, they don't have to worry about the constitutional rights and all that stuff. We do."

Disney can also choose how it handles crimes that occur on its property. It often does fail to pass along reports to local authorities. It's okay if Disney doesn't report crimes against Disney property, because Disney is the victim, says Michael Cofield, formerly a sergeant of the Orange County Sheriff's Office, who worked for three-and-a-half years at the Disney office. The company has the right to want to seek prosecution or not. But it should report crimes involving members of the public, including guests and employees, to the Sheriff's Office, he says.

Attorney Eric Faddis, former assistant state attorney, thinks there are larger issues here. "The overriding theme of their actions is what is convenient for Disney is number one. Everybody else takes second place. Just because you are the victim of a crime, too bad. It's going to cause us more grief to pass that information on than it will if we bury it. And because it is going to be more expedient to us, we are going to bury it. We don't care whether you are going to get justice or not."

It's what you might call Mickey Mouse justice.

● ● ●

HARRY PARSELL, a former investigations manager at Disney World, says that during his tenure he saw thousands of reports concerning accidents and crimes in the parks. Yet very few of these incidents became public. And since Disney is a private company, getting access to these reports is nearly impossible. "There is so much control exerted by Walt Disney World out there that only sensational cases make it through the barrier of secrecy," says Eric Faddis.

Security aside, when things go wrong, don't count on Disney to help. Consider the case of eight-year-old Paul Santamaria. On October 10, 1986, Paul and his family were staying at the Walt Disney World campgrounds for a quiet vacation. Paul went down to the pond with some old bread to feed the ducks. An alligator lunged from the water and grabbed him by the leg. Paul desperately fought to keep from being pulled into the water and eventually freed himself, and survived.

Paul's father asked the company to pay his son's medical bills from the alligator attack. "They flat out refused to admit that Paul had been bit," says Orlando attorney John Overchuck, who represented them. Only after he threatened to make an alligator tooth extracted from Paul's leg "Exhibit A" in a civil suit did the company agree to pay up.

In April 1993 Jaime and Elena Boruchovas, a Uruguayan couple, celebrated their thirtieth wedding anniversary with a visit to Walt Disney World.

On April 8, after a full day in the Magic Kingdom, Jaime and Elena mingled with a crowd near Main Street for the Spectro Magic Parade. All the regulars passed: Donald, Mickey, even Chip 'n Dale. Then came the float carrying Snow White and the Seven Dwarfs, their costumes glittering with electric lights. Suddenly the float careened out of control and headed for the crowd. Dopey flew off the float and landed on Elena: His lights exploded and burned her left leg, seriously injuring it, and she was rushed to nearby Sand Lake Hospital by medical personnel.

After a few days of treatment, Elena received a visitor. Jose Santos was a claims representative from Walt Disney World who spoke flawless Spanish and presented her with a Minnie Mouse doll. He also offered the couple a check for $1,222. According to Jaime and Elena, he said all they needed to do for the money was to sign a "receipt." The document was in English, which neither Jaime nor Elena could read or speak, but Santos told them not to worry and convinced them to sign on the dotted line. He then even drove them to a nearby bank to make sure they cashed the check. Only later did they discover that the document they signed was intended to absolve Disney of any responsibility for the accident.

When the Boruchovases returned to Uruguay, Elena was told by her doctors at the Mutualista Israelita del Uruguay Medical Center that her wounded left leg was infected and would require skin grafts. Since Disney claimed to be absolved of all responsibility, the couple decided to sue to cover the medical costs. A legal battle of mammoth proportions started brewing.

Attorney Spencer Aronfeld represented the Boruchovases and had a difficult time getting any information from Disney. "They were relentless," Aronfeld told us. "And they hide witnesses." While anyone who might have witnessed the event had been duly noted by Disney personnel at the scene, the company was not about to share that information. And Disney employees who witnessed the event were told in a company letter not to speak with Aronfeld under any circumstances.

But one employee was so disturbed by the attempted cover-up that the warning backfired. "I got contacted by Minnie Mouse," Aronfeld says with a laugh. "She said she was a witness. They sent her the letter, and she was upset. The first thing she did was pick up the phone and call me." When the trial began on May 22, 1995, Jennifer Fahey (a.k.a. Minnie Mouse) was the first witness. While Disney's Claims Department, represented by Bill Dammes, testified that Claims Representative Santos had done nothing wrong and was merely following company policy, that wasn't good enough for the jury that had seen photos (which Disney tried to keep out of court) of Elena's injuries. In May 1995 Elena was awarded $100,000.

Elena's case is not unusual. When there is an accident or mishap, Disney Security immediately takes statements from witnesses at the scene and writes a report. These reports, however, can be biased. "They get that injury reported in the light most favorable to them," Orlando attorney John Morgan told us. "You never have a witness in the interim report that has anything unfavorable to say about Disney."

Although Morgan has been involved in at least seventy-five cases involving Disney, he does claim to have a bit of a soft spot for the company for a couple of reasons. The treasurer of the company has dined at his house. And "before I went to law school, I worked at Disney World for seven years," he says with a smile. "I was Pluto."

But some Disney cases are impossible to cast in anything but a horrible light. On October 9, 1989, Patricia Shenck and her eight-year-old son Brian decided to take a spin on a "water sprite," the jet skis at Disney's Seven Seas Lagoon. Shortly before 3:00 PM, the two headed out on the water and scooted along the coastline until they experienced mechanical problems. As Brian told investigators, the water sprite got stuck in the water when his mother couldn't get the gear shift out of neutral. Meanwhile, the ferryboat *Kingdom Queen*, with ninety passengers on board, was fast approaching them. The inexperienced, twenty-three-year-old pilot of Disney's *Queen* blasted the horn to warn the Shencks to get out of the way. According to witnesses, Mrs. Shenck heard the horn and desperately tried to work the throttle, but without success. The two vessels collided, and Patricia and Brian fell into the water. Going against standard instructions, the pilot of the *Queen* put the massive 550-horse-power diesel engine in reverse. Mrs. Shenck was pulled under. Brian and the guests on board the ferryboat could only watch in horror as the propellers lacerated her body.

Just minutes later Sam Bean got a radio call about the accident. A detective with the Orange County Sheriff's Office and a member of the special operations group in the Marine Patrol Division, Beam was responsible for directing the investigation of any water fatalities that happened in the county. When something bad happens, he says, "the Marine Patrol investigator takes control and charge of the boating accident." But when he arrived at the scene at 3:59 PM, he realized right away that he wasn't in charge. The Mouse was.

Disney had sent divers into the water to collect evidence. "I observed divers in the water when I first arrived at the scene," he recalls. There were eight divers in all, six searching for the body and two removing pieces of the victim's clothing snagged to the underside of the ferry. Passengers were unloaded at the scene and put on another boat. This was all being done without Bean's permission, and potentially valuable evidence was being destroyed. But Bean couldn't do anything to get them to stop. Once the Disney divers located the body, they tethered it to a buoy and left it in the lagoon for a couple of hours. Disney managers refused to have the body moved until nightfall.

We've heard a common refrain from law enforcement: Disney is more interested in protecting its image than in allowing local authorities to investigate fatalities. Law enforcement professionals, like Sergeant Harlan Drawdy of the Florida Highway Patrol (FHP), says that Disney officials impede and discourage their efforts to investigate serious car crashes on company property.

Corporal Scott Walter is a traffic homicide investigator and a seventeen-year veteran of the FHP. On August 31, 1994, he was called to investigate a traffic death near Disney World. All he was told, he recalls, was that "Disney Security had been involved in this fatal crash." A Disney Security officer had been in pursuit of two teenagers in a truck, traveling at speeds exceeding ninety miles per hour. The pursuit continued even after the vehicles left Disney property. The truck careened off the road, crashed into a tree, and was consumed by flames. Eighteen-year-old Robbie Simpkema was trapped inside and burned to death. (His friend was severely injured.)

It fell to Corporal Walter to find out exactly what happened. "When I started the investigation I had no eyewitnesses," he says. There was only one person who could fully explain what took place: Susan Buckland, the Disney Security officer who had been in pursuit of the truck. Walter wanted to interview her.

But Disney Security simply would not cooperate. According to Walter, he tried to contact Buckland "many times. I made appointments with her through Disney Security. I tried contacting her at home. She was never available to me."

While Walter was interested in talking to Buckland, he also wanted access to the dispatch tape—a recording of the conversation between Buckland, headquarters, and the other Security personnel involved in the chase. "I tried several times to get a copy of the tapes involved that had anything to do with this particular case. The first time they said that they would make arrangements to get a copy for me. The second time they said that it was being prepared. They also told me that two copies had been made for individuals at Disney and that they shouldn't have trouble getting me one. When I tried again they said that it was unavailable, that it had been taped over."

Walter never got the information he needed. Everything got sucked down into a giant black Mouse hole. The death of young Robbie changed the lives of his parents forever. But it also radically changed their view of Disney. "You always think of Disney as do-gooders," says Robert Simpkema. "Once you lose a son and you become involved, you find out that there is a lot that goes on behind the scenes."

Mr. Simpkema is not alone.

"It used to be difficult to find a jury in Orlando that would find against Disney," says attorney John Overchuck, who has tried numerous injury cases against the Mouse. "But we have done some jury profiling recently. Now the best jury members are those who have had contact with Disney. What you want is a relative of a former employee on the jury. They know what's going on out there. In one recent two-million-dollar case the jury included the spouse of a former Disney manager."

CHAPTER SIX

Disney's Pedophile Problem

In early July 1997 Christopher Laber checked the e-mail on his personal computer. Much to his delight a thirteen-year-old boy named Joe had left a message. The kid claimed to have gotten the address from a friend who suggested that he write Laber, a transportation supervisor at Disney World. Working for Disney was always a hit with kids. But Laber wasn't just a part of the Magic Kingdom: He was also an active pedophile who used the connection to his advantage.

Laber responded immediately to the note from Joe in a July 8 message. He briefly introduced himself and signed it "ISO [in search of] men." Three days later he e-mailed his picture and a note suggesting that the two chat live on the Internet. The next day they did.

Joe started the conversation with a simple "Hi." Laber mentioned that he worked at Disney, an inducement he had used before to lure boys. As the conversation progressed, Laber tried to elicit sexually explicit comments from Joe, and he asked if they could meet within the next few days.

Sure, said Joe.

Laber left his telephone and pager numbers. Why don't you call me on Monday morning, July 14? he asked.

Joe agreed and they signed off. But Laber was so anxious not to lose his thirteen-year-old victim, he sent Joe another e-mail message on Sunday, reminding the boy to call.

On Monday morning Christopher Laber was speaking with Joe. The boy came off as shy and timid. They made some small talk, but Laber became impatient. After only a few minutes of idle chatter, he steered the conversation to the subject of sex. Laber told the boy that he was a "pleaser" who "will do whatever he can to make a person happy."

Joe seemed uncertain about the sexual advance. "I'm sexually inexperienced and confused about my sexual preference," he said. Laber decided to capitalize on his confusion and pressed the boy. "You have to start somewhere. When you do something for the first time it's always new."

There was a pause in the conversation. Joe said he was scared. He also said that he didn't like pain and wasn't interested in any sex acts that would be painful. Sensing things were moving his way, Laber tried to reassure him. He told him that he had recently had sex with another young boy named Matt. "We did just about everything. I mean, I met him a few times, and ah—we fooled around a little bit." Laber then became more explicit and aggressive, and went on to describe the techniques he would use to take away the pain of intercourse.

By now Laber was feeling confident so he decided to pressure the boy to meet him right away. Joe said that Laber could come and visit since no one else was in the apartment. Laber said "great" and hung up the phone. Minutes later he was in his brick red Pontiac Grand Prix, driving toward Joe's apartment on Kirkman Road. He passed the apartment twice, but something made him nervous. After hesitating, he sped off quickly and headed home. Minutes later, three detectives from the Orange County Sheriff's Office were in front of his place.

"What's your name?" one of them asked him.

"Christopher Laber," he said. "Why?"

The trap was sprung. Detective Matt Irwin stepped forward and informed Laber that Joe was not a thirteen-year-old boy, but, instead, a Sheriff's Deputy. "You'll have to come to the station with us."

The deputies followed Laber into his apartment. "The place was filled with Disney stuff, a real shrine," recalls Irwin. There were stuffed animals, characters, and movie posters. They seized his computer as evidence and then took him down to the Sheriff's Investigation Building for an interview. Irwin read him his Miranda rights (which he waived) and then started to question him. Laber said he had chatted with "Joe" on America Online. He also confessed that he had intended to have sex with the boy.

Detectives from the Orange County Sheriff's Office Sex Crimes Unit targeted Christopher Laber with the sting operation because they had been tipped off about his activities just a few months earlier. In May, a mother named Lori Brooks had told the Sheriff's Office that her son, a thirteen-year-old, had been seduced by an adult male. The boy had met him by using a chat room on America Online. They met in person on three occasions, each time engaging in oral and anal sex.

With Laber now in custody, Mrs. Brooks brought her son to the Sheriff's Investigation Building to look at a photo lineup. The boy picked Laber out immediately. The boy's sworn testimony helped lead to Laber's being charged with an attempted lewd act upon a child and possession of computer pornography.

During the investigation, detectives discovered something shocking about Laber's seduction techniques. "He used Disney stuff to curry favor with the boy," says Irwin. "He gave him hats, T-shirts, and other paraphernalia. He used his employee card to buy the gifts at a discount. Disney gifts are good at helping to gain trust."

Christopher Laber is a sexual predator who, as an anonymous Disney employee, used his Magic Kingdom connection to entice young boys. But he is not alone. Disney is a magnet for pedophiles, who prowl in search of kids. While some pedophiles are visitors who come and go, many actually work for the company. This is not a problem unique to Disney. Theme parks and many other businesses that attract kids also attract abusers. The problem is that at the new Disney there is, once again, a lot more concern with covering up the problem than with protecting kids. One result is that some of Disney's pedophiles—unlike Laber, a transportation supervisor—are positioned in high-profile jobs dealing with children. Sometimes they are even Emmy-award winners.

On April 6, 1997, Matt Irwin was searching for pedophiles on the information superhighway by using America Online while posing under the screen name "Niki012." He listed "Nikki" as a twelve-year-old girl and, in his member description, wrote "Looking for something more" in the "Personal Quote" section.

That evening he was in a chat room entitled Orlando, which is one of many chat rooms that allow individuals from around the world to converse with each other in real time using their computer. Suddenly an "Instant Message" appeared on his screen. An Instant Message is a private communication between two members that is independent of and cannot be seen by anyone else in the chat room. It was from "NSWRFL" and he asked "Looking for something more????? What more is there?"

NSWRFL was someone named Chris. He e-mailed a photo of himself. He said he was from Australia and asked Nikki her age.

"Thirteen," Nikki replied.

"Where do you live?" Chris asked her.

"Kirkman/Conroy area" (a suburb of Orlando).

"So... tell me about you."

"5-5, 105, auburn hair and hazel eyes."

"I love hazel eyes," Chris responded. "Have you ever had sex?" he asked.

Irwin thought for a moment before typing in "never gone all the way."

"I'd love to meet you," Chris wrote back enthusiastically, "but I know I'd wind up getting in big trouble." He warned that if they ever had a physical relationship, it would have to remain a secret or he could end up in jail.

A lull emerged in the conversation, but Chris persisted. "How could I meet you? I mean, would we have a chance to be together? If we dated?" There was no immediate response from Nikki, so Chris pressed on. "Do you want to meet me sometime?"

Nikki finally said okay, and Chris left his telephone number. Call tomorrow, he asked.

Nikki told Chris she had to go to bed and said good night. Irwin, however, purposely stayed online. About fifteen minutes later, Chris sent another "Instant Message" reminding Nikki to call and making sure she had the phone number. "I'm probably going to dream about you tonight," he wrote before finally signing off.

The next morning Detective Julia Blackmon, posing as Nikki, placed a call to Chris, with Detective Irwin listening in. Much to their surprise, the detectives discovered that the phone number was to the Animation Section at Walt Disney World. It was Chris who answered the phone.

Hi, this is Nikki, Blackmon said meekly.

Chris said he was glad she had called. "Chris began by telling me he worked for Walt Disney World," Detective Blackmon recalls. "Chris stated he was currently working on the new Walt Disney World movie. Chris stated he drew pictures for the movie." He also told her that he wanted to go on a date that day, "real bad."

I need to call my mom to get permission, Blackmon told him. I'll call you right back.

After Blackmon hung up the phone, the detectives decided to plan the meeting for the next day so they could make sure they were adequately prepared for a bust. Blackmon called Chris back a few minutes later. I can't meet you today, she said quietly. My mom won't let me out.

Chris worked hard to try to convince Nikki that she should allow him to come over to her place regardless of her mother's decision.

You might think that if there were one single crime that Disney would work aggressively to counter it would be child molestation. But you would be wrong.

Since your mom is at work, he said, she'll never find out. For some time, he continued trying to persuade her. "He pursued her relentlessly," recalls Irwin, who was listening in on the conversation. He explained that the age difference wouldn't bother him. "I have talked to many young girls and met with them," he explained.

Fearing that Chris might get suspicious, Irwin decided to proceed and gave Blackmon the go ahead.

"Okay," Blackmon said to Chris. "Why don't we meet today. But pick a location where I can meet you."

Chris said he was at work and chose a parking lot at a nearby Nations Bank for them to meet. He told her he'd be driving a red and silver Dodge Ram pickup and wearing a "Disney" shirt and baseball cap.

After Blackmon hung up the phone, Irwin worked frantically to put together a Felony Squad to make the arrest. Within an hour, they had set up surveillance of the parking lot.

At about 5:50 PM Chris arrived in his truck and pulled up in a parking space. Members of the Felony Squad approached him and asked for his name. Nervously he told them "Christopher Bradley." Detective Irwin then identified himself and placed Bradley under arrest. They handcuffed him and took him to the Orange County Sheriff's Office Investigation Building.

Once in the interview room, Irwin read Bradley his Miranda rights (which he waived) and the detectives began talking with him. Bradley admitted that he was expecting to meet a thirteen-year-old girl named Nikki and that he was hoping to engage in sex with her. "I've never met her; I've never seen a picture of her," he told investigators. "But the thought ah, the thought of it was ah, intriguing but not something I've ever pursued before."

Bradley assured the detectives that this was something new for him—"a big mistake." "I like kids," he explained, "we have a lot of chil—children and older kids coming through the [Disney] studios. We have a wondrous program there that they run through the studios and you know, ah, kids usually enjoy talking to me about my job and it's kind of fun talking to them."

Sheriff's deputies told Bradley that they would need to search his computer, and the animator reluctantly agreed. He got into his truck, and the deputies followed him home. "We could tell he was real nervous about something," Irwin told us. "He pulled over along the roadside a few times and threw up."

Bradley's place was filled with a variety of Disney figures and posters. There was even an ornate certificate on the wall noting that he "had won an Emmy for his work on a 'Winnie the Pooh' cartoon," recalls Irwin. "He showed it to me."

The detectives took his computer back to the office and began working their way through the files on the hard drive. What they discovered was that Pooh apparently wasn't the only image Christopher Bradley was interested in. On his computer hard drive were 286 graphic image files, most of which were pornographic.

Irwin took the files to Dr. Matthew Seibel, a pediatrician for the Child Protection Team of the Sheriff's Office and an expert in determining the age of children in photographic images. Seibel looked through files with names like "10boysis," "!10grl," "!lilsis," "!boy&sis,"

Orange County Sheriff's Office   *Orlando, Florida*
Supplemental Report   *Case Number* **97-138338**

Investigator:	**DET. JULIA C. BLACKMON**
Initial Reporting Deputy:	**DET. MATTHEW IRWIN**
Offense:	**ATTEMPTED LEWD ACT ON A CHILD**
Florida State Statute:	**800.04**
Address of Occurrence:	**AMERICA ON LINE (AOL)** **KIRKMAN RD & CONROY RD**
Date and Time of Occurrence:	**APRIL 6, 1997** **APRIL 7, 1997 1600 HRS.**

<u>Narrative:</u>

April 7, 1997

Det. Matt Irwin advised me he needed me to make an undercover telephone call in reference to an AOL case. Det. Irwin gave me the computer print out of his conversation with a subject "Chris". Det. Irwin stated, he was working on AOL the night before and the subject "Chris" wanted him to telephone him on April 7, 1997, between 1530 - 1600 hrs.

April 7, 1997, at 1600 hrs.

I telephoned 407-560-1617, and asked for "Chris". A male answered and stated, he was "Chris". I identified myself as "Nikki". The male "Chris", had an Australian accent when he spoke. "Chris"

began telling me he worked for Walt Disney World. "Chris" explained, he worked with the movie department. "Chris" stated, he was currently working on the new Walt Disney World movie. "Chris" stated, he drew pictures for the movie. "Chris" asked, me if I can draw. I replied, "No". I told "Chris" he had an accent and he stated, I don't have an accent, you do.

I told "Chris" I enjoyed talking to him on the computer the night before. "Chris" told me he enjoyed speaking to me. "Chris" stated, he would like to meet me, I seemed very nice. "Chris" wanted to meet for a burger. I told "Chris" I would like to meet him also , but I did not know if I could go out. I told "Chris" my mother was not home, she was at work. "Chris" suggested I call my mother and see if I could go out and call him back. I told "Chris" I would do that and call him back. I hung up the telephone and discontinued our conversation.

This Orange County, Florida, Sheriff's Office report describes the arrest of Disney Emmy Award–winning animator Christopher Bradley on child molestation charges and 120 counts of possessing child pornography in April 1997. He pled guilty.

Orange County Sheriff's Office   *Orlando, Florida*
Supplemental Report   *Case Number 97-138338*

April 7, 1997, at 1425 hrs.

I telephoned 407-560-1617 again, and the same person answered the telephone. I asked for "Chris" and he stated, it is me. I identified myself again as "Nikki". I made it sound as if I was upset (crying). I told "Chris" my mother was a bitch and never let's me do anything. I told him I was thinking about running away. I stated, my mother told me I could not go outside. I told "Chris" I would not be able to meet him today. "Chris" insisted he come over and see me. "Chris" wanted my home address and telephone number. "Chris" told me my mother was just trying to do the right thing and when I grew up I would understand. "Chris" stated, his mother still keeps track of him. After speaking to "Chris" for a few minutes, I made it clear to "Chris" I was just mad at my mother and was not really going to run away, I just said that. "Chris" stated, good I'm glad and asked me to meet him for a burger. I began asking "Chris" about what we would do when we meet. "Chris" stated, after we meet we can discuss that. I told "Chris" I was not . looking for a relationship I was just looking for someone to teach me how to have sex. "Chris" said, okay with him. "Chris" again insisted we meet tonight. "Chris" wanted my address and telephone. I told him I gave it out before to someone and told them not to call and they did. I explained, I got in really big trouble with my mother. "Chris" asked again to just meet. I explained again, I could not meet tonight, I did not want to get into trouble with my mother. "Chris" told me that my mother would never know she is at work. I told "Chris" I was afraid she would find out. "Chris" stated, he would just knock on the door and I could answer the door. I told him I have a neighbor that doesn't work and she is my mother's lookout. I stated, my neighbor is a "bitch". If anyone came to the door or I left she would tell my mother. "Chris" stated, I will knock on the door and walk past and you can open the door and I will walk quickly back. I told "Chris" I did not know, I was afraid. "Chris" continued to coerce me into meeting him. I stated, maybe I can act like I am going to the mail box. "Chris" continued on asking if he could meet at my apartment. I continued to tell him no, I was scared.

I asked "Chris" if he was a weird-o and was he going to hurt me. "Chris" stated, he was not a weird-o and would not hurt me. I asked "Chris" if he had a girlfriend and he said no. I asked, if he ever had sex with anyone. "Chris" stated, yes I told you I used to be married. "Chris" stated, he had many girlfriends he had sex with. I asked "Chris" if he was any good at sex. "Chris" replied, I have been told yes. I told "Chris" I never had sex before, but wanted to. I told "Chris", my friend "Suzy" has had sex and she said it was great. I continued to explain, how my girlfriend "Suzy" had a boyfriend and they have sex all the time. I asked "Chris" if he would teach me sex. "Chris" said let's first meet and talk about it. I asked , if he just wanted to see what I looked like. "Chris" said, let's get a burger tonight first and we can talk. "Chris" stated, we would have to be comfortable with each other first. I asked, you mean comfortable like a bed. "Chris" stated, no he would explain when we met. Each time I would begin to have a conversation, "Chris" would have to meet tonight, come on it will be okay. I asked if we could meet tomorrow. "Chris" stated, he did not know when he would be available. I stated, it could be next week. "Chris" stated, he might get busy and knew he could get away from work now. "Chris" stated, he was actually working , but could slip away and no one would know he was gone.

Orange County Sheriff's Office   *Orlando, Florida*
Supplemental Report   *Case Number* 97-138338

I asked "Chris" if he had any diseases. "Chris" stated, no. I explained my girlfriend "Suzy" told me to use a condom. I asked "Chris" if he would uses a condom and bring some with him. "Chris" stated, yes I will. I told "Chris" I almost did it with a boy at school once but he did not have a condom. "Chris" said it was a good idea to use protection. "Chris" again stated, come on let's meet. I stated, my mother might come home and find me gone. I stated, let me call my mother and make certain she stays at work. "Chris" agreed that was a good idea. It was agreed I would call him back at work within a few minutes. I hung the telephone up and disconnected.

I explained to Det. Irwin how persistent "Chris" was about meeting tonight. I further explained The responses "Chris" gave to my questions. Det. Irwin told me to go ahead and advise "Chris" I would meet with him.

I called "Chris" back at the same telephone number. "Chris" answered the telephone. I stated, I called my mother back at work. I explained, my mother's boss was mad at her and that is why she yelled at me. I advised "Chris" I worked everything out with my mother and I am not running away and she is not mad at me. I advised, "Chris" my mother would not be home for a while, and I could meet with him. I advised, "Chris" I could not meet for a burger, I would not have much time. "Chris" was excited, and agreed we did not have to get a burger. I explained, I live in an apartment complex , at Kirkman Road & Conroy Road, Orlando Fl. I told "Chris" to pull into the Nations Bank on the corner, facing the fence. I advised, "Chris" to flash his head lights or beep the horn and I would meet him in the parking lot. "Chris stated, he did not want to draw attention to himself. I asked, "Chris" what type and color vehicle he was driving. "Chris" stated, a silver and red large Dodge pick up truck. I asked, what was he wearing. "Chris" stated, a shirt with "Disney" on it and a red ball cap. "Chris" stated, he was leaving work immediately and would meet me in (20) twenty minutes.

I asked "Chris" if he liked me, would he have sex with me. "Chris" said, "yes". I reiterated, for him to bring condoms, I did not want to get any diseases. I asked "Chris" what size his dick was? "Chris" laughed. I stated, I just want to know, because I don't want it to hurt. "Chris" stated, he could not talk right now. I asked, if I say how many inches could he say yes or no. "Chris" stated, "Yes". I asked, (12") twelve inches and "Chris" replied, "No". I asked, (9") nine inches and "Chris" replied "yes". I asked "Chris" what was wrong, he was not speaking much. "Chris" began to speak in a low voice, "I'm at work and there is another guy in here with me". I asked, "Can you not talk". "Chris" stated, no not really. "Chris" sounded excited and in a hurry to get off the telephone. I asked "Chris" if he was sure the difference in age would not bother him. Chris" stated, no I have talked to many young girls and met with them. "Chris" asked if I had a problem with the age difference. I replied, no not at all. It was agreed to meet with "Chris" in twenty minutes, I hung up the telephone.

I explained, to Det. Irwin "Chris" was going to meet in twenty minutes (20), at Kirkman Road & Conroy Road. Det. Irwin advised, the felony unit of the meeting time and location.

Det. Irwin responded to Kirkman Road & Conroy Road. Upon my arrival, I observed "Chris" in handcuffs, standing next to his silver & red pick up truck. "Chris" was transported to 2450 W. 33rd Street, Orlando, by the felony unit.

Det. Irwin and myself began to interview "Chris" about the above information. "Chris" continued to stated, he was meeting for a burger only. I confronted "Chris" about him agreeing to have sex. "Chris" would put his head down and stated, "I don't understand". "Chris" denied any knowledge of sexual talk. I confronted "Chris" about statements he made to me. "Chris" would state, she was the one that began talking about sex. I asked "Chris" why he agreed to teach me how to have sex. "Chris" stated, I just said I would, I don't know. I asked if he did not intend to have sex with me why did he say he did. "Chris" could not give an answer. I asked, "why didn't you just hang up the telephone?" "Or tell me you did not want to discuss any sexual activities?" "Chris" could not give an explanation. Det. Irwin showed "Chris" the transcripts of there conversation. "Chris" attempted to denied the information. "Chris" stated, he made a bad judgment call. Det. Irwin and myself exited the interview room and Cpl. Caldwell and Det. Webb continued to speak to "Chris".

It was learned after the first telephone contact, the recording equipment was not working properly. The recording equipment was not used for the other telephone conversations.

Det. *Julia Blackmon*
DET. JULIA BLACKMON

Sworn to and subscribed by me, the undersigned authority, this 28*th day of*
April *, 1997.*

Cpl *J. Ml* 0153
Law Enforcement Officer / Supervisor

4

"beth&dad," and "veryyoung." He determined that no less than 120 of the graphic files depicted nude children under the age of eighteen engaging in sexual acts or poses. Detectives arrested Bradley and charged him with 121 felony counts, including an attempted lewd act upon a child, possession of computer pornography, and possession of child pornography. He pled guilty.

Of all Disney's secrets, none is perhaps as dark and troubling as the growing number of active pedophiles in and around the Magic Kingdom. "Disney is having more problems than anyone else," says Irwin, who has cracked several pedophile cases for the Sheriff's Department, including both the Laber and Bradley cases. (He also handled the famous 1997 "baby Jasmine" case, in which a newborn was abandoned in a Magic Kingdom bathroom.)

Irwin is not alone in his views. "All pedophiles are seeking to do is put themselves in a situation to expand their opportunities to offend," says Michael Gibbons, a former Orange County, Florida, prosecutor who has put numerous pedophiles behind bars. "And clearly what better place than Disney? What it's all about for them is winning the trust of innocent children and then striking at the right moment."

The chance to work at Disney World attracts people like John Mushacke. On March 15, 1995, Orange County Sheriff's Deputies arrested the Disney employee on three felony charges: fondling a child, possession of child pornography, and procuring child pornography. Mushacke was charged with fondling a thirteen-year-old girl repeatedly while he worked at Disney. He pled guilty to five counts.

The sheer size of the place means pedophiles can operate in relative anonymity. "Pedophiles are attracted to children, and they go where the children are," says Sergeant Mark Thompson of the Osceola County Sheriff's Department. (Disney territory runs into both Orange and Osceola Counties.) "They are going to search for them, somewhere where they can reach that child. They're attracted to Disney World because it's so big, their chances of getting caught are close to none." Thompson should know. He's both worked the sex crimes beat and done security work at Disney.

Deep-seated psychological motives are another reason pedophiles often pick a place of "childhood dreams" to commit their crimes. "Disney World is the greatest attraction in the world for children and pedophiles," says Professor Jack Enter, a criminology expert at North Georgia College who spent ten years as a detective in suburban Atlanta and has extensively researched sex crimes at Disney. "Part of it is the fact that many pedophiles were abused when they were young, and they get fixated on a certain age. That's one reason why some of them are interested in animation and other things kids are interested in."

Disney can't be blamed if pedophiles happen to choose the Magic Kingdom as their hunting ground. Any large business that caters to children more than likely may have to deal with this particular problem. But what troubles Orlando-area law enforcement officials is Disney's unwillingess to do much about it and the company's resistance to cooperating with police efforts to tackle the problem. As we saw in the last chapter, Disney is willing to cover up crimes to protect its image. You might think that if there were one single crime that Disney would work aggressively to counter it would be child molestation. But you would be wrong.

Orlando is a worldwide entertainment center that attracts people from around the globe. And that reality can present an enormous challenge in dealing with crime, particularly sex crimes. "People come and go," says Sergeant Thompson. "It's hard to track a suspect down even if you have a good ID."

Doug Rehman served until recently as a senior law enforcement official with the Florida Department of Law Enforcement (FDLE). He has a national reputation in his profession, having lectured at the FBI Academy in Quantico, Virginia. While at the FDLE he tried to rectify the problem of catching pedophiles by establishing the Central Florida Child Exploitation Task Force. The first organizational meeting took place in the summer of 1995, and the group now includes every government agency in the area that deals with child molesters: the FBI, Customs, FDLE, Department of Corrections Sex Offenders Unit, and all local county sheriffs and police bodies. "Our goal is to share intelligence and make sure there is no wasted effort," Rehman told us. "The goal is to deal more effectively with pedophiles through better coordination." An important part of the Task Force's work is being proactive. "We don't simply want to sit back and wait for offenses to be reported. We want to go out into the field and prevent crimes from occurring." That requires the cooperation of local businesses—particularly the large theme parks in the area: Universal Studios, Sea World, and, of course, Disney. "Theme parks are magnets for children," he says. "And where the children are, the pedophile goes."

Rehman arranges for detectives to conduct special seminars for private security officers to help them be on the alert for pedophiles cruising their parks. "We give them a one-hour presentation that teaches them about the psychology of a pedophile, how they operate, and how you can spot them. We want them to be aware of things they may not have noticed before."

According to both Rehman and Detective Irwin, who serves on the Task Force, almost everyone has expressed an interest in the training: Sea World, Universal, and even small water parks. "Everyone is interested," says Irwin, "except Disney."

Both Irwin and Rehman say the Mouse was approached several times. They described the Task Force programs to senior Security officials and asked if they would cooperate. "I spoke with a Disney Security person who was all for it," Irwin told us. "It was somewhere in the upper management that it was quashed. It's a shame. The training would have been very relevant and would have been very helpful."

The Task Force also puts agents in the field to run surveillance of suspected pedophiles, again with its major focus on the region's theme parks. But Disney has resisted these efforts, too. "Every one of the theme parks gave us an open door and said whenever you want to come out just let us know," says Rehman. "Everyone, with the exception of Disney."

And even when a sex crime is committed at Disney and a child is involved, the Mouse shies away from calling law enforcement, particularly if a Disney employee commits the crime. On February 25, 1996, a Japanese Travel Bureau (JTB) agent informed a Disney Security investigator that her seven-year-old daughter "witnessed a Spanish man with his pant zipper down, touching himself" at Disney's Blizzard Beach Water Park. According to the JTB rep, it happened twice, first on the morning of February 24 at 8:00 AM, and then at the same time the next day. According to an incident report, a Disney investigator named Stiefel confronted a Disney employee named Lopez who fit the description and asked him about the incidents. Lopez admitted that he did unzip his pants and "adjust" himself in front of the girl both times. Disney fired the man. Yet they waited seven hours— after the girl and her mother had checked out of the hotel—before calling the Sheriff's Office. By then there was no opportunity to make an arrest because both Lopez and the witnesses were long gone.

Sergeant Thompson remembers one case in which Disney simply didn't want to get involved. "We had a guy who would travel around the Disney hotels and go to the pool areas," he told us. "He was taking close-up shots of kids climbing in and out of the pools. These kids were three or four years old, and sometimes the bathing suits were not covering their backsides properly. He was getting close-up shots. You just knew he was going to make a move for a kid. We wanted to go get him, but Disney didn't want to have any part of it."

"The problem comes when they fail to report incidents," says Detective Irwin. "We don't know until it's too late and the case is blown, or we never find out."

Disney's resistance to aggressively dealing with child molestation cases occurs at several levels. Unlike virtually every other major family entertainment establishment in central Florida, it resists training from law enforcement and refuses undercover patrols. But then when its people do stumble across a case, it sometimes fails to notify law enforcement in a timely fashion. This all makes for serious frustrations for those who have worked the Orlando sex crimes beat. As Orange County Sheriff's Office Detective Eric Fortinberry told us: "I would like to think that Disney would take this stuff more seriously."

But the fact is, Disney seems more interested in protecting itself than its young victims. "They do everything they can to minimize their publicity and don't want to deal with the issue," says Sergeant

Thompson. "We're all here to catch the bad guys; you would think there would be close cooperation. But they don't want publicity. One or two cases go by here and there that they perhaps don't worry about, but they don't think about what effect it will have on a child."

Doug Rehman sadly concurs that Disney would rather protect its image and pretend the crimes don't occur than actually deal with them. "It's all about P.R.," he told us. "They don't want the publicity."

It's not that Disney doesn't take crime seriously. As we've seen, it just depends on what category the crime happens to be under. While crimes where children are sexually vicitimized don't seem to get much interest, crimes that cost Disney money do. Michael Gibbons, a former assistant state attorney in Orlando who has prosecuted numerous sex crimes cases as well as theft cases at Disney, says the company has two standards toward crime. "There's a striking difference between the way they deal with sex crimes like child molestation, and petty theft," he told us. "Sex crimes they minimize and try to cover up. But if you steal from the till, they'll throw the book at you."

"They always come down hard on any financial crimes," Sergeant Thompson told us. "They had a maid at All-Star Resorts that was stealing some things. They set up a sting operation to catch her. Suddenly when it's a financial crime that costs them something, they want your help."

Just how much of a problem is pedophilia at Disney? No real statistics are available. But many, like Irwin, believe it is "substantial." Certainly opportunities for abuse abound. Orlando activist Rene Bray says her research shows that more than one hundred kids get lost at Disney World every day. "I've received anonymous calls from people working out there telling me, 'You need to do something about this.'"

And Gibbons believes that the problem at Disney is likely to be even larger than almost anyone can imagine. "Disney personnel and employees have been guilty of this crime, and this crime is historically enormously underreported. We would expect that only a small fraction of cases would actually come to light because of the nature of the crime. And so we're not surprised that there aren't a huge number of cases publicly known."

When it comes to reported cases, the only entity that is likely to know the real number is Disney itself, and the Mouse won't share that information. The company's unique control over how criminal reports and incidents are handled at Disney World is a result of its control over Reedy Creek. If you are the victim of a crime on Disney property—whether at the parks or in a hotel—and call 911, you would expect to be connected with law enforcement. But instead, as we've seen, you are patched through to Disney Security. Supervisors will then make a decision as to whether law enforcement is contacted. The law does not require Disney to report crimes to the Sheriff's Office. The decision is entirely left to Disney's discretion.

Those law enforcement officers who work on Disney property believe the pedophile threat is real. Sergeant Barbara Lewis of the Orange County Sheriff's Office, who runs the Magic Kingdom field office, told us in an exclusive interview: "Pedophiles are going to try to get where kids are—day-care centers and theme parks. If I were a pedophile, this is the type of company I would want to work for."

Former prosecutor Michael Gibbons thinks the problem is so serious that he has formed a group with Rene Bray called Kids in Danger of Sexploitation (K.I.D.S.). Bray helped launch the group after her daughter was molested by a former Disney employee. (She later discovered that the man who sexually abused her daughter had "flashed" customers on the Great Movie Ride at Disney-MGM, but Disney had never reported the crime.)

K.I.D.S. believes that one key in helping to tackle Disney's pedophile problem would be for the company to conduct criminal background checks on its employees. The Florida Department of Law Enforcement offers arrest records for $15. Security checks would undoubtedly be a good idea since a surprising number of Disney employees have serious criminal records that are either unknown or ignored by Disney management (see the next chapter). The result is a revolving door in which serious sex offenders can get hired without any problem.

Consider the case of Jimmie Lee Dennis. On November 15, 1996, the Orlando Police Department arrested Dennis for committing a lewd act upon a child. Dennis had been working at a local middle school as a volunteer when administrators discovered him groping and molesting a fifteen-year-old mentally handicapped child in a closet. After being picked up by the police, Dennis posted a $2,500 bond and was released. While awaiting trial on child molestation charges, he applied for a job at Disney World in the Entertainment Division. The Mouse hired him and put him to work as a costumed character. His job was to roam the park, hug kids, put them on his lap, and pose for pictures. He kept the job until August 21, when he was convicted by Judge Dorothy Russell for his earlier arrest. Linda Drain, the attorney who prosecuted Dennis, says, "I think this case is a pretty good example of the need for Disney to start conducting criminal background checks."

In April 1991 David Wayne Fisher was fired from his job in the Osceola County, Florida, School District after working as a substitute teacher for little more than a year. The axe fell after several incidents were reported in which he had been seen "touching the girls excessively" at Michigan Avenue Elementary School in Kissimee and Dearwood Elementary School in Poiciana. So Fisher went to work at the Fort Wilderness Campground at Disney World. His job included giving kids pony rides. He also served with his wife as a volunteer with local Girl Scout Troops 601 and 628.

In late March 1994 the Fishers took the Girl Scouts camping in Fort Wilderness. On the night of March 28, two tourists called Disney Security to report they had seen David Fisher touching some girls at a bus stop. The tourists later informed the Sheriff's Deputies that one girl had told them they were touched in ways that made them uncomfortable but they were "afraid to say no." Fisher fondled one eleven-year-old girl below the waist, looked down her pants, kissed her lips, and whispered that he loved her.

The Orange County Sheriff's Office was eventually called, and Fisher was arrested. But deputies got an earful from parents when they arrived. "Some of the parents complained about the treatment of the girls by Disney," Detective Fortinberry recalls. "They were separating the girls from each other and initially wouldn't even let them talk to their parents."

Fortinberry was shocked when he discovered that Fisher was back on familiar ground. "His job was placing kids on the pony rides. He would lift kids up by their crotch. Disney claimed they had no complaints about him, but for liability reasons they wouldn't say anything. I didn't expect them to say, 'Yeah, the guy was molesting kids on our property.'"

Would criminal background checks help Disney combat its pedophile problem? Certainly the detectives we spoke to in Orlando thought so. Sergeant Thompson told us, "The first thing to worry about are the people you hire. They are likely to pose the greatest risk." We took the idea to Bill Kelly, a former FBI agent who for more than thirty years specialized in cracking sex crimes. We asked him: If you were running security at Disney, would you conduct criminal background checks? His response was unequivocal: "I would insist on it." But K.I.D.S. has run into a brick wall. It got the same response from the Mouse as the Central Florida Child Exploitation Task Force did: "We're not interested."

Disney used to intensively screen its employees. Spencer Craig recalls when he was hired as a retail clerk in 1971. "I went through sixteen or eighteen interviews over a three-month period, for an entry level supervisor's job," he told us. "I was grilled about my background." When he later moved to human resources he says the hiring process remained intensive. "When it came to hiring, we thoroughly screened everyone."

But that was in the 1970s and early 1980s. Today things are decidedly different. Todd Eversen is an operations host currently working at the Magic Kingdom. He's worked at the park for six years, and his in-laws have worked there for more than twenty. He says Disney hires a lot of people he doesn't trust. "Anybody that walks in the door has a job at Disney, few questions asked," he told us. "The quality of people has deterioriated dramatically."

So why won't Disney screen its employees? Rene Bray raised the idea with Disney officials after animator Christopher Bradley was arrested. Disney denied it had a security problem, and added that the cost of background checks would be prohibitive. "That was just an excuse," she fumes. "Disney would need thousands of security checks done every year. With such a high number, they could negotiate the cost down to ten dollars each. They can certainly afford that."

Others believe this is about more than just the cost of the checks. "If Disney were honest and did criminal background checks," says Michael Gibbons, "we would be shocked and appalled at who's working at their parks and what they have been convicted of. If they started doing checks right now, skeletons would turn up in their closet. It's more than likely going to turn up some horrific offenders, and that is more than likely going to create a legal problem. It all works back to money. And the fact is, besides not wanting to pay for the checks, they certainly don't want any bad publicity connected with such a horrible thing that could cut down on park attendance."

While it's difficult to know just who is working at Disney, copies of the company's security records reveal that numerous employees have arrests for a variety of sex crimes. Detective Eric Fortinberry has a unique perspective on all of this, having both investigated sex crimes at Disney and worked at the park itself. "They probably don't want the criminal checks because it would keep employees out that normally would get through," he says. "They need the warm bodies there." Disney is no longer a highly coveted place to work.

Even if Disney does adopt background checks, that will not make the problem go away. Christopher Laber and Christopher Bradley did not have criminal records, and as long as Disney World remains a magnet for children, it will continue to attract pedophiles. "You are not going to weed them all out," says Irwin, "but you are making a good faith attempt." And beyond security background checks, if Disney acted like any other theme park in central Florida and cooperated with local law enforcement efforts, this would most likely lead to more arrests. Until it does the chances will remain quite low that these child molesters will be caught.

"When they advertise their attractions as a safe haven for children, the least they can do is make a minimal effort to protect those children they are inviting onto their property," Michael Gibbons says. "Right now there are so many incentives for pedophiles to work at Disney."

CHAPTER SEVEN

Peeping Toms

Sometimes the walls have eyes in the Magic Kingdom. Shannon Green was a dancer with Kids of the Kingdom, an upbeat dance group that for years gave highly choreographed performances at Disney World. On June 20, 1991, she was in a bathroom in Cinderella's Castle when she suddenly heard noises coming from the ceiling above. "I had a strange feeling," she recalled later, "so I poked on the bathroom ceiling. When I left the bathroom I heard a noise in the radio room [above me]. I heard the door open and I tried to see who was leaving, but they ran down the stairs too quickly."

By coincidence, fellow dancer Angela Howe was on her way up those very same stairs. "I met this man face to face," she says. "The light was off in the control radio room, and he made a dash for the elevator as it was closing." Howe caught part of his name on his I.D. tag and noticed he was wearing a maintenance worker's uniform. The two dancers immediately checked the service list on a nearby fire extinguisher, identified the man, and reported the incident to Security.

> **Within Disney there is a subculture of voyeurs so large and open that even new employees can get involved fast.**

On July 17, less than a month later, a silent alarm went off in the radio equipment room located inside the penthouse in Cinderella's Castle, right next to the changing room. Disney Security Investigator Mike Crews responded, and, entering the room, found a custodian trying to hide behind an equipment rack. The custodian, Rick Bradley, admitted he had gone into the room to spy on the dancers as they undressed.

Bradley, on the job only a few months, knew where to peep. He told investigators that fellow employees had brought the "secure" room to his attention while they were having lunch in the cafeteria. Within the company, there is a subculture of voyeurs so large and open that even new employees can get involved fast, if they choose to. Jack Enter, a former detective of ten years in suburban Atlanta who now teaches criminology at North Georgia College, has studied the Peeping Tom phenomenon at Disney. He, in fact, appeared as an expert witness at a 1994 civil trial involving Magic Kingdom voyeurs. "One reason that voyeurism is so bad at Disney is that there is almost an underground culture that has been created," Enter told us. "They talk to each other at lunch. Oddballs have a network. They pass along information that things are tolerated."

After Disney Security officials looked over the radio equipment room, they knew they had a problem. Mike Crews noted the Bradley incident in his report: "Investigation revealed that it is possible to look into the restroom and the dressing room from the ceiling accessible from the inside of the radio equipment room. It was also noted that entry into the secured area could be gained by inserting a slim object between the strike plate and bolt."

Surprisingly, Disney Security already knew there were peepholes both in the ceiling of the bathroom and in the walls of the girl's dressing room. It had been warned years earlier by a Disney lighting technician named Terry Lee Neudecker.

For years one of Neudecker's duties had been to secure all the entertainment areas in the Castle. Then one night he stumbled onto a secret: "Someone had poked a little hole in the wall next to a dressing room." He took the information to Rick Harbin, manager of Kids of the Kingdom. "He seemed kind of excited," recalls Neudecker. "It was like this was big news. You know, that, okay, wow, this thing is happening." But neither Harbin nor Disney did anything to correct the problem.

Despite the complaints from Shannon Green and Angela Howe, Disney shrugged off the problem as it had done before. The only action the company took following the Bradley incident was to install a simple flange plate over the radio room door locking mechanism. Incredibly, the company never sealed the peepholes! Charles Senewald is a security professional who formerly headed security for Claremont College and a chain of department stores in California. He inspected the Castle as an expert witness in a Peeping Tom lawsuit. "The action of installing a flange plate as a corrective action is laughable. The door was already alarmed." The real problem was not a security mechanism but a lax attitude about keeping voyeurs out of the Castle.

Disney has a serious problem with voyeurs, employees who secretly watch other employees and guests. It is a new and growing phenomenon. But like so many serious crimes that occur at Disney World, the Mouse seems to take the approach that what you don't know can't hurt you. Indeed, employees caught peeping on guests changing clothes in dressing rooms are not always fired—they can and often do retain their jobs. And employees who are nabbed exposing themselves to guests don't need to fear that the Mouse will contact the sheriff. Disney is far more interested in covering up the crimes to avoid bad press than in protecting its honest, law-abiding employees and guests.

Yes, Rick Bradley was caught peeping and lost his job. But other eyes were still watching.

John Giangrossi worked as a costumer at Cinderella's Castle. His job included bringing outfits to the dancers of the Kids of the Kingdom cast, most of whom were in their late teens and early twenties. He had long heard stories from coworkers about a secret penthouse in the Castle where it was possible to watch the dancers undress. There was a dumbwaiter in a room above King Stephen's, a restaurant located in the Castle, they said. By going through a small passageway connected to a dumbwaiter, he would get a perfect view of the changing area.

Giangrossi decided to do just that. "I had three days off from work, and I came back," Giangrossi recalls. "They had just started their first show, and I went down to say hello to some of my coworkers. Then about ten minutes before the show ended, [I] took the elevator to the penthouse and walked in."

Two weeks later he went back to scope out the room. He brought a flashlight and began to peek through the holes that had already been punched in the wall. Eventually he positioned a dressing room mirror to give himself "a better view." Shortly thereafter he became an active voyeur.

Disney investigators knew that Peeping Toms were still roaming the Castle. Rhonda Morgan, a Disney Security investigator, had discovered peepholes in the Castle and in the Fantasyland Tunnel changing room. This was disturbing news to dancer Alison Swanson, who played Tinker Bell. She regularly used that changing room between performances. And while there had been reports of problems before, Rick Harbin, now Disney Entertainment Division Manager, assured her not to worry because the problem had been taken care of.

How did Disney fix it? The company patched up the holes with duct tape. Jack Enter toured the area several years after these events took place. "It was amazing," he told us. "So many guys had been standing on the ceiling pipes and looking in her room that the insulation was worn off the top of the pipes."

Rumors about the voyeurs were swirling around the Magic Kingdom, and, by now, several of the dancers were really beginning to worry. The dancers approached Disney Security Officer James Hertogs. He was unconcerned. "Boys will be boys," he said. "This has been going on at Disney for twenty years."

Hertogs, however, is only half right. Whenever you have a large work force, you're bound to get some of those "oddballs," as Jack Enter calls them. But during the past ten years, the problem has grown significantly worse. Harry Parsell, until recently an investigations manager at Disney, can recall only one instance of voyeurism that is more than fifteen years old. "In the seventies," he says, "there was a period that somebody was punching a hole in the wall in the dressing room at the Diamond Horseshoe. It was observed, and it was repaired." The rigorous screening process and strict code of conduct that was once required of employees apparently kept peeping to a minimum.

Meanwhile, John Giangrossi became a regular visitor to the secret room in Cinderella's Castle. He even rented a video camera and started recording the dancers in various states of undress. He took videos of them going to the bathroom. By his estimate, he videotaped the dancers five times. And as he began accumulating a library of sorts, he started sharing them with coworkers. He even pulled one out at a bachelor's party for a fellow Disney employee.

As word of the tapes spread around the park and more Disney employees saw them, Giangrossi risked discovery. In September 1991 an employee went to Rick Harbin and told him he had seen explicit tapes, courtesy of Giangrossi. Although Harbin acted surprised, he waited a few weeks before doing anything about it. Finally on October 1, he inspected the dressing room area with Disney Security. Security began taking statements from other employees who said they had seen the tapes and knew that Giangrossi still had them in his home.

But despite the accumulating evidence—including sworn statements from employees that Giangrossi was committing felonious acts—Disney management did nothing over the next three months. Not only did the company fail to confront Giangrossi and contact the Orange County Sheriff's Office, Disney Security didn't even bother to have the existing holes repaired or to secure the room.

A former Florida assistant state attorney familiar with the Giangrossi case is amazed at Disney's conduct. "They had enough to go on," says Eric Faddis, now an Orlando attorney. "They had several sworn statements from witnesses who had been at Giangrossi's home and said that they had seen the videotapes and watched them. Those sworn statements actually identified a suspect and placed the contraband that results from the felony in Giangrossi's hands. Any prosecutor or former prosecutor you can talk to can tell you that's enough information for a search warrant to go into that guy's house and identify the victims on those videotapes." But getting a search warrant would have entailed contacting law enforcement and risking public exposure. That would hurt Disney's well-polished image. So the company decided to wait, apparently with little concern for the safety of the dancers. As with other crimes, Disney elected to keep it covered up.

But by doing so there was the potentially serious risk of bodily harm to the girls. "Voyeurism is a very serious crime," says Bill Kelly, a thirty-one-year FBI veteran who dealt with sex crimes. "It can often escalate to more sex offenses."

Professor Jack Enter agrees. "Seventy percent of rapists are voyeurs. People don't understand voyeurism. It's about power, about viewing an unwilling participant. Disney still doesn't understand that."

While the Mouse didn't stir, Giangrossi kept busy, showing his tapes to coworkers and friends and making copies to give as gifts. He also taped the dancers a few more times, adding to his growing video library.

In early January 1992 Giangrossi borrowed a video camera from coworker Roberto Rivera, who was also with the costume department. The word was, Giangrossi was going to tape again on January 7, 1992, after the 11:00 AM performance. Tipped off about what was about to occur, Disney Security decided it was finally time to take action. But rather than contact the Orange County Sheriff's Office with word that a felony was about to be committed or alert the dancers, Disney chose instead to conduct its own "sting" operation. On January 6 some of Mickey's technicians installed a video camera in the hidden room Giangrossi was using so they could tape him committing the crime.

The next day when Security officials arrived to check their hidden cameras, they were surprised to find Giangrossi already there. He had apparently decided to tape an earlier performance. Fortunately, the Peeping Tom did not notice them and continued his activities uninterrupted. Once the technicians turned on their cameras, they had the evidence that Giangrossi was committing a felony. But rather than apprehend him right away, they waited. And waited. In fact, they watched Giangrossi masturbate and videotape the dancers in partial or total nudity for more than an hour and fifteen minutes. Only after he had finished and the dancers had left for their 11:00 AM show did they nab him.

For Disney the plan was simple: Get the guy to admit to his crime and fire him. They never intended to tell the dancers or contact law enforcement. And it might have worked out that way, except for the indiscretion of a Security employee.

Once Disney had Giangrossi, it took him to an interrogation room

Orange County S..'s Office

S..ATEMENT
FILL OUT IN FULL DETAIL

Date of Statement	Month 01	Day 08	Year 92	Time 1506		Case Number 92-007037

Offense: INTERCEPTION OF ORAL COMMUNICATION

Date of Offense	Month 01	Day 08	Year 92	Time 0940	Suspect (must be initialed) GIANGROSSI, JOHN J.

Location of Offense: PENTHOUSE IN THE CASTLE 4 THE MAGIC KINGDOM   Zone 36

Code	Name (must be initialed) GIANGROSSI, JOHN JOSEPH	Age 21	DOB 8/14/70	Race W	Sex M

Address Res: 6432 N. PLYMOUTH-SORRENTO RD. AAPKA   ZID 32703   Phone 886-1095

Address Business: PO BOX 10,000 - LBV Fl.   ZID 32830   Phone 824-5319

I, __John Giangrossi__ do hereby voluntarily make the following statement without threat, coercion, offer of benefit or favor by any persons whomsoever.

I was getting costumes for Repair and noticed a dumbwaiter door in the Penthouse and I was curious to see inside. I didn't look because I was running late The next day on the bus I heard (2) two maintenance men talking about it, I was even more curious I went back & I took off the cover, It was dark so I couldn't see bottom, so I dropped a penny & hit a concrete floor. And then realized there was a floor. The cover to a volume control was off and light was coming through where I'd been looking. I got an idea to peek at the dancers but put that thought in the back of my mind. It kept driving inside me to do it and so I gave in and did it the first part of Sept. It was there but show of the day in progress and I went up there with a camera seen brief ~~bras~~ Bras and undergarments, they left, I waited (10) ten minutes and left. In the second attempt I did the same but 1 to 2 weeks later in Sept. saw the same But some partial nudity. The (3rd) third time I bought a video camera and recorded the dancers the first time they were Denise Case, Lisa Hickey, Hayley Taylor, Angela Harper, Shannon Green not in that particular order. That tape was accidentally destroyed w/ soda and ~~later~~ later discared. Before it was destroyed it was shown to 3 technicians. I remember (2) two names but not the third. They are ~~Mark Smith~~ Mark Schnallinger, Nick Buzzici and again I do not remember the third.

Sworn To and Subscribed Before Me. The Undersigned Authority, This
8 Day Of Jan, 19 92

Deputy Sheriff ●   Notary Public ○

I Swear/Affirm The Above and/or Attached Statements Are Correct and True:

Signature: John Giangrossi

Arrest Made Yes ● No ○	Miranda Warning Read Yes ● No ○	Will Testify Yes ● No ○	APS Submitted Yes ○ No ●	Will Prefer Charges Yes ○ No ○

10-1181 (11/87)   STATE ATTORNEY   Page 1 of 2

Disney employee John Giangrossi confesses to secretly videotaping female employees changing their clothes. Disney tried to cover up the crime.

SHERIFF'S DEPT.   STATEMENT   ᴶ NO.
ORANGE COUNTY, FLORIDA   (CONT.)   92-007037
.O-1131   (1/76)

After the tape was destroyed I wanted to get another,
So I went again. It was a rented camera as was the First
I went in taped Brief Partial Nudity For about 5-10 minutes
up to 15 minutes. I can't remember I never recored time Nordates. On the
Second tape there were Lisa Hickey, Shannon Green, Hartley Taylor Angela
Have, Denise case, That was in the month of the end of Sept 1st of
October. The 4th time I attempted to record the camera didn't
work I didn't video record nothing That was 14 the end of Oct.
In Nov. I brought an extension cord from my area downstairs
and Plugged it in, by using a Key I then made a hole in the
wall for the other end of the cord. So I could use a constant
Power supply. Through December I didn't tape anything
because I was in Another Part of the park for the entire
Christmas season. And in January I attempted to
tape again. Taped For appraximatly Five (5) minuts the dancers
left. I Stopped

    * In November, I was approached by a coworker named
Victor (that's what his nametag Read) Who seen me bringing the dance
Clothes down on a rolling Rack w/ tights and Bras and asked
me If I wanted to see the dancers naked and I told him no,
thats alright and Brushed Him off. I havent Seen him again

        I gave this statement of my own Free will.

PAGE OF PAGES
 2   2   SIGNATURE

and began questioning him. Not far away, Sergeant Michael Cofield of the Orange County Sheriff's Office was eating his lunch at the Magic Kingdom cafeteria. Cofield was assigned liaison duty at the park and was having a casual conversation with some Security officials. As he tells it, one of the officials leaned over and told him "something to the effect that the guy in the Castle was caught videotaping the girls." That revelation was news to Cofield. Like everyone else in the Sheriff's Department, he didn't know anything about the case. Concerned that a felony was going unreported, he left his plate half full of food and immediately headed over to the Disney Security interrogation room. He briefly knocked on the door and then entered the room, seizing the videotape as evidence. He announced firmly that the Sheriff's Office was taking over the investigation. Although Disney Security was not pleased, there was nothing Disney could do. Had Cofield not had lunch where he did that day, Giangrossi would never have been charged and convicted as a felon.

As word of Giangrossi's arrest spread through the Magic Kingdom, so did the fact that fellow employee Roberto Rivera had knowingly loaned his friend the camera to tape the dancers. That made him an accessory to the crime. Giangrossi told investigators that Rivera had also watched some of the videos. But Disney kept Rivera in his job as a costumer, working with the very girls he had seen on tape. There had been protests about Rivera before. Dancer Angela Harper had complained repeatedly that Rivera would place his hand under her leotards and against her buttocks while pinning a cat tail on her costume.

With Giangrossi behind bars, only a part of the problem was solved. The peeping continued. On May 6, 1992, several of the young women wrote a letter to Disney Manager Rick Harbin. "There still remains on the stairway wall a scrawling which states, 'peep show 25 cents,'" they complained. "We also learned that the video camera seized by the Orange County Sheriff's Department was a camera owned by Roberto and lent to John Giangrossi. We have also been informed that Roberto saw the videotapes of us [at] the bachelor party, and yet Roberto still works as a dresser of the female Kids of the Kingdom. We do not think, based on these facts, Roberto should be

May 6, 1992

LIBERTI

Re: Unfit working conditions

Dear Ingrid and Rick:

This letter is being sent to you to advise you of what we
consider to be unfit working conditions in the penthouse dressing
area of Cinderella's Castle. During the past year, we have
learned of a number of occasions involving "peeping toms,"
who have apparently been watching, and in some cases videotaping,
women members of the Kids of the Kingdom in various states of
undress. In Addition, one or more persons have apparently
observed some of the female Kids of the Kingdom using the toilet
facility located in the penthouse.

To the women members of the Kids of the Kingdom, this invasion
of privacy is extremely distressing, and has caused a great
deal of consternation and concern on our part. As you know,
John Giangrossi was arrested for videotaping several of the
woman unclothed, and it was determined that Mr. Giangrossi's
videotape had become public, and was even shown at a bachelor's
party of a Disney employee.

We treat these violations of our personal security as the
utmost form of sexual harassment. You can imagine the thoughts
that go through our minds every time we think of undressing in
the penthouse dressing room, and when we wonder if these peeping
toms have something more on their minds than just watching.

Unfortunatley, these incidents of peeping toms have not yet
ended. On April 23, 1992, we found new holes in the radio room
which we did not place there.

We Regretfully feel that Disney has not properly responded
to these intolerable conditions, and in fact, actually made
things worse. Instead of sealing off the access to the women's
dressing room upon learning that there was one or more peeping
toms, Disney security chose to use us as "bait" to catch at
least one of the persons responsible for this activity. We were
used as bait without our consent, much to our regret and concern.
We are not pawns to be used to further the efforts of Disney
security or any other part of Disney or law enforcement agency.

*The dancers watched by one of Disney's Peeping Toms complain to their managers that even with
the arrest of John Giangrossi, "holes" keep appearing in the walls. They say Disney's handling of
the case "actually made things worse."*

We were previously told that everything had been taken care
of and there was no need to worry about any further invasive
incidents. However, the most recent discovery of holes leads
us to conclude otherwise.

In addition, there still remains on the stairway wall a
scrawling which states, "peep show 25 cents." We also learned
that the video camera seized by the Orange County Sheriff's
Department was a camera owned by Roberto and lent to John
Giangrossi. We have also been informed that Roberto saw the
videotape of us the bachelor's party, and yet Roberto still
works as a dresser of the female Kids of the Kingdom. We do
not think that, based on these facts, Roberto should be working
in such close proximity to us.

Something must be done immediately to put a stop to these
harassing problems. We request that all access to the radio
room and the crawl spaces be immediately sealed-off, and Disney
increase its security in the areas surrounding our dressing room.
We would also like to see something done to impress upon the
male employees that this type of conduct will not be tolerated.
The recurrence of holes illustrates that the message has not
been loud enough.

Thank you for your anticipated cooperation in this matter.

                        Sincerely,

                        The Female Kids of the Kingdom

cc: Michael O'Grattan

working in such close proximity to us." The letter went on to note that more peepholes had appeared in the walls *after* Giangrossi had been arrested. "Something must be done immediately to put a stop to these harassing problems. We request that all access to the radio room and the crawl spaces be immediately sealed off, and Disney increase its security in the areas surrounding our dressing room. We would also like to see something done to impress upon the male employees that this type of conduct will not be tolerated. The recurrence of holes illustrates that the message has not been loud enough."

Some of the dancers were too upset by the incident to stay with Kids of the Kingdom. Several left Disney. Others, like Angela Harper, asked to be transferred to Mickey's Starland, another dance group. The dancers that did stay with Kids were disturbed that Roberto Rivera was still delivering their costumes. Disney took two months to transfer Rivera, and when it finally did, it assigned him to Mickey's Starland costuming. When Harper learned that Rivera was going to work with her again, she immediately requested he be moved away from her. Again Disney delayed, not transferring him until approximately six months later. Rivera was never even reprimanded by Disney for his involvement with Giangrossi.

Disney's problems with Peeping Toms did not begin or end with John Giangrossi. Its security files indicate that voyeurs seem to thrive at the "happiest place on earth." And while there are still peepholes in Cinderella's Castle, those aren't the only holes in the Magic Kingdom.

In March 1991 Wayne Marshal, a custodial supervisor in the Magic Kingdom, received word that female employees were complaining about a problem with fellow employee Vernon Donaldson. Diane Stidham, who was a hostess on the monorail, wrote a statement saying that when she went to use the ladies restroom during a break, Donaldson was hiding and waiting in a stall. Once she was in an adjacent stall, she noticed he was looking over the top of the partition at her. Nicole Botsford, another monorail hostess, said the same thing had happened to her. On March 27 she was using the same ladies restroom when she saw Donaldson peering over the top of her stall.

Here was another situation in which multiple witnesses claimed a Disney employee was peeping. But what did the Mouse do? He gave Donaldson a written reprimand, but kept him on the job.

On August 27, 1992, Houda Kamari was getting dressed in the EPCOT Moroccan entertainment trailer for an evening performance. It was 9:00 PM and she was looking in a mirror on the wall when suddenly she saw a hand behind her, trying to open the curtain windows. "I was half dressed then," she recalled later, "and pulled the skirt over my breasts and looked down the window and said 'who is it?' I saw this man trying to run away." Someone had climbed up to the window to have a peek.

Fortunately Ali Ajraoui, her lead, was nearby, heard the commotion, and chased the suspect. Houda called security. Ali caught the man and forcibly brought him back to the trailer. When he got a good look at him, Ali recognized him as someone he had chased before. The assailant admitted this wasn't the first time he had looked into the dressing room. He promised, however, that he would never do it again and kept pleading "please let me go."

> **Multiple witnesses claimed a Disney employee was peeping. What did the Mouse do? Gave him a written reprimand and kept him on the job.**

Minutes later Security arrived and Officer Keith Lisenby took the suspect, Essene Feliciano, a maintenance worker, to EPCOT Center Security. Once there, Feliciano changed his story, denying he had peeped through the window. But a check of his record confirmed heavy criminal activity. During the previous eigthteen months he had been arrested four times for felony battery, felony resisting arrest, shoplifting, petty larceny, and loitering and prowling. But once again Disney did nothing and simply returned him to his job. The security report concludes: "No action was taken."

In November 1997 Disney maintenance workers discovered a hidden video camera in an EPCOT changing area. They reported the camera to Disney Security, who took the camera down immediately. Law enforcement found out about it only after it was taken down. "It

05-22-1990

DR: December 05th 1970
SSN: 590-88-0751
DEPT. #: 47N
HOME TEL #: 933-1507

WALT DISNEY WORLD COMPANY
P.O. Box 10,000
Lake Buena Vista, Florida 32830-1000

3382

STATEMENT OF WITNESS/SUBJECT

Person Giving Statement	
Name: HOUDA KAMARI	Place: W158 France Morocco Trailer Entertainment
Department: 47N	Date: August 27th 1992
Origin 60 Ext: 6770	Time: 9:04 PM
	Days Off: Tue/Wed

I started getting dressed at about 9:00 PM. There is a big mirror in the wall. I was looking at the mirror and I saw, in the back window (which was open a little) a finger trying to open the curtains. I was half dressed then, I pulled the skirt over my breast and looked down the window and said "who is it?" I saw this man trying to run away. He probably has climbed to get to the window because it's high from the floor. Ali, my lord, said "what is it"? I told him to go after him, I told him that I saw somebody looking through the window, so he ran after him automatically. I finished getting dressed. After a while, they came together. Ali and this guy named David I think. David was all sweating when they came back. He looked confused. I had already called Security by this time. So Ali started talking to him, asking him why he did that and that this was not the first time and that Ali showed him before for the same reason and looked at his face. That guy said yes. Ali asked him if he remembered him at the bus station that time and he agreed to him. He told him that he comes often to watch the show during his work hours, and he said yes too. He kept saying "please let me go, I got to go now". He kept asking if we called somebody. Ali said "no just to calm him"

SIGNATURE: [signature]

PERSON TAKING STATEMENT: [signature] #9228

WITNESS:

404075

In this confidential Disney security report, an EPCOT dancer complains about a fellow employee who watches her changing through a window. As often with employees caught peeping on guests, Disney took no action against the employee.

CONTINUATION 3382 PAGE 2 OF 2

DATE MO DA YR	Related Report:			
8 27 92	☐ CRIME REPORT	☒ STATEMENT	☐ OCCURRENCE REPORT	☐ S.I.

But still, he kept asking to let him go, that he didn't want to get fired and that he is supporting his stepmother. I told Ali since this is not the first time he will do it again if we let him go, even if he apologized and said he was sorry and that if we let him go he would never do it again. I told him he should have thought of it before. He admitted running and then the security came in. And you know the rest ———.

Signature: [signature]

Report No: 404076

was taken down before we got a chance to look at it," says Detective Tim Anderson of the Orange County Sheriff's Department.

●●●

SOMETIMES, INSTEAD OF EMPLOYEES, Disney's guests are the target of prying eyes or the potentially dangerous acts of Disney employees. Harry Parsell, a former Disney security manager who spent twenty-one years with the company, says he remembers numerous occasions when the company found "holes in the ceiling of women's bathrooms, some going into the pipe casting behind the bathroom, climbing up on the pipe and puncturing holes so that they can look down into [guest] bathrooms."

Take the case of Vincent Amato, another Disney maintenance worker. On August 11, 1992, Harvey Cooper, an employee at the Disney Village Marketplace, saw Amato on a ladder looking into the fitting rooms of the Captain's Tower, where guests were trying on clothes. According to the "confidential" Disney investigation summary, "the fitting rooms were occupied with two female guests approximately fifteen to sixteen years old."

Cooper says he watched Amato for two to three minutes before saying anything. When Amato realized he was being watched, he climbed down the ladder, opened an electrical box and pretended to work. Cooper told investigators he had seen Amato there before, watching other guests as they changed their clothes.

On the same day, another worker in the Captain's Tower, Donald Koepke, noticed Amato on the ladder in the stockroom at another time, peeping into the fitting rooms. And just four days later, a third employee, Tracey Moskala, reported the same thing: Amato was peeping at guests changing their clothes. Moskala said she also saw him doing it a few days earlier.

After these complaints, Disney Security investigated. On August 18, Security Officer Ed Vercamen interviewed Amato and told him three employees had seen him peeping on guests in the changing room. Amato denied wrongdoing. Disney's response? It transferred him to another maintenance job.

H.D: 5-21-88
DOR: 7-17-49
SSN: 288-48-8942

WALT DISNEY WORLD COMPANY
P.O. Box 10,000
Lake Buena Vista, Florida 32830-1000

DEPT. #: 3A4
HOME TEL #: 904-351-1594

STATEMENT OF WITNESS/SUBJECT

Person Giving Statement

Name: Richard Eugene Seeley
22745 Cuele Rd.
Eustis, Florida 32726

Place: WDW Investigations
Date: 1-27-92
Time: 3:10 pm
Days Off: Sat, Sun.

On this date 1-27-92, I was questioned by Randy and Gus about what had taken place at the Poly this past Thursday. They had informed me that they were not law enforcement officers and that the truth is very important in this interview. I told them I was at the Poly to watch the light show at 9 pm. I did see the show and then I was just hanging out on the beach. After a couple of hours I was met by security on the beach. As the result of that meeting I'm here writing this statement.

I have been to the different resort locations (Poly, Cont., H.F. + Cont.) on several occasions. I can't recall the exact dates or times. My purpose for going to the resorts was to expose myself. I don't drink or smoke and exposing myself was a release for me. I have some problems at home with my family and I didn't always want to go home right

SIGNATURE: Richard E. Seeley
WITNESS: 400047

PERSON TAKING STATEMENT: Sworn to and Subscribed Before me
This 21 day of Jan A.D. 1992

Notary Public, State of Florida
My Commission Expires Nov. 19, 1995
Bonded Thru Troy Fain - Insurance Inc.

Notary Public, State of Florida at Large

Disney World employee Richard Seeley confesses in a Disney Security statement that he regularly flashed guests at the park for more than a year. Disney Security knew of Seeley's extensive sex-crimes record, but did not act until he was caught peeping on guest bedrooms at night. Disney fired him, but never contacted the police.

CONTINUATION   PAGE 2 OF 3

DATE
MO DA YR
1 27 92

☐ CRIME REPORT   ☑ STATEMENT   ☐ OCCURRENCE REPORT   ☐ S.I.

away. It was very convenient for me to go
to the resorts and act out. I have acted
out numerous times at different resort
locations. I have been arrested in the
past for exposure. The last time was in
Oct of 1989. The end result of the arrest
was probation (completed) a fine (court
costs) and community service (completed).

I realize I have a problem and
I can't handle it by myself. I have
tried and this is where it has gotten
me. I do have a problem and can't
control it on my own, I have tried!

As I have mentioned I was at the
Poly numerous times. At the Poly I also
noticed, around building 10 a Poly maintence
worker (I believe 2 shift worker) walking up and
down the grass near the beach looking into
windows as he walked by. On a couple
of occasions I have seen him right up to
the window looking between the curtains. I'm
not sure but his name is Jim or Jeff
about 5'10" or just under 6' maybe in his
40's is kind of bald on the top back of his
head, and is stocky built. I think he
may be the one that called security
about me on Thursday.

Signature: Richard E. Weller   Notary Public, State of Florida This 27 day of Jan A.D. 1992

CONTINUATION   PAGE 3 of 3

DATE MO DA YR	Related Report:			
12 7 92	☐ CRIME REPORT	☑ STATEMENT	☐ OCCURRENCE REPORT	☐ S.I.

the same one that showed security when I was on the beach.

I also want to mention that Randy asked me if I wanted a union steward present during the interview, I told him it was not necessary. Randy and Gus were very professional during the interview and did not pressure me into anything I may have said or written.

400049

Sworn to and Subscribed Before me

This ___ day of ___ A.D. 19 96

Notary Public, State of Florida at Large

Signature: Richard E. Smiley

Even repeat sex-crime offenders with criminal records have operated at Disney for years, apparently with the company's knowledge.
On December 30, 1990, a female guest contacted Disney Security from
the Caribbean Beach Resort. When the officers arrived, they noticed
she was visibly upset. She said she had seen a man sitting on a bench,
masturbating. She took them to the exact spot where the incident had
occurred—on the boardwalk between Aruba and Barbados. The
description had the man as 6'2" with reddish hair. She even described
what he was wearing.

The next evening, Security investigators Michael Crews and Diane
Heller saw a man fitting that description sitting on the exact same
bench. They walked by, and he nervously departed. Crews and Heller
followed him to his car in the employee parking lot and then questioned him. He identified himself as Richard Seeley, an employee of
the Disney Florist Department. He explained that he had been jogging
around the lake and had stopped at the bench to rest. But according
to the Security report filed by Crews, "It was obvious that Seeley had
not been running. He was wearing blue jeans, a gray T-shirt and tennis shoes with no socks." They also noticed he was not perspiring.

Crews had caught Seeley before. On August 17 he saw him behind
the Grand Floridian Beach Resort. He looked suspicious then, too.
According to a Disney Security report filed by Crews, Seeley had
"appeared to be looking in the windows" of guest rooms.

Although the Security officers decided to let Seeley go, they ran a
criminal record check on him through the Florida Department of Law
Enforcement (FDLE). What they discovered should have prompted
some sort of immediate action. Seeley had been arrested on four
occasions, with charges of indecent exposure, committing a crime
while wearing a mask, and resisting an officer. In April 1989 he had
been convicted of indecent exposure and was sentenced to six
months in the Orange County jail.

With both a witness who could positively identify him and a
lengthy criminal record, you might think Disney would have questioned Seeley further or turned the information over to the proper
authorities. But, instead, the company did nothing. The incident

report went to Disney's Special Investigative Unit where the Security director just filed it away. While Disney officials later claimed they reported the incident to the Orange County Sheriff, Gabriel Saliba, manager of the Sheriff's Office computer center that keeps all such reports, testified under oath that Disney never contacted the Sheriff's Office.

Seeley kept up his activities. More than a year later, on January 23, 1992, a maintenance worker named Kim Yeats reported a man wandering behind the guest rooms at the Polynesian Village Resort. Investigator Fred Wilcoxson went to the scene and saw a man in dark clothing behind Building 10. He apprehended him. It was Richard Seeley.

Disney has a "zero tolerance" policy when it comes to employee theft. But when it comes to sex crimes, the Mouse looks the other way.

Seeley said that he had come to watch the Water Pageant. Investigator Wilcoxson told him to go home. Yeats, however, told Disney Security that on "numerous occasions" he had seen Seeley dressed in dark clothes, peering in guest's windows.

Five days later, investigators Gus Collins and Fred Wilcoxson paid Seeley a visit. Seemingly weighed down by his guilt, he confessed to his crimes. "I have been to the different resort locations [Polynesian, Grand Floridian, and Caribbean] on several occasions," he wrote in his statement dated January 27, 1992. "I can't recall the exact dates or times. My purpose for going to the resorts was to expose myself. I don't drink or smoke, and exposing myself was a release for me. It was very convenient for me to go to the resorts and act out."

Then in a strange twist, he wrote that he knew about another voyeur. "As I have mentioned, I was at the Poly numerous times. At the Poly I also noticed, around Building Ten, a Poly maintenance worker walking up and down the grass near the beach looking into windows as he walked by. On a couple of occasions I have seen him right up to the window looking between curtains—I think he may be the one that called security about me."

Seeley was a repeat offender with a serious problem. As Security

Investigator Randy Watts said in his Disney Security report: "Seeley stated he was aware that he had a problem and needed to seek professional help. He admitted he knew he was violating company policy and the law, but the problem had escalated to the point that he could not control it by himself." Yet, despite all this, Disney never contacted the Orange County Sheriff's Office to report his crimes. Exposure and public masturbation are misdemeanors in Florida. Had Seeley been sentenced, he would have undoubtedly received court-mandated counseling for a problem he said he "could not control." But ever protective of its image, Disney just sent Seeley on his way, free to commit his crimes elsewhere.

Disney will not release any data concerning how much of a problem it has with voyeurs. In the Walt Disney World security manual, sex crimes are prominent. Some believe it's evidence of how serious the problem really is. "Disney's problem goes much deeper than a few cases," says Professor Jack Enter. "Ninety-nine percent of voyeur cases never get reported. The victims don't know they are victims. You can't go on crime stats to understand the full extent of the problem."

Had Richard Seeley, Vincent Amato, Essene Feliciano, Vernon Donaldson, or John Giangrossi stolen from Disney's till, the Mouse would have pushed for full prosecution. The company has what it calls a "zero tolerance" policy when it comes to employee theft. Yet if an employee peeps on or masturbates in front of guests or other employees, the Mouse often dismisses the evidence as though it weren't criminal behavior that might—or might not—interfere with his duties. "Disney would pull out all the stops, pull in tactical units if anybody tried to give them a counterfeit note, but if someone was videotaping their staff undressing or guests using the bathroom, well—'boys will be boys,'" says Jack Enter. "Their focus is on profit, not their personnel."

CHAPTER EIGHT

Mickey's Firehouse

This is not a story for the faint of heart. In May 1988 John Conway was hired to serve as a firefighter at Walt Disney World. If you are going to fight fires, he figured, what better place could there be to work? He went to work his first day, excited to be part of the Disney Company. But his job with a company that claims it can make dreams come true soon turned into a nightmare.

Most people are unaware that Disney World operates its own emergency service system, which includes firefighters like John Conway and emergency medical personnel. Like the Mouse's security operations, which we discussed earlier, the Mouse has fire and medical stations strategically located around the circumference of the Walt Disney World complex. Behind EPCOT, a secret network of fenced-in roads allows fire trucks to move freely in the event of an emergency. And at the Magic Kingdom, subterranean tunnels and false walls allow emergency service workers to get in, load a patient on a cot, and get out without attracting attention or stirring up much pixie dust.

While the firefighters technically work for Reedy Creek, Disney is their real employer. When someone like John Conway applies for a job as a firefighter, he interviews with people at the Disney Casting Office. Those actually hired receive Disney employee I.D. cards, and are subject to Disney's grooming standards as spelled out in *The Disney Look: Guidelines for Cast Members at Walt Disney World Resort*. Their health insurance benefits are handled by the Mouse. The firefighters have their performance reviews through Disney, and they can work on the job only so long as they have medical clearance from Disney physicians and health-care providers. Firefighters are rewarded for their service and attendance with Disney pins. For perfect attendance, they receive a Mickey Mouse watch.

The Emergency Medical Service (EMS) Division has approximately

160 employees, up from 58 in 1971. Each station houses two ambu-
lances, a fire engine and tower, and specialized equipment to extract
people from confined spaces. While they receive more than 15,000
calls per year, like a lot of 911 systems, the service is abused and most
calls are for minor problems.

But this fire service is unlike any other in the country. To those who
work in the shadow of Cinderella's Castle, the service has become
known not for its heroics, but for the level of sexual and physical
abuse that has occured in Mickey's Fire Department in recent years.
And like so much crime that has occured in the Magic Kingdom, the
Mouse has seen fit to cover up the problem rather than actually deal
with it.

John Conway had been assigned to the Magic Kingdom Fire Station
in the summer of 1988. While on duty one afternoon, he was walking
around the day room of the station still getting accustomed to his
new job when "it" happened. All of a sudden a group of firefighters
began pushing the sofas out of the way and then grabbed him and
forcibly restrained him. "They undid my pants," he recalls in a sworn
deposition, "took down my pants and my underwear, and they forced
me to bend over." Next, with his legs kicking and his screams rever-
berating throughout the station, a firefighter named Vince Byrd
walked into the room. "[He] had a medical gown on, a white lab coat
and latex gloves and surgical mask and all that kind of stuff," recalls
Conway. Before the ordeal was over, they probed his rectum with the
eraser end of a pencil. His assailants had a name for this method of
attack: a "sphincter view."

But they weren't through having "fun" with him: Conway was then
forced to walk through the fire station with his pants and underwear
around his ankles. He was taken to the laundry room, where he was
handcuffed to the laundry racks with another firefighter named
Michael Tucker, who had also just been attacked. They stood in the
dark for twenty minutes screaming to be let out before they were
freed.

Conway was horrified and reported the abuse to Lee Wilson, the
assistant chief on the next shift. "I was shocked, and I couldn't believe

what happened," he recalls. "I told him that I was 'sphincter viewed.' I said that's outrageous." But according to Conway, Wilson just laughed and reminded him that as a new employee he was on probation and could be fired for any reason. The assistant chief also apparently shared the news of Conway's complaint with some other firefighters because days later some of his assailants reportedly threatened him, saying repeatedly, "I heard you have a family."

Conway was not alone in being "sphincter viewed," and over the next several years, he saw other coworkers attacked in the same cruel manner. In fact, this fire station, which sits in the shadow of Cinderella's Castle, was the site of numerous attacks on other unsuspecting victims. And as many of those who were assaulted tell it, management not only tolerated these attacks, but actually condoned them.

John Henderson was also hired as a firefighter in 1988. He clearly recalls in a sworn deposition when "it" happened to him. It was 1989 and he was relaxing in a recliner in the day room when suddenly he was "taken from the chair to the linen room and handcuffed on what was the clothing rack." One person reached around him and undid his belt, "while the other one put the handcuffs on." By the time the incident was over, Henderson remembered he was "sobbing." Like Conway, he reported the incident to his superior, Lieutenant John Howe. Howe said Henderson was "being too sensitive."

Within only a couple months of being hired, firefighter Carl Stutes claims he was violated in the same way. Stutes says he was sitting in the day room when he was attacked by fellow firefighter Charlie Forsyth and another man. They held Stutes down, undid and pulled down his pants, and then ripped off his underwear. Forsyth threatened to insert a laryngoscope into Stutes's rectum, but in the end didn't do it.

A couple of years before the attacks on Conway and Henderson, firefighter Jay Phillips began to experience what he says were years of nightmarish abuse by his coworkers. Born in St. Augustine, Florida, the son of a biologist, Phillips joined the Navy out of high school in 1974 and stayed in for five years. Uncle Sam put him aboard the U.S.S.

Saratoga and trained him to be a firefighter. After he left the service, it seemed the obvious next step was to find work as a civilian in the same field. He passed his fire standards test at Ocala Community College in central Florida and in 1980 was hired at the Tavares Fire Department. When an opening became available at Disney World, he got the job. The memory of his first shift at the Mouse is one he will carry with him for the rest of his life.

He was working at Station One, the B shift. "When I got to the double doors," he recalls in a sworn deposition. "I was jumped from behind, and my pants were ripped from my body, including my underwear. I was placed in the prone position by a few firefighters, and Driver Operator [Bruce] Johnson began probing my rectum with his ink pen."

The attack continued for several minutes. When they were finished with him, his assailants just laughed and walked away. Phillips thought the attack was some sort of initiation rite and hoped it wouldn't happen again. But unfortunately, it was only the beginning of what would, for Phillips, be a prolonged, horrendous experience.

A few days later his attackers came after him again. Phillips took refuge in the ceiling rafters, clinging to beams. He thought he had found a safe hiding place. But as he tells it, he was inevitably discovered and ordered down by his commanding officer, William Campbell. When he reached the floor, he was jumped. And as his assailants removed his pants, Campbell simply stepped over him, refusing his request for help. The commanding officer told him, "It's your problem."

Since it usually took three or more people to hold him down, he often received bruises on his legs and arms from trying to resist his attackers. "Even the holidays were open to abuse," recalls Phillips. "One day near Christmas, Bruce Johnson called himself 'Sphincter Claus' and proceeded to attack me again." Johnson and the other firefighters who were a part of these attacks became known as "the Wolf Pack." According to firefighter Jim Mix, who had been with the department since 1982, the name came from the fact that when somebody "started picking on one person, everybody would kind of join in like a pack of wolves would do with an injured animal."

The assaults on Phillips continued over the next several years. According to Phillips, he was attacked about once a month, perhaps a total of twenty-four to thirty times. He often tried to hide from his tormentors. "I know that Jay used to run and hide all the time," says Conway.

One obvious question is, Why did the abused firefighters choose to stay employed at Disney? Several of them explain that they were too embarrassed to share their stories with anyone. Many never even told their wives. Some, like Phillips and Conway, explain that they were threatened by colleagues and told "I heard you have a family." Phillips says that because he worked in the Navy and then the fire service, he was accustomed to "chain of command" reporting. And when no one in the chain of command would help, he simply assumed he had no right to do anything else and had to endure the abuse if he wanted to keep his job.

You would think that numerous cases of sexual abuse reported by half-a-dozen employees would warrant action by management at the "happiest place on earth." You would be wrong.

Clinical psychologist Edmund Bartlett of Winter Park, Florida, examined firefighter Phillips and characterizes the assaults as "ritual attacks." The attacks were designed by senior firefighters to be part of "character-building" exercises. (How they expected them to build character is anyone's guess.) They were well-planned and executed with elaborate—if bizarre—preparation.

Jim Mix reports witnessing fellow firefighter Danny Akers being assaulted. "Several people were chasing Danny Akers to 'sphincter view' him because he was new," he says in a sworn deposition. Three firefighters "grabbed him, [and] bent him over the back of the couch." One "was sitting on his head and pushing his chest into the couch," while two others pulled his pants down, and prepared him for penetration. And all this time, Akers was screaming, fighting, and "trying to get away." Fortunately for Akers, fellow firefighter Scott Lyons intervened, and the assault was halted. Jay Phillips says Akers "told me that was the most humiliating, degrading thing he had ever been

14

```
 1                (Discussion held off the record.)

 2      A.    I'm going to tell you -- and you can put

 3   this on the record -- exactly how I feel about this

 4   once and for all.

 5              This has caused me great mental stress.

 6   I'm going to end up back in the hospital again if

 7   these proceedings continue.  I went under the most

 8   tragic things anyone could ever do, and right now

 9   I'm shaking.  My insides are tearing apart.

10              This is not a subject I will discuss.  The

11   only answer you're going to get from me is "no

12   comment", case closed.  If you want to take me into

13   court, you want to do whatever you want, you do it,

14   but I'm about to call an ambulance.  Do you

15   understand that?  I cannot go through this again.

16      Q.    All right.  All right.

17      A.    Have you ever heard the term "rape"?  Do

18   you understand what rape is?

19      Q.    Yes, sir, I do.

20      A.    All right, then.  Then leave me alone,

21   because that's what I feel like every time you

22   people call me in to do this stuff.

23              MS. SWANSON:  Let's go outside.

24              (Discussion held off the record.)

25
```

Former Disney firefighter Dante Battilla, who filed a complaint against Disney because of the sexual attacks he experienced, discusses under oath the pain the attacks caused him. Disney quietly reached a confidential settlement with Battilla.

through in his life." Akers told Firefighter J.R. Murphy the same thing. Still, Akers was afraid to report what was going on for fear of possible retribution. He later died of cancer.

Dante Battilla, another firefighter, filed a Charge of Discrimination with the Florida Commission on Human Relations against Disney in January 1995. Battilla charged that coworkers "held me down and shoved a penlight up my rectum." Disney eventually settled with Battilla, who, as part of a confidential settlement, can no longer discuss the attacks.

But "sphincter viewing" was not the only abuse that occurred; there was also the threat of a "fullering" attack. In a sudden, unprovoked attack, the heaviest firefighters would jump on top of someone all at the same time. "There was the 'Fuller Nine' or the 'Fuller Eight,'" says Conway, "and it was a group of guys out at the station, and they were the heaviest, biggest guys at work."

Fullering attacks were naturally not as intrusive as "sphincter viewing," but they could be painful. Firefighter Dante Battilla reports in his complaint that coworkers "who were the largest on duty would take a running jump and land on me while other firefighters were holding me down, until about one thousand pounds of men were on top of me and caused me to bleed in my urine for two days."

Disney claims in court documents that they had no knowledge that "fullering" ever took place. Yet the firehouse management clearly knew. At one point the Reedy Creek management even tried to regulate "fullering." Commander Van Kirkpatrick placed a four-person limit on "fullering," according to Phillips and Conway. Firefighter Carl Stutes says Van Kirkpatrick told him that "fullering" should be limited to about "2,000 pounds."

You would think that numerous cases of abuse reported by half-a-dozen employees might warrant action by management, especially at the "happiest place on earth." Certainly fire department supervisors and Disney management knew about the problems. Firefighter John Henderson says he recalls Jay Phillips raising the subject of the sexual attacks in front of the Fire Department's deputy chief of operations, Gene Rivers, at a shift meeting. Henderson also claims that Rivers

Dep. of John Conway
3/19/97   27

1	sphincter viewing; is that correct?
2	A. That is correct.
3	Q. I am asking you a fairly broad question.
4	I will probably come back and ask you some specifics
5	later because I'm taking notes and I may come back
6	and ask you some specifics, but I would like for you
7	to describe to me what occurred on the day when you
8	believe you were sphincter-viewed.
9	A. They cleared the couches in the dayroom,
10	moved the couches back, because the couches were in
11	the middle of the room there, and they restrained me
12	and put their arms around me. And I couldn't move
13	or go or, you know, walk or, you know. I'm going:
14	What the heck is going on? What are you doing. Get
15	away from me, you know, leave me alone.
16	And they put me out in the middle of the
17	floor of the dayroom. They handcuffed me. They put
18	handcuffs on me. They undid my pants, took down my
19	pants and my underwear, and they forced me to bend
20	over. Vince Byrd --
21	Q. Who?
22	A. Vince Byrd, Gerry Vincent Byrd, had a
23	medical gown on, a white lab coat and latex gloves
24	and a surgical mask and all that kind of stuff, and
25	they were all wearing gloves, and they exposed my

LIBBY LESTER REPORTING SERVICES
ORLANDO. FLORIDA (407) 425-6543 or (800) 525-3994

Firefighter John Conway describes the sexual attacks he experienced in a March 19, 1997, sworn deposition. Disney quietly settled with Conway a civil suit he brought against the company.

28

1   anus to everybody in the room.

2   Everybody was laughing, carrying on. They

3   took a pencil, I believe it was a pencil, the eraser

4   end of a pencil, and they forced -- they pushed it

5   around in my butt.

6   Q.   In your anus?

7   A.   Yes.

8   Q.   Now, during this time --

9   MR. REID: Move to strike his narrative.

10   Q.   During this time you indicated that your

11 hands were handcuffed. Were they handcuffed

12 together? Were they handcuffed to something else?

13 Describe for me how you were handcuffed.

14   A.   My hands were handcuffed behind my back.

15   Q.   And you've referred throughout that they

16 physically forced you and they all were wearing

17 gloves. Can you describe for me specifically,

18 giving me the names of who they were?

19   A.   Yes.

20   Q.   Who is that?

21   A.   Dennis New. Gerry Vincent Byrd. David --

22 God, I can't think of his last name. How horrible.

23 Gary Armstrong. Greg Lang.

24   MS. SIGMAN: Is that Lane or Lang?

25   THE WITNESS: Lang, L-a-n-g.

1   A.   Not David Grifis. Not David Grifis. I

2   can't think of his name right off. How could I

3   forget his name?

4   Q.   Okay. But another individual also?

5   A.   Yeah.

6   Q.   If the name comes to you during the course

7   of the deposition, if you'll just let us know, I'd

8   appreciate it.

9   Anybody else?

10   A.   No.

11   Q.   Now, the names of the individuals that

12 you've just given us, are those the individuals who

13 actually participated in either physically

14 restraining you or sticking a pencil, eraser end of

15 a pencil, into your anus?

16   A.   Yes.

17   Q.   Were there other individuals in the

18 room --

19   A.   Yes.

20   Q.   -- when this occurred?

21   A.   Yes.

22   Q.   Can you give me the names specifically of

23 those individuals, the ones that you recall?

24   A.   All I can recall, Butch Dougherty and

25 Jimmy Puterbaugh. And the others, I can't even

30

```
 1   remember.  I was shocked.
 2       Q.   Had you been warned that this was going to
 3   happen to you?
 4       A.   No.
 5       Q.   Had you heard that it might happen to you
 6   because you were a new man on the job out there?
 7       A.   Yes.
 8            MR. REID:  Objection, leading.
 9       Q.   Who had you heard that from?
10       A.   I can't remember individual names at this
11   time.  I was not the only one sphincter-viewed that
12   day.  They took another individual.
13       Q.   Okay.  Wait just a minute and we'll get to
14   that.  I'm going to ask you a specific question
15   about that.
16            Well, do you know which individual of the
17   ones that you named was the one who stuck the eraser
18   end of a pencil into your anus?
19       A.   No, I can't.  I don't.  At that point I
20   was in shock.
21       Q.   After this occurred, what happened next?
22       A.   They forced me to walk around the station
23   with the handcuffs on, my pants down around my
24   ankles, and my underwear down around my ankles.
25   They led me back to the -- there was two little
```

31

1   rooms in the back of the bunk room. One was a

2   laundry room and the other room was a bunk room.

3   The laundry room, they put me and the

4   other individual in, and they handcuffed us to the

5   laundry racks that were in the room. These were

6   metal laundry racks that they hung the uniforms on.

7   As a matter of fact, the laundry racks are still out

8   at the station at this time, or they still use those

9   same laundry racks.

10   They closed the door, turned the lights

11   off.

12   Q.   Now, let me stop you there for a minute.

13   When you say "they", are you talking about the same

14   individuals that you identified earlier?

15   A.   Yes. However, in the laundry room, it was

16   Gerry Vincent Byrd and Dennis New.

17   Q.   Just those two?

18   A.   That I can recall.

19   Q.   I mean, do you believe that there were

20   more individuals that you can't recall specifically

21   their name or do you simply recall there only being

22   two other people doing this to you, Vincent and

23   Byrd? I mean Byrd and New?

24   A.   Right.

25   Q.   After they closed the door and turned the

actually threw him out of a later shift meeting when he brought the subject up.

As deputy chief of operations from 1984 to 1995, Rivers was responsible for supervising all of the assistant chiefs on the various shifts, enforcing the policies and regulations of the department, assisting in making new policies and procedures, and receiving information on incidents of physical harassment of employees. Yet Rivers claims he never heard about the attacks until 1995, when a formal investigation was launched.

John Conway says he reported the attacks to Fire Chief Pete Thomas numerous times beginning in 1988, his first year on the job. In 1992 he went to the Florida Psychiatric Group and reported the harassment to a Disney manager who worked at the Florida Psychiatric Group part-time. He told Disney Labor Relations Manager Jerry Montgomery about the attacks in July of that same year. And on January 13, 1993, he even filed a request for a formal investigation by the Reedy Creek Improvement District. The request was denied. Finally, in April 1994 Conway says he reported the harassment to Disney Labor Relations Manager Ralph Mitchell. No one took action.

Union officials, however, were seriously troubled by these reports and raised the matter several times during contract negotiations with Disney. Jim Puterbaugh, the union president, addressed the subject in negotiation sessions attended by Bill Ward, a Disney labor relations attorney; Jerry Montgomery, Disney's labor relations vice president; and Mickey Shiver, a Reedy Creek administrator. Larry Jessup, the firefighters' hired union negotiator, says Disney management knew about "sphincter viewing" and "fullering" because he brought the matter up during labor negotiations in both 1989 and 1992. "I recall a very specific conversation I had with Jerry Montgomery, Jim Puterbaugh, and Don Helenthall at the bar in the hotel we were negotiating at," he recalls in a sworn deposition. "And the specific purposes of our after-hours, if you would, conversations was on these issues of the 'sphincter viewing' and using those forms of harassment." Firefighter J.R. Murphy was present at the negotiations and says he remembers Jessup raising the subject.

Disney's knowledge of these attacks was apparent. In a class on sexual harassment attended by the firefighters at EPCOT in 1990 or 1991, Sandi Adams (a Disney employee) brought up the subject of "sphincter viewing." Both Jay Phillips and John Conway claim that former Chief Pete Thomas was in that class at the time.

These attacks didn't occur quietly in the dark corners of the Disney firehouse. Instead, they took place in open areas. Sometimes they were even announced in advance over the public address system. According to both Mix and Phillips, these announcements would allow the commanders and lieutenants to leave the day room before the sexual assaults began. John Howe, former deputy manager of administration at Reedy Creek, admits that these attacks were not dark, department secrets, but part of "general talk around the department."

Still Disney and Reedy Creek did nothing to halt these attacks or punish those who carried them out. "With all of the harassment that was occurring, there was no action by the upper management," says Phillips. "They chose to ignore the problem and hoped it would go away."

It was only after Phillips sent a twenty-one–page report to Tom Moses, top administrative officer for Reedy Creek, in August 1995 that an investigation commenced. The investigation was launched to determine whether indeed the attacks had taken place. A.W. "Tony" Coschignano of the Orlando Fire Department conducted the inquiry, interviewing thirty-five different witnesses. But he had limited resources. Moreover, some managers were not keen to cooperate, given their knowledge of and sometime involvement in these attacks. Still, Coschignano persisted, and in January 1996 he finally presented his results to management. Fire Chief John Best, Mickey Shiver, and Tom Moses attended the meeting. Coschignano concluded that Phillips, Henderson, Stutes, and Conway "had in fact been subjected to 'sphincter viewing.'"

Disney and Reedy Creek took no action.

Reports of sexual harassment and abuse are not entirely new ground for Disney and Reedy Creek. In 1994 a group of female firefighters successfully sued the Mouse for sexual harassment.

Firefighters Barbara Brown and Pamela Lang and Training Captain Michelle Bartley alleged Disney and Reedy Creek condoned 140 incidents of sexual harassment by male firefighters and their supervisors between 1988 and 1992. The male firefighters posed naked in front of the women, urinated in front of them in the women's restroom, and regularly watched "pornographic videotapes at the station." The women noted that they repeatedly reported the incidents to superiors, but the complaints fell on deaf ears. Disney lost the case in court, and ended up paying the women millions.

Phillips and Conway both filed civil suits against Reedy Creek and Disney. (In July 1998 Disney quietly settled out of court with Conway for an undisclosed sum of money. The Phillips case is still pending.) Other firefighters talk about the

To date, no one has been punished for these attacks. Instead, several of the most persistent perpetrators have been promoted.

case only reluctantly. There was deep shame in admitting that they were victims and had been violated by coworkers. When several firefighters who were not part of the lawsuit were forced to give depositions, they wept during cross-examination. Most were embarrassed about the attacks and had shared them with no one, not even their spouses.

Disney refuses to comment in official court documents on these attacks or the Coschignano report. Several of the accused have denied the allegations. The company claims that the problems are Reedy Creek's and not Disney's. And it argues that the Magic Kingdom has nothing to do with the management of the Fire Department.

Yet when these firefighters were hired, they were interviewed by officials from Disney's "Casting Office," and all received Disney employee I.D. cards, were subject to Disney's grooming standards, and were given copies of *The Disney Look: Guidelines for Cast Members at the Walt Disney World Resort*. The firefighters have their performance reviews through Disney, and they can work on the job only so long as they have medical clearance from Disney physicians and health-care providers. The company also rewards them with

Disney pins for their service and attendance. For perfect attendance, they receive a Mickey Mouse watch. Even their health insurance benefits are handled by the Mouse.

In his *Standards of Business Conduct*, Michael Eisner says that "Upholding legal standards of conduct, while mandatory, is not enough. We are also responsible for maintaining ethical standards. These standards govern how we treat everyone we have contact with. These are standards of integrity—trust—respect—fair play—and teamwork." But not, evidently, at Mickey's Firehouse.

To date, no one has been punished for these attacks. Instead, several of the most persistent perpetrators have been promoted.

PART III
The Children's Idea Factory

CHAPTER NINE

Animation

I n 1994 Warner Brothers decided to conduct a unique experiment. The company was preparing to release a new animated movie called *Thumbelina*, based on the old Hans Christian Andersen fairy tale about a tiny girl. As motion picture companies almost always do, it held a test screening to gauge audience interest. The reaction to the first screening was flat. Frustrated and disappointed because it felt it had a good product, Warner decided to try something that had never been done before. The company stripped the Warner Brothers logo off the lead-in segment and replaced it with Disney's name. The results were startling. Although the film remained the same, test scores soared.

Thanks to the rich history of Disney films like *Cinderella, Pinocchio, Sleeping Beauty, Bambi,* and *Fantasia*—and the decline in Hollywood's golden era when Warner Brothers, Paramount, and the rest had definable styles and stars that made each studio's work instantly recognizable—the Mouse has become the only real brand name in movies. When people hear about an upcoming Disney animated film, they flock to the theater to see it, not because it features a big star, but precisely because it is a *Disney* film. "Disney's brand name is impossible to beat," Philip LaZebnik told us. He cowrote the scripts for Disney's *Pocahontas* and *Mulan.*

Disney is the undisputed champion of animation. John Lasseter, director of Disney's *Toy Story*, is only half kidding when he says, "You can have an hour and a half of blank film leader with the Disney name on it and people will go see it."

Max Howard, who worked in Disney animation from 1986 to 1995 and now heads Warner Features animation, agrees. "People will go to see a Disney movie even if it's not good. They've earned that."

And when it comes to generating company profits, no division of

Disney can match the financial returns from animation. Forget all the talk about live-action movies, Miramax Films, ABC, or even the theme parks. The Mouse's heavy profits come from animation. Consider:

- Without animated hits like the classic *Fantasia* and *Beauty and the Beast*, Disney's film division would have lost $100 million in the early 1990s.
- The rerelease of *Fantasia* and the 1961 version of *101 Dalmatians* alone contributed more than $415 million to the bottom line, more than half the company's income in one year.
- In 1993, when Disney released a videocassette version of the classic *The Jungle Book*, it actually took in more money in sales than the blockbuster *Jurassic Park* took in at the box office. (And of course it cost a lot less to put *The Jungle Book* on videocassette than it did to make *Jurassic Park*.)
- In 1992 home-video sales of *Beauty and the Beast* provided roughly one-third of the full year's earnings for all of Disney's filmed entertainment.
- According to the *Los Angeles Times*, animation and its ancillary income (merchandising, etc.) may account for 70 percent of all Disney profits.
- *The Hunchback of Notre Dame*, which had only a fair showing at the box office, added an estimated $500 million to Disney's bottom line—about a quarter of Disney's entire annual profit in a given year.
- *The Lion King* alone has made more in *net profits* ($1.5 billion) than the entire Miramax Films Division is worth (estimated at $1 billion).

Disney executives have told the Associated Press that animation is more than twice as profitable as all of the studio's live action films combined—with a fraction of the risk and effort. "In an average year," writes Associated Press reporter John Horn, "Disney may release two animation films and 60 live-action titles (including Miramax films) and yet those two animated movies dwarf the 58 other releases."

Yet while Michael Eisner is almost universally regarded as the brilliant captain who piloted the Disney ship back to profitability, he actually considered killing the animation studio in the mid-1980s, when he became chairman. The Chief Mouse thought animation was an expensive and slow way to make films, and he favored live action. He gave the animation studio a reprieve, but handed control over to Walt's nephew, Roy E. Disney, Jr. , who had never worked in the Animation Department. Soft-spoken, laconic, and lanky, Roy Disney had helped make Michael Eisner chairman in 1984.

Walt's nephew inherited an animation studio in the doldrums. Films like the *The Black Cauldron* were expensive to produce and were generating very little at the box office. Over the next half-dozen years, animation was considered "the stepchild" of the company, according to Roy Disney. His office was on the third floor of the old animation building, a long walk from the center of company power. In February 1985 Michael Eisner had the animation depart-ment moved off the studio lot. The division was placed four miles across town in a nondescript tilt-slab warehouse by the Glendale Freeway. Any new television animation work was sent overseas. "[The new management] are stressing the live action more so than the ani-mation," said animator Jane Baer at the time. "The animators have been made to feel like second-class citizens."

Michael Eisner is regarded as the brilliant captain who piloted the Disney ship back to profitability, but he almost killed the animation division when he took over.

But Roy Disney remained committed to seeing animation succeed. He brought in new talent and supported their creative ideas. Absent his efforts, it's unlikely Eisner would have stuck with the company's biggest money-making division. Will Finn, who has worked on numerous Disney animated features since the late 1970s, told us Roy Disney was "the Godfather and saving saint of Disney animation. Without him, Michael Eisner probably would have shut it down."

Even though animation survived, Eisner's attention in those early years was focused on live-action films. Reporters at the business pub-lication *Barron's* recall that when they paid a visit to the Mouse in

June 1991, Eisner and Disney executives were touting the success of *Pretty Woman* and talking up *Billy Bathgate* (a film that eventually bombed at the box office), and were making wild predictions (which turned out to be sadly wrong) about the profitability of Euro-Disney. Although it was just six months before the release of *Beauty and the Beast*, they had little to say about it. Actually, according to *Barron's*, company executives were downright surprised that the reporters even expressed an interest in talking about animation. But six months later, after *Beauty and the Beast* proved immediately profitable, Eisner suddenly took an interest. *Beauty* made nearly double at the box office what *Little Mermaid* had made in 1989. As it turned out, without the success of Disney's neglected Animation Division, the company would have lost money under Eisner's tenure.

The cash flow from animation stems not only from new films, but also from the continued appeal of the Disney classics. The video release of the animated version of *101 Dalmatians* sold 15.9 million copies in one year. *Fantasia* sold 9.6 million in the same amount of time. Pinnochio sold 13.4 million copies in 1993 alone, and *Snow White* a whopping 36 million worldwide in 1994. In fact, Disney animation has the five top-selling home-video titles in history, which generate an immense cash flow no other entertainment company can equal. Lisbeth Barron, an entertainment analyst at S.G. Warburg and Company, estimates that Disney *nets* $7 on every video it sells. Who else can release a thirty-year-old film on videocassette every seven years or so and make that kind of money?

The success of Disney animation can still be traced to the tremendous commitment Walt Disney made to perfecting his craft, to achieving the highest quality of detailed animation artistry. Walt would willingly toss out twenty minutes of animation, which might represent hundreds of hours of expensive work, if it did not help a film. Animator Jack Kinney worked for Walt for more than twenty-seven years on films like *Pinocchio*, *Dumbo*, and *Peter Pan*. "Walt set his goals high and expected everyone around him to do the same," he recalls. "To say a thing was impossible was un-Disney."

Walt developed animated film into an art form. From the first

Mickey Mouse short to the technical brilliance of computer animation used in *Toy Story*, no one can surpass Disney's ability to generate excitement and interest through visual images.

But fans are also committed to Disney because they trust in the Disney story. As writer Richard Schickel puts it, Walt Disney positioned himself as a friend of the "family market" and as a purveyor of "largely innocent fantasy." Parents trust their kids to Disney—so much so that the Mouse has become America's most popular baby-sitter. Most parents feel confident that popping in a Disney animated video means innocent, clean entertainment.

Walt earned that trust over decades by placing strong restrictions on what could and couldn't happen in his cartoons. The old Disney produced a "Comic Book Art Specifications" manual that provided artists with strict guidelines for drawing Mickey and his friends. Disney characters could not partake in drinking, smoking, off-color humor, or swearing. And, of course, the relationship between Mickey and Minnie, or Donald and Daisy, was "platonic," according to the manual.

The reputation of the characters was protected not only by controlling how they would be drawn but also by how they were marketed. When someone at the company authorized the use of Disney characters in a beer commercial in exchange for a nice royalty fee, Walt was outraged. He immediately put a halt to it. When a watch-maker produced a wristwatch with Mickey and Minnie embracing, Walt yanked the licensing agreement, fearing that the scene was too sexual. And when the Disney Studio was working on names for the Seven Dwarfs, there was a long, intense discussion about using the name "Dopey." Some thought it sounded too modern and connoted narcotics addiction. Only after Walt found the word in Shakespeare did the dim-witted dwarf get his name.

There were numerous rewrites of the story *Pinocchio* because of concerns about how the little stick-boy might come off to parents. Unlike the original version of the story, Walt decided to present the boy as someone easily swayed by bad influences, rather than a determined delinquent. He felt parents would prefer it that way.

Every effort was always made to protect the innocence of Disney characters, a quality Walt felt was central to their appeal. "Mickey's a nice fellow," he once said, "who never does anybody harm, who gets into scrapes through no fault of his own but always manages to come up grinning." In a 1935 internal memo Walt laid out six qualities he believed made a good animator. One of those was "Knowledge of story construction and audience values."

But the company that once prodigiously guarded the *mores* of Mickey and friends no longer exists. Today, Disney films are fundamentally different. Like the changes at Disney World, the company's animation is no longer what it once was. Driven by both a short-term profit motive and a lessened concern about conveying troubling messages to children, recent animated releases have a more adult orientation. Tom Sito is an animator who worked at the Mouse for eight years before jumping to Dreamworks. At Disney he played a central role in several recent films. He led the story team for *Pocahontas*, was a member of the story team for *The Lion King*, and was an animator on *The Little Mermaid*. "Animation started changing at Disney in the late 1980s," he told us. "The emphasis moved away from producing traditional kids' fare. For marketing purposes, they wanted a more adult product in animation, something that would attract both kids and adults."

Philip LaZebnik, who co-wrote *Pocahontas*, told us the same thing. "The natural tendency from *Little Mermaid* on is that you didn't want to concentrate on little kids. There was a real desire to break away from simple kid audiences and to make movies that appeal to adults."

But often, to attract the interest of adults, a film must tackle mature subject matter and incorporate imagery parents may not have in mind for their kids. According to Professor Ronald Ostman in the *Journal of Popular Film and Television*: "Disney routinely might try to produce a multi-level film that appeals to children on a basic level and titillates accompanying adults on a different level (for example, sexually)."

Adult elements enter the animated features in ways both small and large. *Toy Story*, for example, includes plenty of action for children and lots of merchandise made for little consumers. But the film also includes dialogue that is unquestionably geared for adults. When the cowboy Woody pooh-poohs Buzz Lightyear's high-tech gadgets, he's accused of "laser envy." Face it—this Freudian connotation is not directed at four-year-olds.

In *The Hunchback of Notre Dame*, cute Quasimodo the Hunchback is clearly a character designed for the enjoyment of kids, and Disney sold millions of toys bearing his image. But in reality the movie is intended more for adults. Will Finn, head of the film's story team, says he enjoyed working on *Hunchback* but had some misgivings. "The film includes incredibly dark and mature subject matter," he told us in an exclusive interview. "It's about the complexity of a religious figure who is torn between good and evil, chastity and lust." *Snow White* this is not.

There are also deep undercurrents in the film related to the Catholic Church. The film's most dynamic figure, Judge Frollo, teaches Quasimodo the alphabet by having him recite the words: "Abomination, blasphemy, contrition, damnation." Finn said that the Disney story team intended for Frollo, the archvillain of the film, to be a priest as he was in Hugo's book. But executives figured that it would be "too controversial. So we had to secularize Frollo," he says. "But we did everything visually to indicate that he was supposed to be a priest."

The songs for the film are also really not intended for kids. Alan Menken, the Oscar-winning composer of *Hunchback*'s music, admits, "In one song, we have Frollo sing the church liturgy but also sing of twisted sexual fantasies." Lusting after Esmeralda, Frollo says, "Hellfire, hellfire, there's a fire in my skin. This burning desire is turning me to sin." Clearly this is new territory for Disney. Can you imagine Captain Hook doing anything of the sort?

But Disney Chairman Michael Eisner was an early and consistent champion of *Hunchback* and these controversial story elements. At one point during production, when animators got nervous about the film's content, he reportedly told them, "We can't make Dumbo forever."

This duality in the new Disney animated films—appealing to both children and adults—creates real confusion, even for those intimately involved with these projects. While the new Disney animated features have the same commitment to visual excellence, the stories are edgier. "Disney is both the same and different from before," LaZebnik told us.

Actor Robin Williams, who has voiced for several Disney animated films including *Aladdin*, puts it this way: "Disney is still Disney, the one ingrained in the American memory. But it's a different Disney, doing different things."

Actor Jason Alexander, who played George on *Seinfeld* and provided a voice for *The Hunchback of Notre Dame*, recounts his excitement when he first got involved in the project and his realization later on that this was a different Disney. "Disney would have us believe this movie is like the Ringling Brothers for children of all ages," he said about *Hunchback*. "But I won't be taking my four-year-old."

Disney has already received plenty of public criticism concerning the supposedly hidden messages in its animated movies. In August 1996 three Texans filed suit against the company, claiming there were veiled sexual messages in recent family-oriented features. The suit centered on three films: *The Little Mermaid, The Lion King*, and *Aladdin*. It is alleged that during a wedding scene in *The Little Mermaid* (1989), the presiding official becomes sexually aroused and a protrusion appears in the general genitalia area. In *The Lion King* (1994) the word "SEX" supposedly appears in a cloud of dust. And in *Aladdin* (1992), Aladdin flies to Princess Jasmine's balcony on his magic carpet and attempts to win her back after a fight. When her tiger Rajah threatens him, Aladdin tries to shoo the tiger while the genie cracks jokes. It is at this point that Aladdin allegedly whispers to Jasmine "Take off your clothes."

Are such messages actually in these films? The Disney animators we spoke with say there are some hidden images that do make their way into animated films—but not in these instances. Tom Sito, a straight-talking animator who drew the wedding scene, insists "the protrusion you see is his knees." And in *Aladdin*, the script at least calls for Aladdin to say: "Scat! Come on, good tiger. Take off and go. Down kitty." The dialogue is hard to distinguish even when one knows what to listen for, and it can easily be mistaken for a similar-sounding phrase such as "Take off your clothes." Sito also says the hazy letters that appear in the clouds during *The Lion King* really spell SFX—for special effects. Someone on the animation team wanted to leave a little "calling card" in the film.

Sito has spent more than a decade in animation. Before joining Disney, he drew other characters, including He-Man. Sito told us he's a bit surprised by the controversy over "hidden images" in *The Lion King*. The scene he thought would draw the most objection from critics was not the one with a subliminal message in the clouds, but a later scene in which the cubs Simba and Nala play together. "He's basically straddling her, if you know what I mean."

Disney spokesman Steve Feldstein, however, dismisses the notion that the company would ever put objectionable material in any children's animated program. "This is the Walt Disney Company," he says. "Why would we do something like this?"

But according to some Disney animators, it does happen. Animators insert the images as an inside joke to be shared with their colleagues. The 1988 Disney animated/live-action film *Who Framed Roger Rabbit?* is a treasure trove of hidden images. In one scene Jessica Rabbit's dress opens during a quick shot of her flying through the air. There is also a single frame of Betty Boop exposing herself to the camera while adjusting her garter. "With Betty Boop, you actually saw pubic hair," animator Dave Spafford, who worked on the picture, says proudly. And Spafford gleefully admits to having drawn other unexpected images in the film: Daffy Duck with an erection during the piano duel scene, and Bugs Bunny flipping off Mickey Mouse. The film also features graffiti suggesting that a good time can be had with someone called "Allyson Wonderland."

Then there is the case of the mysterious symbol on the video box for *The Little Mermaid*. The image is supposed to be a castle, but it seems to look more like what *Variety* calls "a phallic-shaped center spire." Whether the artist intended such a resemblance is not known. According to some Disney animators, the cover artist was reportedly disgruntled with the company and included the drawing as an act of defiance. While Disney contends that the symbol is not a phallus, it did discreetly repaint the spire for the laser disc cover.

In 1995 WDIV-TV Detroit reporter Emory King discovered that Donald Duck sometimes quacks out four-letter words. In a short, animated feature called "Clock Cleaners," a clock version of Donald Duck comes to life and begins to taunt the real Donald. The famous Disney fowl responds with a simple "F—- you!" When this was discovered, WalMart pulled the video from its shelves, and Disney promptly edited the film.

Although these pranks are usually drawn by animators interested in leaving their unique mark on a Disney film, that doesn't mean the company is unaware of them. Major characters in Disney animated features will have a team of ten to fifteen artists drawing them. Lesser characters still have five to seven artists. "Most people have the impression that one animator snuck these things in," LaZebnik told us. "But the fact is, each scene goes through hundreds of people and is edited. They all know the images are there."

Sometimes these "calling cards" even find their way into children's live-action films. Early on in the movie *The Santa Clause*, the character played by Tim Allen gives his wife an 800 number to call. The number he reads off is real: it belongs to a phone sex service. Disney claims that it did not know that it was a working number. Tanya Maloney, Disney's vice president of home video distribution, says, "Parents do need to take responsibility to prevent their children from calling any number they see and hear." Somehow, the fact that today's parents need to screen Disney movies before their kids see them was lost on her.

Most of the criticism Disney has received concerning its animation has been about the hidden messages. Yet the real change in Disney animation is more direct and visible than any subliminal message: The Disney characters created today are different. Mickey Mouse might have enjoyed innocent fun in Walt's day, but the new Disney has changed his mores. In the 1995 short Runaway Brain, the usually lovable mouse is a video game addict who forgets that it's the anniversary of his first date with Minnie. He intends to make it up to her by proposing a round of miniature golf, but Minnie somehow mistakes his offer for a $999.99 Hawaiian cruise. To pay for the cruise, Mickey agrees to serve as a subject in a sci-fi horror experiment. He ends up with a transplanted brain and become a drooling, fanged creature. He even attacks Minnie.

Consider the evolution of the new Disney heroine. Cinderella and Snow White were upstanding and good-hearted. "They lived by the Golden Rule," says Will Finn. "If you are good, goodness will come to you. That is what *Cinderella*, *Snow White*, and *Sleeping Beauty* are all about." Perhaps the last Disney heroine to fit that mold was Belle in *Beauty and the Beast*. Belle was independent and strong-willed, but also childlike and innocent.

More recent Disney heroines, however, are rebels who live on the edge. They are also full-figured, well-endowed, and sexually charged. For example, in *The Hunchback of Notre Dame*, the heroine Esmeralda sings a sexy and frothy song while doing a pole-dance that could have come out of *Showgirls*. Kirk Wise, the director of the film, called Esmeralda "a departure from the traditional Disney heroine because she's—a little more street-smart, a little more cynical, a little more dangerous. I think she's the first Disney heroine to carry a concealed weapon. We're proud of that fact."

In *Pocahontas* the Indian princess wears an off-the-shoulder dress that displays her figure. Company cochairman Roy Disney described the character as the most "incredibly beautiful and sexy female cartoon" in the company's history. The *New York Times* added that Pocahontas amounted to "an animated Playboy Playmate." And in fact she was designed that way. Animator Glen Keane drew Pocahontas with the aid of posing supermodels.

The great physical maturity and beauty of the new Disney heroines are mostly about attracting adult audiences (in this case males) to what used to be considered children's animated films. Bugs Bunny and other animated characters are also designed to attract adult audiences, but they do it with wit, not overt sexuality. In its review of *Hunchback*, *USA Today* noted that when it came to the voluptuous gypsy dancer, "Heaven knows most dads in the audience" will certainly notice.

And according to LaZebnik, that is precisely the point. In *Pocahontas*, he says, the shape and form of the princess was "designed to appeal to everyone, children, mothers, and adult males."

Disney's new heroines are different not only in looks, but also in deed. According to Will Finn, who worked on *Beauty and the Beast*, and on *The Little Mermaid* and as head of story on *The Hunchback of Notre Dame*, there is a bit of the feminist twist in the new Disney films. "Disney female characters are very strident," he says with a laugh. "For Disney heroines, the problems are always external. Someone is causing them problems, usually a male character or two. But the male heroes always have problems of their own making. The Beast had anger; Ali in *Aladdin*, his rudeness."

In *The Little Mermaid*, sixteen-year-old mermaid Ariel is tyrannized by her father Triton, who is unreasonably prejudiced against "humans." He calls them "barbarians" and "fish eaters." When his daughter falls in love with human Prince Eric, Triton condemns him. "Daddy, you don't even know him," Ariel whines.

"Know him! I don't have to know him," Triton responds. "They're all the same."

He goes on to destroy Ariel's entire collection of human artifacts she has collected over the years. When Ariel finally runs away from home and tries to unite with her true love, it is Triton who is repentant—not Ariel. And in the end, it is Triton who learns from the crab Sebastian: "Children have to be free to live their own lives." An unusual perspective on parenting.

In *Aladdin* Princess Jasmine also defies her father in order to be with her love, Ali. And like Triton, her father is constantly causing her problems and seems to learn more from his daughter than the other way around. And of course in *Pocahontas*, the princess has to defy her overprotective father to meet with John Smith. All three of these heroines must cope with patriarchal fathers who are narrow-minded and get in the way. "There definitely is a gender politics here," says Finn with a laugh. "It's almost illegal at Disney to create a character flaw in a female heroine."

Gender politics even entered into Disney's recent release *Mulan*. "In *Mulan*," Phil LaZebnik, who co-wrote it, told us, "there was a conscious effort to get away from the overt sexuality of Pocahontas or Esmeralda." But the feminist twist he mentions is firmly in place. As Janet Maslin noted in her review for the *New York Times,* "*Mulan* rails against gender prejudice by trotting out every storytelling stereotype in the Disney playbook.... Reverent as it is in the depiction of Mulan as a woman warrior, the film presents most of its male characters as buffoons." The "political correctness" of the film, she notes, is "intense."

Feminism is not the only form of sexual politics to enter Disney's animated films. In 1988 Thomas Schumacher joined Disney to take over production of *The Rescuers Down Under*. Being openly gay, he was concerned about being accepted when he joined the company. Today, however, he says that for homosexuals the Mouse offers "a supportive environment." Tremendously gifted as a storyteller, Schumacher was eventually promoted to vice president of the Animation Division and now plays an important role in the creative development of all the animated features.

Schumacher says he wants the animated films to have a message. "Hate comes up a lot," he says bluntly. "Probably the strongest message that comes up in all of our films is the notion of self-discovery and the power to be who you are.

To attract the interest of adults, a film must tackle mature subject matter and incorporate imagery parents may not have in mind for their kids.

That's what makes our films resonate. In each of our films there is somebody endeavoring to be who they want to be, who they can be." Does his view of self-discovery extend to sexual preference? Schumacher is coy when answering that question. "I am loath to say there are characters who are gay in our movies because people will want me to go backward and point them out."

But Ernie Sabella and Nathan Lane are not so shy. The two accomplished stage and screen actors provided the voices for the lovable Timon the Meerkat and Pumbaa the Warthog in *The Lion King*. "Timon's a feisty little cheerful fellow. He and Pumbaa seem to have a very nice arrangement—though I couldn't say what the extent of their relationship is," Lane says with a grin.

"I know what Nathan says about them," Ernie Sabella says laughing. "These are the first homosexual Disney characters ever to come to the screen. You can call Timon a gay character."

Animators say that "gay humor" has also found its way into the animated films. Andreas Deja is a talented animator who has worked in feature animation for more than fifteen years. Like Schumacher, Deja is openly gay, and he proudly lists the not-so-subtle gay characterizations in recent films. In *Aladdin*, he points out, the genie, whose voice is supplied by Robin Williams, coos to his master, "I'm getting fond of you, kid—not that I want to pick our curtains out or anything." He also notes that Gaston, the conceited hunk in *Beauty and the Beast*, at one point throws his legs over the arms of his chair and proclaims, "I do all my decorating with antlers!" Deja says he modeled Gaston after "preening West Hollywood muscle clones" he sees at his gym.

During production on these features, there were real debates over some of these characterizations. According to Schumacher, Jeffrey Katzenberg, then chairman of Disney Studios, was worried about the genie scene in *Aladdin*. "Jeffrey asked if those [scenes] offended me— which might surprise people, because apparently we weren't worried about offending Arabs," he recalls. "I thought it was all in good fun. I know we all argue among ourselves [in the gay community], but why try to deny the fact that swishy fashion designers exist? They do! What are we running from? Show me ten hairdressers: I'll show you eight gay men. What is the surprise?"

Disney's animation is changing at its very core. Each animated film has an underlying message that is central to the project. The values and truths each film projects are intentional and well-planned. Peter Schneider, president of Feature Animation, describes the process of developing a film this way. "First we come up with a core value for each story. I hate calling anything a mission statement but I suppose it could be called that. The core value puts process in creativity. It's written down, and we all talk about it. It's not mysterious or ethereal. It's a value that we hang on to in terms of judging whether we're doing a good job."

But do these "core values" really influence children? It's a debate that continues to rage in discussions over television, the movies, and music. Disney animators certainly think it does. Will Finn, for one, says he hopes the films he worked on "influence kids in a positive way."

LaZebnik adds that the message of each Disney film he worked on was methodically developed, "precisely because the company understands that entertainment can have a powerful effect on children."

Tom Sito agrees. "We like to say that television or films should not be where children should find their values and history, but it would be naive to think they don't."

Some research does indicate that children try to imitate what they see. According to the *Journal of the American Medical Association*, 74 percent of children say they want to copy what they see in movies and on television programs. As far as "hidden images" are concerned, the Federal Communications Commission (FCC) has outlawed their use in television advertising, claiming that subliminal messages are not a "fair business practice."

The most compelling element of Disney films used to be tapping into the heart of the human struggle: our day-to-day relationships with one another and our tattered but unshakable belief in goodness. Sometimes that core value was something basic and simple, like teaching a child about responsibility. While those elements still do appear in the films—for example, Simba in *The Lion King* learns about growing up and taking responsibility, and Hercules learns about proving himself—Disney's animation is increasingly designed to address complex social issues like racism, oppression, and religious intolerance. "I don't think you'll find deep social undercurrents in *Little Mermaid*," LaZebnik told us. "With each successive film it's apparent that the hope is to promote a deeper morality." Of course, the natural question is: Whose morality?

CHAPTER TEN

The PC Princess

Mike Gabriel remembers when the idea first came to him. It was Thanksgiving day, and he was spending time with his family. While he was still in the throes of completing *The Rescuers Down Under*, a charming film that helped to revive the animation industry, he was also mulling over what his next project might be. He had wanted to do a western, a big-scale epic that would lend itself to the kind of Broadway-oriented animated musicals that Disney had recently revived. But he just couldn't get the pieces to fit. So what he was now searching for instead was a quintessentially American story, something out of history and folklore that every schoolkid would know.

In the midst of the traditional holiday festivities, his mind was wandering through the stories he had heard as a child. Suddenly, he recalled the story of Pocahontas, the daughter of the powerful leader of the Powhatan nation who protected explorer Captain John Smith from certain death. To Gabriel it seemed like a perfect fit for Disney. When he got back to his office after Thanksgiving, he immediately took the idea to Michael Eisner, then–studio Chairman Jeffrey Katzenberg, and Thomas Schumacher, Disney's vice president for Animation. They loved it.

At first glance, *Pocahontas* seems to fit the mold of recent Disney successes. Like *Beauty and the Beast, Aladdin*, and *The Little Mermaid*, it could very easily work as the story of a heroine who deals with issues relating to coming of age and romance. In the past, Disney films had always hung on several moral lessons young children could take with them from the theater. And as Will Finn, who worked on *Beauty and the Beast* and *The Little Mermaid*, puts it, most often the lesson was "Disney's version of the golden rule: If you are good, goodness will come back to you." While the *Pocahontas* project undoubtedly started out that way, in the end, the story of the Indian princess was no ordinary Disney animated feature. The Mouse wanted to do more. And what it ended up creating tells us a lot about the new Disney.

After receiving the go-ahead from Disney executives to explore *Pocahontas*, Gabriel began working with animator Joe Grant to develop conceptual art. They played around with how the princess would be portrayed. Early on they became impressed by the notion of unity with nature and began consulting Native American writings on spiritual matters. While historians believe Pocahontas was twelve years old when she first encountered Captain John Smith, they transformed her into a "regal young woman in perfect harmony with the wind, trees, sky and water around her." The historical Pocahontas—who converted to Christianity, married an Englishman, and is buried in England—was transformed into a cover girl for Native American philosophies and present-day ecological concerns.

The early concept art was deeply animist—the Native American belief that rocks and trees, like humans, have spirits. Early on Grant drew Pocahontas with a mystical or spiritual quality. "Joe Grant's magnificent work was all about enchantment, magic," Schumacher recalls. "At that point, though, it seemed like icing for a cake that had yet to be baked. Yet, over time, it became clear how astounding his impact on the movie would be. His work spoke to an aspect of the movie that no one but he had understood: the spiritual side."

Soon after Grant drew the first sketches of the Indian princess, Disney tapped Oregon-based artist Bruce Zick to make the preliminary drawings of the natural setting. Zick, who worked on *The Rescuers Down Under* and *The Lion King*, recalls, "What I did was delve into the music, the philosophy, the spirituality, the symbols of that world as well as researching American historical landscapes." His artwork stressed the cycles Native Americans believe dominate natural life.

Meanwhile, other members of the growing *Pocahontas* team started making trips to Virginia, where the story takes place, to meet with Native American activists. The purpose of these trips, according to Stephen Rebello, who wrote the official history of the film, was to "learn from them tribal history, philosophy, beliefs about ecology" and "the spirit systems."

Strongly influenced by what they were learning about Native American philosophy, the Disney team began to reinvent Pocahontas. "In the beginning of developing this movie," recalls codirector Eric Goldberg, "we were going down the traditional Disney path. We had some yuks, some serious stuff, some light and frothy stuff—the Disney soufflé. But as we were trying to hash out the tone of the movie, the more cartoony we thought, the less it played. The basic subject matter of the movie could not be treated in a cavalier way."

Throughout the film, Native Americans and Englishmen are classified by race—into good and evil.

Instead, the spiritual basis of Native American life and their views of ecology deeply affected the Disney team. Suddenly, gone was the idea of a poignant story of love and maturing into adulthood. "The love story was what I'd come into this project most concerned about," recalls Gabriel. "But the ecological themes dropped in because the Native Americans are so ecologically based in their beliefs."

The tone of the film was also influenced by intervening external events. As the *Pocahontas* team went to work structuring the story, the 1992 Los Angeles riots erupted. The violence and destruction left a powerful imprint on the team, heightening its awareness of and concern for racism. Such intolerance became an important contemporary subject that needed to be addressed. So *Pocahontas* also became a drama about race relations. Schumacher remembers, "We knew that we were making more than just a love story or entertainment, but a story fundamentally about racism and intolerance."

How to incorporate the influences of Native American spiritualism and tackle complex racial issues in the same film—and an animated children's movie at that—was not easy. For months Gabriel and the others wrestled with how to merge the two themes. Finally the right chord was struck, and it didn't come from the story team but instead from the music team. Lyricists Stephen Schwartz and Alan Menken had been hired months earlier by Disney to weave apt music for the film. And in this case, their music set both the tone and direction of the entire movie. The first song they wrote was "Colors of the Wind."

You think you own whatever land you land on
The earth is just a dead thing you can claim
But I know ev'ry rock and tree and creature
Has a life, has a spirit, has a name
You think the only people who are people
Are the people who think and look like you
But if you walk the footsteps of a stranger
You'll learn things you never knew
You never knew.

Schwartz says the lyrics were inspired by Chief Seattle's famous speech to the United States Congress challenging white ascendancy in America and the appropriation of American Indian lands. And as it had done to the script, Native American spiritualism inspired much of the music. "From a lot of research into the writings by and about Native Americans," he says, "a whole pattern of thought began to emerge. I was not sure at first how 'adult' I could go with the songs, but the attitudes toward nature and the world contained in Native American philosophy impressed me."

Menken and Schwartz envisioned Pocahontas singing "Colors of the Wind" to the pale-faced explorer Captain John Smith. It was intended as a response to Smith's views of her ways as "savage." Composer Menken thought the piece skillfully merged the issues of race and the environment. "With every first song on a new project, expectations are high; there are a lot of implications for a collaboration based on a first song. Within the context of a Native American speaking to an Englishman, we wanted to capture a relationship, something that expressed our contemporary hopes for the environment and the world. I don't know if I've ever seen a reaction to a song like Stephen and I did with 'Colors of the Wind.' It was dizzying."

For Mike Gabriel and the rest of the *Pocahontas* team, "Colors of the Wind" truly brought everything together. "'Colors of the Wind' perhaps best sums up the entire spirit and essence of the film—this song was written before anything else," recalls producer James Pentecost. "It set the tone for the movie and defined the character of Pocahontas. Once Alan and Stephen wrote that song, we knew what the film was about."

Inside Disney, the song generated a near-euphoric religious feeling. *The Art of Pocahontas,* the company's official history of the film, describes "Colors of the Wind" in deeply reverential terms. "In the song, Pocahontas, resentful of Smith's perception of her as an 'ignorant savage,' voices her philosophy and her spirituality, in a celebration of the world's ordinary miracles, its natural wonders—the very wonders that so-called 'civilized people' may at times take for granted or view only as a means to profit and exploitation. Nothing less than a humanist credo, 'Colors of the Wind' passionately underscores the theme of the interdependence of every living thing and sounds a ringing plea for tolerance and empathy. For Captain John Smith, it marks a turning point in his racist world view, a further opening of his heart. For Hollywood feature film animation, the musical sequence marks a coming of age in its rousing endorsement of brotherhood and understanding." "Spirituality," "exploitation," and "racism"—*Bambi* this was not.

The script for *Pocahontas* grew out of "Colors of the Wind." In January 1993 screenwriter Carl Binder began work on a viable screenplay, and four months later, fellow writers Susannah Grant and Philip LaZebnik joined him. They took their direction from both the music composition and the work the visual artists had done on the characters. The Disney method for writing an animated feature involves detailed, laborious work. Screenwriters attend frequent story conference sessions that often include no less than ten highly creative artists and writers, along with producers and directors honing and perfecting ideas in a collaborative process that often descends into nasty disagreements. Yet, somehow, the spirit on this film was different. The spiritualism of the Native Americans seemed to rub off on everyone involved. "Like an Indian council," claims Carl Binder, "we wrote by consensus."

What they created was a script about religious conversion—but not to Christianity. In the Disney version, it is Captain John Smith who experiences a politically correct religious conversion. "His plotline in the movie is that he's living an unexamined life, is afraid to see the hole in himself," says John Pomeroy, supervising animator of Captain John Smith. "So, to escape, he seeks one adventure after another. Until he meets Pocahontas. She gives him her philosophy of what life, religion, and spirituality are all about and he gives her his strength, originality, and bravado." Captain John Smith embraces animism, and it defines the entire film. Disney animated films have often made use of magic and given human qualities to animals. But Pocahontas was different because of the message is sought to convey. This was not simply a movie about tolerance, but about achieving tolerance through a particular spiritual channel.

In the movie, a tree named Grandmother Willow is a living soul-being who teaches humans spirituality and understanding. Nature's wisdom is superior to man's. "The idea of the character came into the picture very early," says Stephen Schwartz. "For me, she became the voice of the Native American shaman or wise person. So many of them emphasize using one's senses in a different way, being open to things around you, in the air. She sings, 'Quey, quey, natora,' which means, in Algonquin, 'Now I understand.'"

"Nature was to become as much a character in this movie as anything else," recalls Eric Goldberg. "Respect and disrespect for nature, for each other's cultures, would fuel much of the action, the drama, and themes of the movie." *The Art of Pocahontas* reads, "There is more than a touch of religious fervor, of spirituality, in the artist's imaginings of seventeenth-century Virginia as a vast wilderness of rampant flower and wildlife on the banks of the Chesapeake."

The Indian princess was remade to conform to the spiritual demands of the film and to make it more appealing to adults. The historical, twelve-year-old girl who met Captain John Smith didn't offer much drama. (William Strachey, secretary of the Jamestown colony, reported that she was doing cartwheels "all the fort over.") So Jeffrey Katzenberg, then studio chairman, charged Glen Keane, supervising animator, with reshaping Pocahontas as "the finest creature the human race has to offer." Pocahontas was to become more a goddess than a princess. Keane used four successive women for inspiration. Although he first glanced at a few paintings of Pocahontas herself, they obviously had little influence on what would finally appear. Next Native American consultant Shirley Little Dove Custalow McGowan offered him a view of her "Native American features." But, his real inspiration came from drawing twenty-one-year-old Filipino model Dyna Taylor and American supermodel Christy Turlington.

As "the finest creature the human race has to offer," Pocahontas became a spiritual creature, and the animators wanted to generate a special spiritual presence. "Pocahontas is first introduced with wind and leaves rising, blowing through the forest to a waterfall where she's standing, then they continue to blow around her and her billowing hair," explains animation supervisor Don Paul, who also worked on *The Little Mermaid* and *Aladdin*. "We put subtle Indian hieroglyphic shapes sparkling in the wind and based the leaves on Native American graphic shapes, especially arrowheads. These are visual ways to convey her closeness to and celebration of nature."

> "If we want to be absolutely historically accurate, do you know what happened to the real Sir John Ratcliffe? When the Indians captured him, he was nailed to a tree and skinned alive. That would have been a choice Disney moment. Maybe a good song sequence."

The color schemes the animators chose for the film were a reflection of how they believed the Native Americans and the English settlers each dealt with the land. Every effort was taken to clearly convey the interconnectedness Native Americans supposedly had to the land and the exploitative nature of the English. Softer palette colors were used to convey the spiritual serenity Indians found in nature, while the English settlers were depicted in dark and grim color schemes. "We tried to envision and create an ideal world for the Native Americans," recalls artistic coordinator Dan Hansen. "A world in which [Sir John] Ratcliffe, in his bright purples, would look totally out of place and Smith, in blues and grays, would look only slightly less out of place. By contrast, Pocahontas would be the jewel of this world, the Native Americans' skin tones and colors of their clothing are in perfect harmony with the beautiful greens and browns of their world." There was no subtlety. Smith was granted the privilege of seeming less out of place only because of his relative willingness to learn from the Native Americans.

Throughout the film, Native Americans and Englishmen are classified by race—into good and evil. The artist who drew Ratcliffe for the film, Duncan Marjoribanks, says animators depicted Ratcliffe as a "fascist. Obese and obnoxious, he is the antithesis of what Powhatan stands for." And songs are used to reinforce this powerful categorization. Pocahontas is the symbol of Native American congruence with the natural world, while the colonist Ratcliffe symbolizes white exploitation. "Colors of the Wind" is a melodic and moving piece; in contrast, Ratcliffe presents the materialistic, Western point of view in songs such as "Mine, Mine, Mine."

The gold of Cortez
The jewels of Pizarro
Will seem like mere trinkets
By this time tomorrow.
The gold we find here
will dwarf them by far—
Oh, with all ya got in ya, boys,
Dig up Virginia, boys.

"In the song 'Mine, Mine, Mine,' Ratcliffe is comical, boisterous and almost silly," says Marjoribanks. "But as his frustration builds and his truly nasty, evil nature comes out, by the time of 'Savages,' he's turned into a fascist."

What can you expect
From filthy little heathens?
Their whole disgusting race is like a curse
their skins a hellish red

they're only good when dead
they're vermin, as I said
and worse
They're savages! Savages!

Although the film distinctly personifies Ratcliffe's evil nature, there is little interest in the corresponding evil nature of the Native American tribes. Chief Powhatan also sings about savages. But the impression the artists convey is that his hatred springs from being threatened by an invading alien culture. The chief is resonant and dignified. According to story head Tom Sito, part of this characterization is "political correctness." "If we want to be absolutely historically accurate, do you know what happened to the real Sir John Ratcliffe? When the Indians captured him, he was nailed to a tree and skinned alive. That would have been a choice Disney moment. Maybe a good song sequence."

Sito recalls that the only real concern Michael Eisner expressed about the movie was the fact that Pocahontas didn't have a mother. "Michael Eisner called a special meeting and wanted to know why Pocahontas did not have a mother," Sito remembers. The Disney chairman wanted to avoid any criticism about dysfunctional Native American families. But the story team had researched the Pocahontas lineage, and they had a very good reason for not including her mom in the film. "The reason Pocahontas doesn't have a mom in the film is that her father, Mamwatowick (Chief) Powhatan, was polygamous and had one hundred and forty-nine wives." Although Eisner wanted to rewrite that story element, too, the animators stood firm and the film remained as it was.

Once the theme, setting, story, and script had fallen into place, the last, major element to be determined was the voice talent for the characters. And for the voice of Chief Powhatan, Disney made a highly symbolic choice. They didn't choose a struggling Native American drama student but, instead, Russell Means. As you may recall, Means led a group of armed activists from the American Indian Movement (AIM) and occupied Wounded Knee, South Dakota, for 71 days in 1973. Two people died in the standoff and 12 were wounded, including

2 marshals. Nearly 1,200 people were arrested. Means's views on racial and ethnic issues are best summed up in what he regards as his most important speech ever, a July 1980 address he delivered in the Black Hills of South Dakota, entitled "For America to Live, Europe Must Die." Although over the years he has remained committed to Native American causes, he has also dabbled in the entertainment world, releasing an album entitled *The Radical*, which includes songs like "Nixon's Dead Ass" and "Waco, the White Man's Wounded Knee."

When Disney first approached Means about reading for Powhatan, he was somewhat reluctant. After all, he was still a committed activist, and the political undercurrents of the film were as important to him as the drama. He promised, however, to read the script and think about it. His decision didn't take long. "When I first read the script," Means recalls, "I was impressed with the beginning of the film. In fact, I was overwhelmed by it. It tells the truth about the motives for Europeans initially coming to the so-called New World. I find it astounding that Americans and the Disney Studios are willing to tell the truth."

Participating in *Pocahontas* was not simply a professional opportunity for Means, but a chance to promote the cause he had championed for decades. He clearly understood what Disney was trying to do. "For Hollywood and for the Indian People, 'Pocahontas' has started a revolution," he wrote in an open letter he released after the film came out. "Before this film, movies have absolutely refused to entrust the historical truth of our people. At last, Disney has told the truth to children all over the world. They have admitted that the real reason the European males came over here in the first place was to rob, rape, and pillage the land and kill to gain respect from the other sacred colors of the human race." The spiritual and ecological elements of the film were also not lost on him. He praised the portrayal of Pocahontas and the other Native Americans as being "in a four-dimensional fashion which includes spirituality with the environment. [T]he film shows how human beings historically interacted and integrated with the environment spiritually, and otherwise suggests possibilities for today."

Disney turned to the talents of Native American actress Irene

Beddard for the voice of Pocahontas. While Beddard did not have the activist tradition of Means, she was committed to the project because it corrected the typical white man's presentation of history. "Now, with this film, Pocahontas can reach a larger culture as a headline," she said when the film was released. "No, it doesn't make up for five hundred years of genocide, but it is a reminder that we will have to start telling our own lives."

What began as a characteristically American story about an Indian princess's rescue of an English captain, became an anthem about spiritualism, ecology, and racism. In the words of Glen Keane, supervising animator for *Pocahontas*, Disney viewed the film "not just as entertainment, but as an attempt to convey things in which we truly believe."

CHAPTER ELEVEN

The Lyin' King

I f animation is the most profitable segment of today's Disney, the crown jewel of the department is *The Lion King*. To date, the film has netted more than $1.5 billion. But did the new Disney, hailed as a creative enterprise, really come up with the characters and unique plot elements on its own? Or did the Mouse steal it from a dead Japanese animator?

On a pleasant Saturday evening in June 1994 a group of Hollywood's elite was gathering at the Academy of Television Arts and Sciences Theater for the premiere of a greatly anticipated Disney feature. Comprised of approximately eight thousand members who have contributed their creative talents to the enhancement of the industry, the academy is the professional body that grants the well-known Emmy awards each year. It also regularly offers private screenings to celebrate highly regarded films just about to be released to the public. On that particular night, the screening was of a much talked about Disney animated film called *The Lion King*, the story of a coming-of-age lion who has to overcome adversity and learn about responsibility.

Fred Ladd and his wife were among those at the screening. A long-time member of both the academy and the American Film Institute, Ladd has spent more than thirty years in animation as a producer, director, and screenwriter. In 1974 he cowrote the animated *Journey Back to Oz* for Warner Brothers. Based on pieces of plots from several of L. Frank Baum's Oz books, the movie features a multitude of Hollywood's best talent. Milton Berle was the voice for the Cowardly Lion, Paul Lynde provided the voice of the silly Pumpkinhead, and Ethel Merman was Mombi. Rounding out the impressive cast were Liza Minnelli, Mickey Rooney, Danny Thomas, and Mel Blanc as the Wizard of Oz.

Ladd got his start in the animation business in the early 1960s. He began by dubbing foreign animated short features (shorts) into English. After developing a solid reputation in this specialized field, NBC tapped him to remake Japanese animated stories for the U.S. market. Although Japanese animae (pronounced annie-may) was in its infancy at the time, it showed great promise as a medium.

NBC became involved when a field representative in Tokyo saw a cartoon character named Tetsuwan Atom ("Mighty Atom") on Japanese television in 1963. The adorable little robot boy had an irrepressible charm. The representative immediately contacted NBC Enterprises in New York with news of his find. NBC producers agreed that the cute, tiny character had star quality, and they contacted Ladd to produce a U.S. version. "Tetsuwan Atom was a natural," recalls Ladd. "We renamed him Astro Boy, and we just knew he would be a big hit." Indeed, the futuristic tyke was a big success, and, soon after, Ladd was producing other Japanese animated stories like Gigantor, the story of a lovable but powerful robot remotely controlled by a boy.

Fred Ladd had several reasons for wanting to see *The Lion King* on that June night. No doubt he wanted to enjoy the Disney Company's incomparable animation capabilities and vision. But he was also curious to see how it would handle the story. He, too, had produced an animated story about a lion back in the mid-1960s. And it was also a coming-of-age tale based on the work of the same man who had invented Astro Boy. *Kimba the White Lion* had both fascinating characters and interesting moral values. It was enormously popular in Japan and had been syndicated by NBC throughout America for more than ten years.

When Ladd had first learned in 1993 that Disney was producing an animated feature about a lion cub named Simba, he was amused. But as he sat down in the Academy Theater and the film began to run, any sense of amusement quickly vanished. In fact, Ladd was "shocked and amazed" at what he saw, he told us. Minutes into the movie, he remembers whispering to his wife, "For crying out loud, this looks like Kimba." And as the story unfolded he kept mumbling the same thing. "My God, I can't believe this," he said every few minutes as the characters were introduced. At one point Ladd blurted out, perhaps just a bit too loudly, "Don't tell me we're going to see the father in the clouds!" Minutes later, the audience saw Simba doing exactly that. Not surprisingly, he left the screening upset.

When you compare *Kimba the White Lion* with *The Lion King* you can more fully understand Ladd's outrage. In both stories, the wise lion king is killed, and the young prince is driven from home. He later returns to find that in his absence the throne has been occupied by a brutal, older lion with a scar over one eye, whom he must now defeat in battle to become king. The young lions are named, respectively, Kimba and Simba; the older, evil lions are Claw and Scar. Even the climactic fight is similar. Kimba kicks burning sand into Claw's eyes, while, in *The Lion King*, Scar scoops a pawful of hot coals into Simba's eyes.

But there is more. In both stories, a wise, elderly mandrill baboon, who had been the old king's friend, becomes the prince's sardonic but kindly mentor. And a comical, excitable bird of about the same size in each film—a parrot in *Kimba*, a hornbill in *The Lion King*—plays the role of a herald, or informer. Both accounts have a scar-faced lion villain supported by a team of comic-relief cowardly laughing hyenas. In *Kimba* boss Claw has a black-panther henchman serve as his intermediary to the lower-class hyenas, whereas in *The Lion King* the evil Scar gives orders directly to the hyenas. Claw is a hot-tempered, brutal thug, and the black panther, Cassius, is suavely sinister with an upper-class British accent. Disney's Scar is also played as suavely sinister, with an upper-class British accent.

> **Although Disney animator Sadao Miyamoto says his superiors privately admitted to him the influence of Tezuka's work on *The Lion King*, he clearly is uncomfortable about publicly discussing the reality that Disney may have stolen key elements.**

Both stories have the prince as a cub meeting a young lioness who becomes his playmate. In *Kimba* there is a clear implication that Kimba and Kitty will wed when they grow up. And in the sequel, they do. In *The Lion King* Simba and Nala marry when they become adults, and the lioness bears his child to carry on the dynasty. Both young lions survive by eating bugs. Kimba eats locusts, and Simba is taught to eat bugs so he can hang out with herbivores Timon and Pumbaa.

If that's not enough, consider the unusual plot elements that appear in both works. Kimba and Simba both see images of their fathers in the sky. In the TV cartoons Kimba has a vision every few episodes of his mother or father in the stars, in the clouds, or over a full moon. In *The Lion King*, King Mufasa tells young Simba, "Look at the stars. The great kings of the past look down on us from those stars. So whenever you feel alone, just remember that those kings will always be there to guide you." Later the adult Simba is inspired by Mufasa's image in the clouds.

In both stories a stampede is a key event in the hero's life. In *Kimba the White Lion* Kimba and his friend are threatened by an antelope stampede. Kimba must save Bucky Deer, who is clinging to a tree in the midst of the stampede. Later, Kimba is so despondent he could not stop the antelope that he declares himself not fit to rule and runs off to sulk. In *The Lion King*, King Mufasa is killed while rescuing Simba from a tree in the midst of a wildebeest stampede. Overcome by anguish and guilt, Simba is tricked by Scar and flees into exile.

Fred Patten is a long-time fan of both Disney and animae, and serves as a columnist for *Animation World* magazine. He has seen both programs numerous times and notes some of the common scenes and when they appear.

KIMBA: Opening title credits and theme song: from the adult King Leo posing majestically on a cliff, panning down over birds flying over the savannah, showing a panorama of all the animals of Africa. 0:01 to 1:57
THE LION KING: Opening scene: "The Circle of Life": pan over birds flying over the savannah, showing a panorama of all the animals of Africa, sweeping up to King Mufasa posing majestically on Pride Rock. 0:40 to 1:51

KIMBA: Prod. #66-24: Pauley Cracker flies to Bucky Deer clinging to a tree in the midst of the antelope stampede and tells him to hold on, Kimba is coming.

THE LION KING: Zazu flies to Simba clinging to a tree in the midst of the wildebeest stampede and tells him to hold on, his father is coming. 33:08 to 33:14

KIMBA: Prod. #66-42: Lightning starts a fire, and rain puts it out. 13:37 to 13:52
THE LION KING: Lightning starts a fire, and rain puts it out. 79:58 to 80:05

KIMBA: Prod. #66-8: During a fight in the hot desert, Kimba kicks burning sand into Claw's eyes. 22:32 to 22:37
THE LION KING: During a fight in the midst of the big fire, Scar scoops a pawful of hot coals into Simba's eyes. 78:30 to 78:35

KIMBA: Prod. #66-24: After Kimba protests that he cannot handle the responsibilities of becoming king, Dan'l Baboon gives him a pep talk including a spanking to get his attention. 13:49 to 14:23
THE LION KING: After Simba protests that he cannot handle the responsibilities of becoming king, Rafiki gives him a pep talk including a sharp rap on the head to get his attention. 67:11 to 67:32

KIMBA: Prod. #66-1, 66-9, 66-3: Kimba sees his mother's image in the stars, he sees an idealized image of himself with his father, Caesar, in the clouds, and he sees his father, King Caesar, superimposed over a full moon.
THE LION KING: King Mufasa tells young Simba to "Look at the stars. The great kings of the past look down on us from those stars." Simba sees Mufasa's image in the clouds. 69:06 to 69:11

KIMBA: Prod. #66-5: The cubs Kimba and Kitty playing. 21:35 to 22:15
THE LION KING: The cubs Simba and Nala playing. 17:07 to 17:30

So there clearly are similarities in six major characters, in key elements of the story line, and in the unique plot twists and setting. Does this sound curious? It should. Actor Mathew Broderick, who provided the voice for Simba, admits that he was confused when cast for the part. At first he thought he was playing Kimba, "the white lion in a cartoon when I was a kid." But Disney claims it is all coincidence.

Since the academy screening in June of 1994, *The Lion King* has become the most successful movie of all time, reaping Disney a fortune. Walt's nephew Roy E. Disney, Jr., heads up animation at the studio. He's proud of the film and rightfully calls it "the most profitable movie of all time." While its great popularity stems in part from the technical excellence of its animation, its real strength is the characters and the story of the maturing lion prince Simba, who grows from an insecure cub into a strong ruler of all the animals of the jungle.

The Lion King is considered the prize jewel in the Disney animation crown not just because of the money it made for the company, but also because of its artistic scope and reach. In a subtle slap at Walt, Disney promotional material proclaims that the film is different from the Disney classics, which were based on European fairy tales. The company heralds *The Lion King* as the "the first Disney animated feature to be based on an original story idea." Story head Brenda Chapman maintains that is what made producing the film so difficult. "Writing an original story is definitely more challenging because there is nothing to fall back on," she says.

When asked about the many parallels between *Kimba the White Lion* and *The Lion King* Disney's only explanation is that it's sheer coincidence. "No one associated with *The Lion King* has ever heard of *Kimba* or seen it," claims the company in an official statement.

Howard Green, spokesman for Walt Disney Pictures, goes even further, diminishing the professional reputation of the Japanese animator who created Kimba. "None of the principals involved in creating *The Lion King* were aware of Kimba or [Osamu] Tezuka."

But the truth is otherwise. Like the little wooden boy Pinocchio it made so famous, Disney is having trouble being honest. As we shall see, the team that created *The Lion King* included numerous individuals who knew about both Kimba and Tezuka. Indeed, Disney even hired a Japanese animator very familiar with Tezuka's work to develop elements of its "most successful movie of all time." It appears Disney animation has changed not only the way it presents its animated stories and characters, but also how it acquires them.

● ● ●

OSAMU TEZUKA WAS BORN in Toyonaka City in Osaka, Japan, in 1928. His parents loved the arts and encouraged their development in their son. Tezuka's father was a film buff and constantly ran his film projector, showing numerous American animated shorts and Charlie Chaplin movies. As a young boy, Tezuka took to sketching and doodling, at which he soon became quite adept. In 1946, barely eighteen years old, he published his first comic book, *New Treasure Island*. The work incorporated many techniques from American animation, creating a fast-paced story with a stunning visual style. Tezuka went off to medical school, but the book became a national sensation and sold more than 400,000 copies at a time when many people in war-ravaged Japan barely had enough to eat. When he completed medical school and obtained his physician's license only a few years later, he was forced to make a career choice: medicine or drawing cartoons. He chose the uncertain path of the early Japanese cartoon industry. Thus, Tezuka became one of its founding fathers. Like Walt Disney, he began by drawing cartoons that appealed to both children and adults. One of his earliest successes was *Junguru Taitei (The Jungle Emperor)*, the story of a family of lions. It was serialized in *Manga Shoneu (Boys' Comic)* from November 1950 to 1954 and remains popular in Japan to this day. Indeed, even in the United States *Junguru Taitei* is carried in bookstores that stock Japanese-language books.

Tezuka eventually hooked up with an American animation company named Disney and produced the authorized Japanese comic book versions of *Bambi* in 1951 and *Pinocchio* in 1952. He had enormous appreciation and respect for Walt Disney. So did the Japanese people, who dubbed Tezuka the Walt Disney of Japan. The two animation masters met only once in a chance encounter at the New York World's Fair in 1964. As Tezuka loved to tell it, he approached Disney as a fan. Much to his delight, Walt said he not only knew who he was, but also liked his work. There was no higher compliment for an animator who idolized this American genius.

As his popularity as a cartoonist blossomed, Tezuka decided to expand into television animation. With the money he had made producing comics, he created Japan's first TV animation studio in 1961. Following Walt Disney's lead, his formula was simple and familiar. He concentrated on characters rather than on gags, action, or flashy visuals, and created wonderful characters like Mighty Atom and Kimba the White Lion. According to Fred Schodt, Tezuka's translator in the United States, Atom was designed to be a 21st-century Pinocchio, a nearly perfect robot who strove to become more emotive and human.

Mighty Atom was an instant success in Japan and was a tribute not only to Tezuka's talent, but also to his daring, bold nature. Designing a cute, boy-like character was one thing. But who would believe that Japan, a nation with a recent memory of atomic destruction, would fall in love with a robot character with an atomic heart? Several years later, when Atom was introduced to America as Astro Boy, he won the hearts of millions of American children.

Shortly after his chance meeting with Walt Disney in 1964, Tezuka began working on the animated television series *Jungle Taitei*, or *King of the Jungle*. It was based on his earlier comics printed in *Manga Shoneu*, which told the story of three generations of lions. It was a laborious project in part because, like Walt Disney, Tezuka was a perfectionist. His efforts, however, were well rewarded. The final product was a huge artistic accomplishment for its day. *King of the Jungle* became one of Japan's most widely watched animated works and was originally broadcast on television from 1965 to 1967. Thirty years later, the characters from *King of the Jungle* are still enormously popular in Japan. The adult lion from the series is the cartoon mascot-logo of the Seibu Lions, one of the country's top baseball teams.

To produce the program, Tezuka had presold it to Japan's Fuji television network. But he also wanted access to the U.S. market. So he struck a deal with NBC television, which liked the concept of a friendly, altruistic lion. NBC offered Tezuka enough money to film

Jungle Emperor in color rather than black and white, if he would agree to some changes. In the earlier, comic-book form, *Jungle Emperor* covered the entire life of a lion named Leo—the death of his parents, his contact with humans, his maturation, and eventually his death. NBC felt those scenes were too much for young children and insisted Leo remain a cute cub who never grows up, sort of a feline version of Peter Pan. What NBC wanted was an upbeat series with minimum violence and no deaths, which might be too traumatic for children. For marketing purposes, it insisted that every episode be self-contained so the series could be shown in any order.

The challenge of taking 533 original pages of comic books and keeping them in line with NBC's requirements fell to director Eiichi Yamamoto and producer Fred Ladd. And to accomplish that task, they shifted the focus of the story to character development. Yamamoto combined most of Leo's various animal antagonists into a single villain: a brutish, one-eyed lion who had seized the vacant jungle throne after Leo's father's death. Next he transformed this villain's assistant, Tot (a comical black panther), into a much more sinister henchman. And he gave Tot's old comedy-relief role to two new stooges—a couple of laughing hyenas.

Yamamoto and Tezuka then created a large supporting cast of Leo's friends, several of whom had been minor characters in Tezuka's comic books. There was Mandy, an old baboon father figure and adviser, and Koko, the comically pompous parrot who appoints himself as Leo's herald and news-gatherer. To ensure a rich use of color and scenery, Fred Ladd arranged for Tezuka and Yamamoto to send an animation team from Japan to work at Ladd's New York office. There they were instructed in color production by Preston Blair, a veteran Disney animator.

The Americanization of *The Jungle Emperor* fell to Ladd. Having just recently reproduced Mighty Atom as Astro Boy, he was familiar with Tezuka's technique. One of the first things he did was work on a name for the series. In the Japanese version, the main character was Leo the lion. But that name was deemed too stereotypical for American audiences. There was also the additional problem that Leo was the name of MGM's trademarked lion logo-mascot. So Ladd figured the name had to be changed to something more original. After tossing around a few bad ideas, someone finally suggested Simba, which is Swahili for lion. "We liked the name Simba, but it was an actual name or word for lion, so we couldn't protect it legally as ours by getting a copyright on it," Ladd told us. "Someone on the staff suggested the name be changed to Kimba. We liked it. Thought that was cute."

Along with the new name came changes in character design, and *Kimba the White Lion* was born. The final product was an impressive production for its day. The artwork was solid, and the story line was commended for its positive moral values. Kimba was a strong role model with a willingness to fight for good causes. NBC syndicated the program nationwide, and it first appeared on Los Angeles's KHJ-TV, Channel 9, in September 1966 in a 5:30 late-afternoon time slot. In late 1966 and early 1967 it spread to other American cities. During the next decade, Kimba aired in numerous cities across the United States, with its last run being in Los Angeles on KBSC-TV, Channel 52, from August 1976 through July 1977. The contract for the American rights expired in September 1978 when NBC had to close its NBC Films subsidiary because the federal government had issued an anti-trust directive forbidding television companies from both broadcasting and syndicating programs to other broadcasters.

Osamu Tezuka remained active during the next dozen years and was revered in his country as a national treasure. It is difficult for Americans to fully understand the high status Tezuka enjoyed in his country. In a 1983 profile of Japan, *Time* magazine included a survey of Japanese cartoons. Art critic Robert Hughes observed: "The top artists, with, at the very top, Osamu Tezuka, known as God of Manga, are treated by their adoring public of all ages with an enthusiasm unknown to Stan Lee or Garry Trudeau; they are stars in the way that Mick Jagger or Norman Mailer are stars, and are credited with some of the properties of both." Tezuka's celebrity status even led to some interesting television appearances. In a 1980 Japanese national television special on Disney World, he played a bumbling tourist working his way through the park.

But Tezuka was also well-known in the small world of American animation. In the early 1980s he visited both Disney World in Florida and the Disney Animation Studios in Burbank. He also stopped by the house of Disney animation luminary Ward Kimball. And when he appeared at the 1980 Comic-Con industry convention in San Diego, he was mobbed by fans who had him draw several sketches of Astro Boy and Kimba. He received Comic-Con's Inkpot Award "for excellence and achievement in: comic arts; cinematic arts; animation arts; science fiction; adventure fiction; and fandom service." His short experimental films, *Broken Down Film* and *Jumping*, were shown at animation festivals around the United States.

Unfortunately Osamu Tezuka's life was tragically cut short when he succumbed to stomach cancer. He passed away on February 9, 1989, and all of Japan mourned. The prestigious newspaper *Asahi* published an emotional editorial the day after he died: "Foreign visitors to Japan often find it difficult to understand why Japanese people like comics so much. Reportedly, they often find it odd to see grown men and women engrossed in weekly comic magazines on the trains during commute hours. One explanation for the popularity of comics in Japan, however, is that Japan had Osamu Tezuka, whereas other nations did not. Without Dr. Tezuka, the postwar explosion in comics in Japan would have been inconceivable."

The impact of his life and work has been felt worldwide. In December 1990, ASIFA-Hollywood, the Hollywood chapter of the international professional animation community, presented its Winsor McCay Award "for lifetime contribution to animation" to Osamu Tezuka, posthumously, at a gala banquet. He received a glowing three-page tribute in the program book, and the text included an illustration of Kimba. Interestingly, none of that year's other award recipients received more than a one-page tribute. The award was presented by June Foray, a noted animation voice actress whose roles included Granny Gummi in Disney's *Gummi Bears* TV cartoons.

Still, the Disney corporation says it never heard of Tezuka, despite all of this and the fact that Disney executives regularly visit Japan and Disney animators regularly attend conventions where his work is displayed. As far as the Mouse is concerned, Tezuka never existed. But the truth is, Disney has numerous individuals well acquainted with his work, and they apparently used it when they produced what became Disney's own sensation.

●●●

WHEN OSAMU TEZUKA passed away, Disney's work on *The Lion King* was well under way. Sometime in the late 1980s Jeffrey Katzenberg, then chairman of Disney Studios, sat down with Peter Schneider, vice president of feature animation, and suggested the possibility of a movie that was focused entirely on animals in the wild. Katzenberg suggested an African setting with lions as the primary characters, and also suggested that the central theme be woven around a young lion coming of age and learning to take on responsibility. Roy E. Disney, Jr., was enthusiastic about the idea and put Thomas Schumacher, fresh from producing *The Rescuers Down Under*, in charge of the project. The working title became *King of the Jungle*, and development work began at a time when the majority of the studio's animation resources were still deployed on *Beauty and the Beast*.

Work on *The Lion King* began when there was enormous pressure on the Disney Animation Department. Michael Eisner and Jeffrey Katzenberg had decreed that the studio would release a new animated feature every eighteen months. Michael Eisner outlined the furious pace in his 1992 letter to shareholders: "Next up, 'The Lion King' followed by 'Pocahontas.' And after that we are aiming for three animated releases every two years!"

It was an extremely challenging task: Walt himself would never have worked under such deadlines. Walt felt that tight deadlines and a focus on quantity would destroy the quality of the animated movies. But Michael Eisner believes that animation was driving the company financially. It helped push up profits at the box office, provide new toys for merchandising, and new attractions for the theme parks. This pressure to perform meant that Disney animators needed to develop remarkable characters and meaningful stories—and do it fast!

It is difficult to say who knew what about Tezuka and Kimba at Disney's executive level. It is likely Michael Eisner had been exposed to Kimba earlier in his career. In the early 1970s he spent two years at ABC with prime responsibility for children's programming. This happened to be at the same time NBC was aggressively marketing Kimba. In his words, Eisner spent most of his working hours watching children's cartoons. He likes to joke that he saw so many cartoons so many times he can still sing the theme songs of *Bugs Bunny* and *George of the Jungle.* Can he hum a few bars from *Kimba the White Lion?*

But Michael Eisner had little involvement in the development of the film. For that task, Disney tapped two animation veterans, Roger Allers and Rob Minkoff, to make their directing debut with what eventually became *The Lion King.* Allers was the first to join the project in October 1991. He had enjoyed a two-decade career in animation that included everything from character design and animation to story supervision. Curiously, he had worked in the small world of Japanese animation and had lived in Tokyo for two years. In 1982 he provided character design, preliminary animation, and story development for the Japanese-produced feature *Little Nemo: Adventures in Slumberland.* As one of the animation directors, he oversaw the Japanese artists. The company he worked for, Tokyo Movie Shinshu, is a major Japanese animation studio, and it would have been impossible for Allers not to have been exposed to Tezuka's work. "The Japanese animae community is tight-knit," says Fred Patten, who was unaware of Allers's background until the authors told him. "Everyone knows everyone. It would be impossible for him to not know about Tezuka. To not have been exposed to Tezuka would be the equivalent of working in the Hollywood animation industry and never to have heard of Walt Disney." Indeed, several of the Japanese animators who worked on *Little Nemo* had previously worked for Tezuka. And while Allers was living in Japan, *Kimba* was regularly airing on national television. (Allers declined to be interviewed for this book. And curiously, any mention of his work in Tokyo has been excised from his Disney biography.)

Development of *The Lion King* was a complex, difficult process.

The key early work on developing the characters, theme, and plot took place during an April 1992 brainstorming session. Allers played a central role in the meeting, since the other director, Rob Minkoff, had only recently joined the team. For two days the directors met with producer Don Hahn and story head Brenda Chapman. Also attending were Kirk Wise and Gary Trousdale, the directing and story-savvy duo responsible for *Beauty and the Beast*. The meetings were intense but productive. "Our stories are built from clear-cut characters, heroes and villains, and more ambiguous characters who provide comic relief," says Hahn. "That brainstorming session clarified the characters and provided us with the movie's central theme. What emerged was a character makeover for Simba and a radically revised second half of the film." Several months later screenwriter Irene Mecchi was brought on board to help further develop the characters and define their personalities.

Allers and Minkoff then brought together a story team to chart themes, characters, and plots. Meanwhile, the first animators started to fully develop the artwork. And at this point, several other people—who not only had been exposed to Japanese animation, but who also had direct, detailed knowledge of Kimba—joined the project. One member of this story team was Mark Kausler.

A gifted artist, Kausler had seen Kimba several times during the late 1970s and early 1980s. At that time Fred Patten had been involved in organizing a Japanese animation club in Los Angeles. The club held several screenings of Japanese animated features around Los Angeles County, first in downtown Englewood at a photographic studio and later at several other locations. The club, which remained active from 1979 to 1989, showed Kimba "numerous times," says Patten. "A lot of animation students at Cal Arts used to come to the screenings. Several later went to work in Disney animation and have credits on *The Lion King*."

Kausler was a frequent attendee and used to have detailed discussions with members of the club on the value of the character Kimba. "He was always arguing about the merits of Kimba," Patten recalls. "He knew the stories very well."

Another Disney animator who showed up at those screenings was Sean Keller, a talented artist who was such a fan of Kimba that he made a Kimba bodysuit and wore it to animation conventions.

Disney also hired Japanese animator Sadao Miyamoto, who became closely involved in the creative work behind the film *The Lion King*. Miyamoto is now a senior staff artist in the Planning Department at Disney. "When I first saw the storyboards," he admits, "I was taken aback, because they did look like *The Jungle Emperor*." Although he says his superiors privately admitted to him the influence of Tezuka's work on *The Lion King*, he clearly is uncomfortable about publicly discussing the reality that Disney may have stolen key elements from *Kimba*. "It's one thing to be influenced by the film," he says cautiously. "How much people referred to it is an altogether different issue."

"Disney is concerned about their squeaky clean image. For them to admit they stole something is seamy and sleazy. Without their image they would have nothing."

Another veteran Disney animator remembers *Kimba* being used during the development of the film. Tom Sito worked at Disney for eight years and did everything from illustrations for *The Little Mermaid* ("drawing a lot of singing fish," in his words) to serving as story head of the epic *Pocahontas* before leaving for Disney's rival, Dreamworks. While with Disney, Sito also played a crucial role as a member of the story team for *The Lion King*. He recalls how fellow artists referred to artwork from Kimba during production. "They would hold up the artwork next to storyboards and compare the two," he told us.

Disney is littered with other individuals who know about Tezuka and his work. Wendell Washer, an artist and animator who works for Disney Television, was a founder of the Animae Fan Club of Los Angeles in 1977. And according to Fred Patten, Washer owns perhaps the most extensive collection of Japanese animation in the United States, including several copies of Tezuka's work. In addition, Disney animators regularly show up at animation conventions and buy copies of Tezuka's work. "For Disney to claim they never heard of Tezuka is ludicrous," says Patten.

In Japan, Tezuka's production company, Tezuka Production Co., LTD., has been more than a little disturbed about the whole affair. President Takayuki Matsutani told us in a letter: "It is true that the actual shape and coloring of *The Lion King* characters are different from those used for both *The Jungle Emperor* animation and comic book. Nonetheless, there are enough similarities that we believe the Disney staff who worked on *The Lion King* clearly had *The Jungle Emperor* in mind during production." But Matsutani also said the company has no plans to litigate, at least not at this point. "We believe that lawsuits contribute neither to culture, nor to mutual understanding among the various people actually involved in production of creative works such as animation." The door, however, may still be open. Matsutani writes: "We have no intention at this time of filing a lawsuit against the Walt Disney Company. That stated, we are nonetheless always prepared to act resolutely to protect both the works of Dr. Osamu Tezuka and his honor."

The reluctance to take on Disney is not evidence of a weak case but of respect for the creator of the company. As so often has been the case, and especially in recent years, the company that bears Walt's name is protected in part by the rich legacy and apparent reservoir of affection he left in many circles around the world. "Tezuka was always free in admitting that he was inspired by Walt Disney personally," says Fred Patten. "It would be very difficult for Tezuka Productions to sue a company that bears the name of a man Osamu Tezuka considered his idol."

Fred Schodt, a friend of Tezuka, agrees. "Litigation is socially frowned upon except as a last resort in Japan," he told us. "And the Tezuka family, which still controls Tezuka Productions, is not interested in confronting or suing Disney. Tezuka, after all, had himself been a Disney fan."

Fred Schodt believes most of the problem is a result of the Disney Company's attitude. "How the late Walt Disney would have handled the [Tezuka] dispute is anyone's guess. But one suspects he might have been more sensitive to the underlying emotions than is his company." What Schodt and other Tezuka supporters desire is not that

Disney cough up money, but that it simply acknowledge the inspiration Tezuka's work provided for *The Lion King*.

While that may seem a fair enough request, it's doubtful it will happen anytime soon. *Kimba* producer Fred Ladd, who says he has no legal claim to make against Disney because he does not own the rights to *Kimba*, thinks even a simple acknowledgment is unlikely. "Disney is concerned about their squeaky clean image," he says. "For them to admit they stole something is seamy and sleazy. Without their image they would have nothing."

Yet in the tight-knit world of animation, Disney's image has been tainted. And creative animators are taking their licks at the Mouse. Matt Groening, creator of *The Simpsons*, got a few laughs at Disney's expense in one episode of the show. Lisa Simpson's saxophone teacher, an old jazz musician known as Bleeding Gums, dies unexpectedly. After the funeral, Lisa goes to a hilltop to play a last tribute to him when suddenly his head appears in the clouds, à la *Kimba* and *The Lion King*. But before Bleeding Gums can speak, he is interrupted by a lion's head that appears and says, "You must avenge my death, Kimba... I mean, Simba!"

At American comic conventions you can find plenty of T-shirts showing Tezuka's Kimba in front of a mirror seeing a reflection of the face of Disney's Simba. Underneath, the caption reads, "The Lyin' King: Mirror, mirror, on the wall, who created me after all?"

CHAPTER TWELVE

Tinseltown Theft

D isney's propensity for borrowing ideas from others goes beyond *The Lion King*. Sometimes the Mouse will even steal pixie dust.

In 1988 Daryan Faeroe thought he had a brilliant idea. The self-proclaimed inventor and Disney gift-shop employee had been tinkering with various ideas for years. But finally, while it appeared simple, this idea seemed to be a sure thing. As part of the Disney employee suggestion program, Faeroe submitted his idea: bottle and sell pixie dust—the magical stuff used by Tinker Bell in the Peter Pan story. He suggested putting the dust in a bottle and then wrapping the whole thing in a velvet pouch. Faeroe met with representatives from Disney's Product Development Division in California for a half-hour, but they told him Disney didn't want the idea.

So, when he stumbled across a Disney mail-order catalog just four months later, Faeroe was completely surprised to see that Disney was selling pixie dust for $6 a bottle. And like his dust, the Disney stuff consisted of glitter in a bottle. The only difference: The bottle wasn't in a velvet pouch.

When Faeroe confronted the company, the Mouse denied stealing his idea. "They completely ignored me, as if I didn't exist," he recalls. But little did Disney know,

Disney has even threatened "twelve-year-old kids with Mickey Mouse on the Web sites" with legal action.

Faeroe was serious about his inventing: In September 1987, months before he approached Disney, he had received state and federal trademarks for his pixie dust.

When Disney attorneys found out about the trademarks, they sent Faeroe a letter in October 1989 saying the company "was willing to place some nuisance value on this matter." In short, they offered him

$10,000 for the trademark rights and his silence about the whole affair. But Faeroe figured that the dust, marketed along with the Tinker Bell character, could be a big-seller at the theme parks, in mail-order catalogues, and the dozens of Disney stores throughout the country. So he counteroffered for $15,000, but Disney smugly refused. And that's when things got a bit nasty.

In February 1990 Disney sued Faeroe, claiming he and his attorney had accepted a $10,000 settlement. Both Faeroe and the attorney denied the claim, and after a brief nonjury trial, the judge ruled in Faeroe's favor. Disney then appealed to the 5th District Court of Appeals in Daytona Beach, Florida, where in May of 1995 a judge again ruled against Disney.

Fearing further litigation, Disney eventually settled the case for an undisclosed amount of money. The whole affair left Faeroe a little glum. "There's a lot of things I love about Disney," he said at the time. "It was set up by somebody I really admire. I don't want to see a lot of adverse publicity about Disney. They could have had this for very little. But they did something they shouldn't have done."

Daryan Faeroe is not the only one Disney has trampled over. For more than twenty years Terry Olson has kept SAK Entertainment, a performing troupe, alive. While today it is an Orlando entertainment institution, the critically acclaimed troupe had humble beginnings when Olson founded it in 1977. "Most of us were doing other things to make ends meet," he recalls. "We brought everybody together and asked them what do you need to make it. Whatever anybody said, that's what we started paying them. I just figured that if we're going to get ahead in this, we've got to put all our energies into it."

In its early years, SAK (the name comes from, "We've got a sack full of costumes") played for the developing Renaissance Festival circuit. But then in 1982 Walt Disney World signed the group to perform street theater at the recently opened EPCOT Center World Showcase. Olson and the SAK players enjoyed working at the park. All day long, seven days a week, they would pull people from the audience and con-script them as performers. "EPCOT was a great place to perform because people were there to have a good time," Olson recalls. "You'd always go out there and get a huge crowd. We felt very true to Walt Disney and his ideas."

But of course Walt was no longer running the company, and when SAK's contract came due seven years later in 1989, the Mouse turned into a rat. Disney offered to end the contract agreement and have the SAK players become full-time cast members, for less pay and no creative control. SAK wasn't interested and politely refused. As Olson tells it, Disney quietly began to send out people to videotape the SAK performances. Then it used the tapes to train its own employees, and when the contract ended, SAK was canned and replaced by Disney employees doing essentially the same shows. "We definitely considered suing them for copyright infringement," Olson says. But it cost too much to find attorneys willing to go against Disney.

"The year 1989 was a terrible time," Olson says. "There was a handful of us who stuck around and collected unemployment." Eventually the SAK players planned a comeback, and today perform at their own theater in downtown Orlando. Even though they didn't sue the Mouse, they did get the sort of revenge only a stage actor could appreciate.

In August 1997, on the twentieth anniversary of the group's founding, Olson and SAK performer Andy Anthony visited EPCOT carrying their "sack full of costumes." After changing in the bathroom near the Italy pavilion, they performed "The Menace of Venice," one of their favorite skits. They drew a large crowd, but to their utter disappointment, not one Disney official noticed. "We figured if I got arrested for entertaining people," says Olson, "it would be good publicity."

Undoubtedly, Paul Alter loves his job. For years he has been the director of *The Price Is Right*, the famous game show on CBS Television. Every morning at 10 AM he meets with the producers in the Green Room of Stage 33 at CBS-TV City. There he reviews where all the prizes will appear on stage and how the cast will help display them. At 11 AM the rehearsal begins for the taping of the first show. Just hours later the guests are let in and the fun begins.

Alter, however, is more than a television director. He also generates ideas for movies. In 1977 he sketched out the basis for a screenplay about a toddler who turns into a towering, destructive giant thanks to a genetic accident, and called it "Now, That's a Baby." Alter said he got the idea while baby-sitting his granddaughter and watching her knock over toy buildings and pick up toy cars. Three years later he submitted it to Disney as a story idea. It was a refreshing idea for a movie, but Disney Vice President Tom Wilhite rejected the story. Several years went by, and all was soon forgotten. At least by Paul Alter.

Thirteen years later the new hit Disney movie *Honey, I Blew Up the Kid* appeared. It was the story about a scientist father who accidentally blows up his children to enormous size. Alter dusted off his old treatment and script of "Now, That's a Baby" and discovered seventeen major areas of similarity between Disney's movie and his ideas, including specific scenes, such as when the villain tries to shoot the giant toddler with missiles.

Perplexed by what he found, Alter approached Disney for an explanation but got nowhere. The company didn't even acknowledge much of his correspondence. At one point, he even wrote Disney to say that he would forswear all financial claims if the Mouse would simply give him a letter of apology. But Disney refused. So Alter took the company to court.

Attorney Tom Girardi argued there was ample evidence that Disney had taken critical elements from Paul Alter's storyline. Not only were there similar scenes in the movie, but the early Disney drafts of the film demonstrated even more parallels. "In Paul's treatment, the baby grows to its giant size because of a genetic type of accident," says Girardi. "In the movie, the baby grows to giant size because of a machine in a laboratory. Unfortunately for Disney, one of the first drafts of the screenplay shows the baby growing to gigantic size because of a genetic-type accident. Paul's footprints were all over the film." The trial was brief, and in November 1993 a jury awarded Alter $300,000 in damages.

What makes Disney's thievery so interesting is the fierce defense it makes of its own trademarks. Certainly the Mouse can and should protect itself from those who are making money by using its images and trademarks without permission. But sometimes Disney goes over the edge.

White River is a tiny lumber mill town in northern Ontario, Canada. Although there is little remarkable about the nondescript village of 1,200 residents, it has its place in history: White River is the birthplace of Winnie the Pooh, the heavy-set, honey-loving bear made famous by children's author A.A. Milne. As the local story goes, Harry Colebourn, a veterinarian from the City of Winnipeg, was on his way to London to serve in the army during World War I. As he passed through the area, he bought a bear cub for $20 from a trapper at the White River train station. In memory of his hometown, the vet named the bear Winnipeg. When Colebourn reported for duty in London, he was forced to give up his bear. Winnipeg went to the London Zoo, while Colebourn shipped out to France.

> In 1989 Disney threatened to sue three Florida day-care centers that had five-foot likenesses of Mickey and friends painted on their walls.

The zookeepers quickly shortened the bear's name to Winnie, and he became a hit with the public. Warm, bumbling, and curious, Winnie captured the hearts of hundreds of English children, one of whom was Christopher Robin Milne. Author A.A. Milne learned about the lovable bear from his son, and soon after began to work on his endearing tales about Pooh Bear and his friends.

By 1990 White River was on hard times, and the town's elders decided to erect a sixteen-foot statue in honor of Winnie to commemorate the famous bear's 75th birthday. For White River, it would be the ideal way to celebrate its place in history, and at the same time, the tall bear statute might even bring in some tourists. With the timber industry in decline, it would be a nice source of much-needed revenue.

But soon after the town began construction, it realized that its bear had a lot to fear from a Mouse. Executives at Disney headquarters in Burbank got word of the Canadian town's plans, and they were not amused. Within weeks, Disney lawyer Robert Ogden dispatched a sternly worded letter to the town elders of White River. He warned that they could not make any reference to the fabled bear since the Walt Disney Company had bought the rights to Milne's character in 1961. He argued that White River was violating Disney's copyright, and a lawsuit was in the offing.

White River Mayor Ollie Chapman was stunned and wasn't sure how to respond. But when word of the Disney letter was leaked to the media, the Mouse in Burbank was flooded with letters and postcards in support of White River. People even started calling the small Canadian mill town to offer their support. "We got calls from people as far away as Australia who said, 'Go for it. Give it the good fight,'" recalls Chapman. "Show them they're not God."

Embarrassed by the bad publicity, Disney backed down and approved the statue. Still, the Mouse insisted upon some restrictions. Ogden told White River that it could base its statue only on the drawings by British illustrator Ernest Shepard, which had appeared in Milne's books, and not on the later drawings made famous by Disney's animators.

Always relentless, in 1989 the Mouse threatened to sue three Hallandale, Florida, day-care centers that had five-foot likenesses of Mickey and friends painted on their walls. Arguing that the use of the characters suggested Disney had given a stamp of approval to the day-care centers, the company gave the centers one month to scrub the walls clean. When the story hit the newspapers, the centers found people nationwide rallying to their support. "I've gotten so many telephone calls from people angry at Disney that I bet Walt Disney is turning over in his grave right now," said Erica Scotti, who ran Very Important Babies Day Care. Hallendale Mayor Gilbert Stein added that he was "appalled at the harsh politics of a corporate giant that was built with the nickels and dimes of kids. I'd like to ban Mickey Mouse from the city limits."

But Disney wouldn't back down. So the characters were wiped clean from the centers' walls and were replaced with characters belonging to Hanna-Barbera, who gladly allowed them to be drawn.

For Michael Eisner, this is simply part of doing his job. "One of my jobs is protecting the Disney image," he says, "and being a little bit of the 'No, you can't do that' voice." As a result, Disney files hundreds of lawsuits a year to protect its copyright. No doubt, many of these cases are justified. But sometimes the Mouse seems to have trouble distinguishing between protecting its rights and bullying. According to Thomas McGlynn, vice president of marketing for DecoPak Corporation, which owns the rights to Disney characters for cakes and ice cream novelties, the Mouse is unrelenting. He says Disney has even threatened "twelve-year-old kids with Mickey Mouse on their Web sites" with legal action.

PART IV
Mickey's Flicks

CHAPTER THIRTEEN
Circus Miramax I

*"We don't want to grow up and
be another Walt Disney."*

—Bob Weinstein, Miramax Co-Chairman, 1989

I t was Monday, January 22, 1996, and the snow had just stopped
falling on the nearby Wasatch Mountains. Australian Director
Scott Hicks, his agent Jonathan Taplin, and two others were sitting down for a celebratory meal at the Mercato Mediterraneo restaurant in Park City, Utah. The Sundance Film Festival, *the* meeting and
deal-making place for independent cinema, was in full swing. Just
hours earlier, in a long meeting at a nearby condominium, Taplin had
sold the distribution rights for Hicks's latest film, *Shine*, to New Line
Cinema for more than $2 million. The movie tells the poignant story
of Australian pianist David Helfgott's childhood abuse at the hands of
his tyrannical father, his subsequent descent into madness, and then
climaxes with his triumphant return to the concert stage.

The evening started out pleasantly, but just as they raised their
wine glasses in a toast, a burly 250-pound man, who looked like a
longshoreman in an Italian suit, suddenly stormed up to the table and
screamed, "You [expletive]! You tried to [expletive] me!"

The man continued, bellowing threats at the top of his lungs. Out of
control, he grabbed lapels and made several crude anatomical references that caused nearby patrons to blanch. Finally, the maitre d' and
a muscular waiter intervened and evicted him from the restaurant.

This was no anonymous lunatic. It was the head of one of the most
important pieces of the Disney empire—Miramax—which Disney
acquired in 1993. The acquisition wedded the film industry's most
provocative producer and distributor with Hollywood's squeakiest-

clean, family-brand studio. The new Disney is no longer interested in simply providing entertainment for families. In 1997 Disney's film companies—Disney Pictures, Hollywood Pictures, Touchstone Pictures, and Miramax—released fifty-nine movies. Of those, thirty-eight, almost two-thirds, were R-rated. And the film company that has garnered the most attention is Miramax.

In the mad world of Miramax, the fracas at the restaurant was just another typical day for its cofounder, Harvey Weinstein. A bad temper is Harvey Weinstein's specialty. He once fired an employee for making an error while playing on the company softball team. Flying phones, foul language, and kicked over furniture are common hazards in his office. To those who work with Harvey and his brother Bob, their formula is simple. "This business is about ego and greed," Patrick McDurrah, former director of Miramax International, told us. "Harvey is ego, Bob is greed."

Actor Robert Redford, the guiding force behind the Sundance Film Festival, has dealt with Miramax since its earliest days. "Harvey is an impresario-merchant," he says. "He pushes and sells and grabs you by the throat. He takes product to the audience's throat. You don't want to close your eyes around Harvey. You don't know what article of clothing will be missing."

Yet, in little more than a decade, Harvey Weinstein and his brother Bob have built the company into a powerhouse. Much of that success has come from controversial films with X ratings. And while most film producers and distributors rush to find mainstream movies that appeal to a wide audience, the Weinsteins promote films about incest, ghastly violence, and strong sexual themes, with Disney's support. "We're very happy they're part of our team," says Joe Roth, Chairman of Disney Studios.

The Weinstein brothers—sons of a diamond cutter—grew up in Flushing, Queens, in the shadow of Shea Stadium. When they were children, their father Max would take them to the movies every Saturday while their mother, Miriam, got her hair done. "They used the local theater as a baby-sitter," says Bob Weinstein. "They'd drop us off at the triple feature and pick us up six hours later." This early form of benign neglect sparked a love for films, and given the fact that neither was particularly interested in school, became an early focus of their lives. "We went to the University of 47th Street," is how Bob puts it.

The Weinsteins proudly recall when as teenagers they went to see the French film *400 Blows* by Francois Truffaut under the mistaken impression that it was a porno-graphic movie. Instead, they were introduced to the esoteric, but occasionally profitable, world of independent cinema.

In 1978 the two brothers bought a dilapidated movie house in downtown Buffalo and booked

> **Miramax promotes films about incest, ghastly violence, and strong sexual themes. "We're very happy they're part of our team,"**
>
> —Joe Roth, Chairman of Disney Studios.

music acts like the Grateful Dead. To make money between concerts, they ran film festivals. "We'd show *Alice's Restaurant* at seven, *The Sting* at nine, and *Jimi Plays Berkeley* at midnight," recalls Harvey.

They kept an eye on independent cinema, catching films by foreign directors like Truffaut, Luis Brunuel, and Philippe de Broca. They especially took notice of New Line Cinema, which started in a fifth-floor walk-up apartment in New York. The company produced a Rolling Stones concert film called *Sympathy for the Devil* and rereleased—as camp—the 1983 anti-drug movie *Reefer Madness*, both of which made good money. The key to New Line's success was acquiring cheap films with high shock value. "The moment when a 300-pound transvestite ate an all-too-real dog turd on camera in 1972 really put New Line on the map," says independent film producer John Pierson, who now works for Miramax. The moment was not lost on the Weinsteins.

The brothers formed Miramax, named after mom (Miriam) and dad (Max), and bought the rights to their first film in 1979. It was a concert tape from Britain that featured performers like Sting and Phil Collins. Although the film came from a six-hour Amnesty International benefit concert, the Weinsteins cut it down to two hours and retitled it *The Secret Policeman's Other Ball*. The film grossed more than $6 million at the box office.

Bob and Harvey were not producers or directors, but distributors. To acquire films, they attended festivals where they could bid on the work of hopeful directors. But unlike other independent distributors, the Weinsteins heavily edited the films they bought. In fact, Harvey became known as "Harvey Scissorhands."

The brothers thrived by distributing minor foreign films like *Crossover Dreams*, *Erendira*, and the Danish *Twist and Shout*. To market them, they played to the lowest common denominator—sex. *Erendira*, for example, is a surrealistic Brazilian film scripted by Gabriel Garcia Marquez, the Nobel laureate. The Weinsteins picked it up for about $50,000. The original Latin American ad campaign for *Erendira* featured the film's star, Irene Papas. But the Weinsteins didn't think an actress in her fifties would generate much at the box office. "She appealed to an older audience," recalls Bob Weinstein. "We figured we'd try another element." His solution was a publicity campaign that focused on Claudia Ohana, the young costar who had a relatively minor role in the movie. They persuaded her to come to the United States to do a publicity tour, and arranged for her to sit for a rather provocative spread in *Playboy*. The film ended up grossing nearly $3 million.

The first big Miramax success came in 1986 when they secured the rights to distribute *Working Girls*, a film about prostitutes in a bordello. It was shot in Super 16mm and partially funded by Alternate Current, a lesbian-owned production company. This film was controversial, even for independent cinema. At the Toronto Film Festival, director Lizzie Borden had to block out (with tape) several graphic masturbation scenes, and the New York Film Festival chose not to run the film at all, after deciding the Lincoln Center was not ready for graphic images of prostitutes inserting diaphragms. But when Harvey Weinstein saw the film, he fell in love with it.

Producer John Pierson recalls being cornered by "two very insistent rug merchants" while talking with Lizzie Borden. Even though they desperately wanted the film, the Weinsteins applied tough negotiation tactics. The discussions dragged on for several months. Eventually Borden and Pierson signed, because there was little interest from anyone else. (After all, if the New York Film Festival wouldn't show it, who would?) The Weinsteins agreed to pay $200,000 for the distribution rights. "They certainly deserved credit for not being intimidated by the clinical depiction of sex, power, and money in *Working Girls*," says Pierson. "Other men, especially certain male distributors, definitely felt threatened. In fact Harvey and Bob might have been too unintimidated, because they'd already determined how to sell the sex in a film that was utterly, demonstrably unsexy."

The film is a documentary-style feature that allows audiences to be invisible guests for a day and part of an evening in a Manhattan brothel staffed by about ten prostitutes who work two shifts. Borden claims the set she built in her loft in New York was based on a real house of prostitution where she did research for the film, which presents prostitution as simply another career choice. "Borden neither glamorizes, romanticizes nor condemns anything or anybody connected to the brothel," *Variety* noted in its review of *Working Girls*.

To avoid being slapped with an X rating but still capitalize on the film's lurid nature, the Weinsteins released *Working Girls* as "unrated" by the Motion Picture Association of America (MPAA) and ran an advertising campaign with the tag line: "The two things I love most in life are sex and money; I just never knew until much later they were connected."

The film ended up grossing about $1.8 million at the box office, and 35,000 videocassettes were shipped. For the producers it eventually earned about $750,000—half domestically, the other half in foreign revenue. While it was not a great commercial success, it gave the Weinsteins reputations as innovative marketers willing to take on the most controversial films.

• • •

IN SEPTEMBER 1989 BOB WEINSTEIN attended the Toronto Film Festival, where he saw a new film by director Peter Greenaway. It begins with a pack of stray dogs eating bloody hunks of rotten meat. Two refrigerator trucks pull up, loaded with dead fish and hanging pig carcasses. Then, a gang of thugs tear the clothes off a struggling, terrified victim so the thugs can smear his naked body with excrement, before they force it into his mouth and rub it in his eyes. They pin him to the ground while the leader gleefully urinates on him.

From that episode, this strange new film entitled *The Cook, the Thief, His Wife and Her Lover* "builds." There is a brutal sex scene in a toilet stall; there are French kisses and tender embraces with a bloody, mutilated cadaver; and a nine-year-old boy's navel is hideously carved from his body. A restaurant patron's face is scalded by a tureen of vomit-colored soup, and two middle-aged lovers have sex in the back of a truck filled with rotting, maggot-infested garbage. The film climaxes with the main characters slicing off—and swallowing—a piece of carefully seasoned human corpse.

Recalls John Pierson, "Bob Weinstein sat in a screening of the Greenaway film, observed nearly half the audience walking out in disgust, and called his brother to insist they must buy the film. It's a standard chapter in the annals of Miramax."

By 1989 Miramax was bumping along. Montagu Ventures, an arm of the London-based Midland Bank, offered the company a $25 million debt/equity package. With the money now in hand, the Weinsteins expanded their operations. They bought *The Cook, the Thief, His Wife and Her Lover*, which they marketed as a film about "Lust, Murder, Dessert." They also released *Scandal*, dubbed by Harvey Weinstein as "a perfect Miramax title." The movie tells the tale of Christine Keeler, a woman whose affair with government minister John Profumo rocked the British government in the early 1960s. To market *Scandal*, the Weinsteins produced print advertisements featuring a nude Joanne Whalley-Kilmer (the actress who played Keeler) snaked strategically around a black chair. The film *sex, lies, and videotape* was distributed using a similar sex-appeal approach.

"We spend a lot of time making movies look more provocative than they really are," says Miramax marketing official Mark Gill. "Our cheap cliché is: 'Sex, betrayal, murder.' People want to see things that are provocative. You'll see a lot of women with no clothes on their backs in our ads. We'll put a gun in the ad if we can. It works. You can scorn me for this. But it works."

Because the material the Weinsteins were releasing was often controversial, they perfected another publicity-seeking tool. When the MPAA slapped an X rating on Pedro Almodovan's *Tie Me Up! Tie Me Down!*, Miramax sued Jack Valenti, head of the Motion Picture Association, and the association. Miramax lost the case—but it used the controversy to generate even more interest in the film.

The company has distributed some moving films like *My Left Foot*, the story of the late Irish artist Christy Brown who triumphed over cerebral palsy to become one of the country's most respected poets and painters. They also released *Cinema Paradiso*, an Italian movie about a film aficionado and his joys growing up in Sicily. But these films are the exception. Miramax is determined not to lose its provocative edge. In 1989 Bob Weinstein proclaimed, "We don't want to grow up and be another Walt Disney."

When the merger was announced, Katzenberg was asked if Walt wasn't spinning in his grave. "I don't know," he said, dryly. "I haven't been over to the grave lately."

Buoyed by the success of *Scandal* and *sex, lies and videotape*, the Weinsteins relocated their offices to Robert De Niro's TriBeCa Film Center on Greenwich Street in Los Angeles. Although the move brought them geographically closer to established filmmakers and stars, it didn't change their unconventional approach to distributing films. They stuck with their formula of buying inexpensive productions they could dress up and distribute for a profit, while always factoring in the benefits of some controversy.

In 1991 they bought and distributed *The Pope Must Die*, the story of a pope who illicitly fathers the world's most famous heavy-metal rock star. The film includes sultry nuns who serve as the pope's harem and cardinals who control illicit arms deals and cooperate with organized crime. When Catholics protested, the Weinsteins enjoyed the added attention, and even promoted the supposedly comic film as having a high-minded purpose. "*The Pope Must Die* is a film that urges an end to the corruption that threatens the Catholic Church," read the company's press release for the film. "And its head is a priest who cares enough about the Church to risk his life to save it." Miramax did, however, wilt slightly under pressure and changed the film's title to *The Pope Must Diet*, but by then its notoriety was already assured.

At the same time, they acquired the rights to a documentary called *Paris Is Burning*, about the world of dancing drag queens. They also distributed *The Grifters*, a story about the sexual tensions between a mother and son who both work as con artists. Near the end of the movie, the mother (Anjelica Huston) actually tries to seduce her son (John Cusack) in order to steal his money.

But by the early 1990s, the formula wasn't working. Not only had Miramax gotten into financial trouble, but the major studios were encroaching on this business. A lot of big companies became involved. Sony Pictures had opened Sony Classics, and October Films was started. "The landscape was rapidly changing," says Patrick McDurrah, former head of Miramax International. "Where once Miramax had been able to pay hundreds of thousands for an acquisition of an independent film, suddenly they were going to have to pay a million or more for that same film if they were lucky enough to be able to bid for it."

Facing a cash crunch, the Weinsteins began looking for a buyer for Miramax. Initially discussions were held with Sony, but Sony wanted more creative control than the Weinsteins were willing to give. But in the spring of 1992, Harvey Weinstein received a call from Jeffrey Katzenberg, chairman of Disney Studios. The Mouse was interested in buying Miramax.

Disney was interested in acquiring film companies that could generate profits and help it build a library of films that could appear on the growing number of cable TV channels. Michael Eisner and Jeffrey Katzenberg were familiar with the Weinsteins' work and aggressively pursued them.

Negotiations began on two central points: price and creative control. Eventually a price was agreed to: some $60 million in cash and stock options. And much to Bob and Harvey's surprise, Disney promised to give them the freedom to run the business as long as they didn't release a movie with an NC-17 rating. For its part, Disney got its hands on Miramax's library of some 200 films, everything from *Working Girls* to *Cinema Paradiso*. Had the Mouse not called, Miramax might have simply faded away. "I used to go into Chase Manhattan Bank," says Bob Weinstein, "on my knees, to start out with, then I'd be on my belly, begging for money." Reportedly, the Weinsteins were $12 million in debt when the deal was finally sealed in May 1993.

To many in the entertainment world, it was an improbable marriage. They felt that the mix of Weinstein bravado and Disney's corporate conservatism would only end in mutual frustration. But they underestimated the Weinsteins and exaggerated Disney's link with the past. When the merger was announced, Katzenberg was asked if Walt wasn't spinning in his grave. "I don't know," he said, dryly. "I haven't been over to the grave lately."

In the Miramax deal, Disney was willing to grant the Weinsteins something even Sony wasn't willing to give: carte blanche on creative issues. Why did the company do it? "Acquiring Miramax was a business decision to expand the presence in the marketplace and expand acceptability to the filmmaking community," producer Ralph Winter, who has worked on several Disney feature films, told us by cellular phone from the set of Disney's *Mighty Joe Young*. "These are the main reasons. Miramax is an avenue to produce and make movies in an area that Disney has not traditionally made money."

Disney, which still promotes itself as a fount of family entertainment, was now actively pushing to liberalize the R rating through Miramax.

From Disney's perspective, this deal was above all about money. Joe Roth, Chairman of Disney Studios, admits that Disney and Miramax are "odd bedfellows from a content standpoint, but from a business standpoint, we're terrific partners."

As if to test the true level of their independence, the Weinsteins continued after the acquisition to sign up the sort of controversial films that had made them successful. The first film they bought was

Exotica, the story of a man obsessed with a stripper who dresses up as a young school girl on stage.

Next came *Fresh*, a movie about a young boy involved in the drug trade. The film begins with twelve-year-old Fresh showing up late for school because he ran behind on his morning rounds as a drug courier. The young entrepreneur delivers heroin for a local kingpin and does freelance work for a crack dealer. While *Variety* said the audience could expect to "feel a queasiness about the spectacle of a little boy setting other people up for the kill," the Weinsteins were not deterred.

Young people and death also pervade another 1994 Miramax film. *Heavenly Creatures* is a story about two teenagers, Pauline and Juliet, who imagine all sorts of fantasy murders. When a priest talks to Juliet about Jesus, he is dragged off and beheaded. Pauline, sent to psychiatric counseling for a precocious proclivity for sex, imagines her shrink disemboweled. The two teenage girls become so immersed in each other they have a fantasy love-making scene. The film climaxes when Juliet's parents' pending divorce threatens to force the girls to live apart. The girls respond by hatching a lethal plan.

In 1994 Miramax's *The Advocate* received an NC-17 rating for what the MPAA called "a scene of graphic sexuality." So in classic, self-promoting style, the Weinsteins hired attorney William Kunstler to challenge the decision. Kunstler's attempts failed, and eventually they cut twelve seconds of nudity—the "bare" minimum to get an R rating.

Another Miramax release, *Clerks*, ran into ratings trouble. Among its interesting characters are Veronica, who tells Dante (her boyfriend) how many men she has had oral sex with—in great detail. The scene earned the picture an NC-17 rating. Miramax responded by hiring super attorney Alan Dershowitz to argue that the MPAA was trying to "censor the voice of a generation." Miramax planned to take the MPAA all the way to the Supreme Court if necessary. "This is a perfect case to challenge the ratings procedure in the courts," said Dershowitz. Disney, which still promotes itself as a fount of family entertainment, was now actively pushing to liberalize the R rating through Miramax. And it worked. In the end, the MPAA, fearing rising legal costs, backed down, and Disney's Miramax released *Clerks* with an R rating, unaltered from the MPAA NC-17 version.

Miramax ended the year with *Pret-à-Porter*, a Robert Altman film about the fashion world, marketed with the campaign: "Sex. Greed. Power. Murder. Some Things Never Go Out of Style." ("What more could you ask for in a movie?" Harvey asks.) The MPAA again stamped a Miramax film with an NC-17 rating. Within a year, the Weinsteins became adept at what one Disney executive calls "Miramax line-dancing," straddling the NC-17 and R rating line. Perhaps they even moved it over a few notches in their favor. *Pret-à-Porter* ended up with an R rating.

But all the line dancing in the world wouldn't get them an R rating for a movie about some kids.

CHAPTER FOURTEEN

KIDS

In late January 1995 just past midnight, Harvey Weinstein was nervously shifting in his seat. He was in the fusty Egyptian Theater in Sundance, Utah, for the first public screening of the latest Miramax film. There were already rumors circulating that *KIDS* would be unlike any of their other movies. "This is like old Miramax," Harvey said at the time. "I used to be nervous at screenings. But what's scary is also exhilarating." Despite a title befitting classic Disney children's programming, the children in Miramax's release aren't members of the Mickey Mouse Club. These prepubescent children are not tap dancing, they're lap dancing.

As the lights dimmed, Disney's newest release began to roll. A seventeen-year-old boy named Telly is smoothly seducing a sweet-faced girl who is barely out of puberty. At first the two kiss, and he then promises her that he really cares. Before you know it, they are having intercourse, with every graphic noise and motion recorded for the audience. When Telly is finished, he nonchalantly leaves. The "virgin surgeon," as he calls himself, has just notched another conquest, and minutes later he's with his friend

> The children in *KIDS* aren't members of the Mickey Mouse Club. These kids aren't tap dancing, they're lap dancing.

Casper, sharing all the intimate details. "Virgins, I love 'em," he tells his friend. "No diseases, no loose as a goose p——, no skank, no nothing. Just pure pleasure." By now it's clear no one in the cinema audience has ever seen anything quite like this.

Further on in the film, Telly and Casper go skateboarding, get some drugs in Washington Square Park, and prowl for more sex. Along the way, they beat up a man, who merely bumped shoulders with Casper, with their skateboards. Fifteen or so of their friends also help. Telly,

Casper, and friends then visit a neighborhood swimming pool, where a black friend of Telly's tries to entice a girl into sex by gyrating his pelvis and swinging his penis back and forth so that she (and the audience) can hear it go slap-slap-slap.

As the story proceeds, we learn that not only is Telly bent on seeking and actively seducing prepubescent girls, he's also HIV-positive. Jennie—who had sex with Telly once at age thirteen and has been abstinent since—learns she has tested positive for the AIDS virus. She begins a frantic search for him to tell him the frightful news. She finds him at a party in an apartment where a young girl, passed out on drugs, serves as a symbolic backdrop to the unfolding story. As Jennie walks through the apartment, she finds kids sprawled all over, dead drunk, in various states of undress. She then goes into the master bedroom, where she finds Telly having sex with his latest young virgin. She realizes she is too late to save this girl, and Telly yells out "shut the door!", so she wanders into the living room. High on drugs, Jennie passes out. To end the film on a high note, while she is unconscious, she is raped by Casper in a painfully long and graphic sequence.

The Associated Press called *KIDS* "voyeuristic and gratuitously violent both in its dialogue and action." A reviewer for the *New Yorker* called it "nihilistic pornography." But the night went as well as could have been expected for Harvey Weinstein, who stood near the back rows of the theater. When he had first seen the film, several months earlier, he hailed it as "a masterpiece. I had to have this movie," he recalls. "That's all that matters." The fact that Disney let him acquire *KIDS* tells us a lot about the direction of the company.

To understand *KIDS* you need to look behind the celluloid to the man who guided it from a warped idea to its final production. Larry Clark is in his mid-fifties and pulls his graying hair back into a ponytail. Although he could pass for a college literature professor, Clark has spent most of his life photographing kids in various states of undress. Calm and slightly shy, he calls *KIDS* "a realistic film about what's going on when kids have their own world. It's a private world and adults are not allowed in. I was granted access to that world." This is the world according to Larry Clark—where children are intertwined with morose themes like drugs, exploitation, and sex. And it's a view Harvey Weinstein and some Disney executives call art. Undoubtedly, you have other words for it.

Clark began taking photographs as a kid growing up in Tulsa, Oklahoma. In fact, he was introduced to the world of photography at an early age. His mother made a living taking photos of babies, and she would often take her son along as she traveled from door to door. His father was a traveling salesman who was never around. When Dad was home, he spent most of his time in his room eating ice cream. Clark was awkward and had few friends at school. When he reflects on those years, he invariably turns to the subject of his slow-developing sexuality, which he sees as the root of his problems. "I was the kid who didn't go through puberty until he was sixteen [expletive] years old," he says. "And everybody else is going through puberty in the sixth or seventh grade, right? By the time I got to the point to experience that, everybody is already three years past me." He was apparently so disturbed by his arrested development that he thought, "I'm going to kill myself."

Frustrated by this, Clark began to inject amphetamines at age sixteen with some kids in the neighborhood, thus starting a drug habit that would plague him for decades. A few years later he was off to the Layton School of Art in Wisconsin to study photography. He was a good student, and when he returned home, he was ready to photograph the world as he saw it. Almost all of the images he shot were disturbing photos of friends shooting up, having sex, and posing as tough guys. He snapped hundreds of pictures that were collected for a book entitled *Tulsa*. Although many of his friends in these photographs died of complications from drug abuse before the book came out, he kept on using them. "Once the needle goes in it never comes out," he wrote. The book includes one self-portrait with Clark backed against a corner, topless, with fuzzy and crazed hair, his eyes zoned out and his arm wrapped tight with a tourniquet. Dark blood is dribbling down to the floor.

When the book finally came out in 1971 Clark was seriously hooked on drugs. Still he was receiving some attention for his provocative work. The National Endowment for the Arts (NEA) gave him a grant to produce another book of pictures, this one entitled *Teenage Lust*. (The book took him twelve years to finish, but the NEA didn't seem concerned about the delay or the title.) He was busy snapping photos for his new project when he got sidetracked by legal trouble. In 1979 Clark was in a Quaalude-induced haze and shot someone in the arm. He spent nineteen months in an Oklahoma maximum security prison for "assault and battery with a deadly weapon with intent to kill."

After leaving the state pen, Clark moved to New York and threw himself into completing *Teenage Lust*. The result was an autobiographical scrapbook of sorts, with plenty of photos of Clark naked—with women and friends. There is also a photo of a naked boy with an erection pointing a gun at the figure of a naked, bound girl. He titled the shot *Brother and Sister*. In another photo, a street kid is fondling himself and displaying his body as if for sale. Yet another photo shows a boy in a fedora having intercourse with a girl who appears to be in some chemical-induced fog. In the mirror, you can see another man waiting his turn. "They met a girl on acid in Bryant Park at 6 AM and took her home," reads the caption.

Teenage Lust wins high praise from D.H. Mader in *Gayme* magazine, a publication that caters to pedophiles and features nude and seminude photographs of boys. Mader believes the images are designed to arouse those who look at them. And he warns, "Clark will not follow the child protectionists' party line that they are 'innocent victims' of the sex trade. High-minded leaders of the gay movement, whose response to attacks on gays as 'child molesters' is to deny that there is an erotic attraction between men and boys and to seek to put sexuality into the straightjacket of 'consenting adults,' may also be offended [by the book]." Harvey Weinstein, however, calls Clark's work "brilliant."

After *Teenage Lust* Clark started to work with collages, carefully arranging his photos around a particular theme, although never straying from his interest in boys and sex. When New Hampshire teacher Pamela Smart was charged with sleeping with student Billy

Flynn and then encouraging him to kill her husband, Clark became obsessed with the infamous case. He was particularly intrigued by young Billy. "There was a rash of teenage killers," he said at the time, "and they all looked kind of like nerd kids. But Billy Flynn—I saw a picture of him coming out of the police car, and I said, 'That's the way a kid killer should look.'" Clark made an "artistic collage" about the case, with Billy Flynn at the center of it.

Clark eventually got bored with collages and returned to producing books. In 1992 he released *Larry Clark 1992*, an obsessive work about a sixteen-year-old boy he met at a punk club. Clark actually got permission from the boy's parents to take some revealing pho-

Children intertwined with drugs, exploitation, and sex. And it's a view some Disney executives call art.

tographs. He shot dozens of pictures with the kid in a white undershirt, white athletic socks, and white boxer shorts just loose enough to display his private parts. For added effect, in several of the photos Clark had the kid put a gun in his mouth.

The subsequent year he followed up with a book of photographs called *Die perfecte Kindheit*, which featured numerous photos of naked kids and an equally naked Larry Clark cavorting with them in public fountains. As D.H. Mader puts it, *Die perfecte Kindheit* is about "the violence, both physical and sexual, done to boys, and their violence against others." If you want to pick up a copy in the United States don't bother. Fearing seizure by customs or law enforcement, the Swiss publisher won't ship copies stateside.

Up until the early 1990s, Clark's career was as a still photographer, capturing gritty and lurid images of kids. But he longed to make movies. When Gus Van Sant made a picture about Clark's life called *Drugstore Cowboy* in 1989, the director encouraged him to pursue his dream. Only a few months later, Clark found himself a partner for his cinematic project. He ran into some kids one day in Washington Square Park in New York who were riding around on skateboards. He approached a thin teenager named Harmony Korine and told him he was planning to produce a movie. Coincidentally, Korine told him that he had already written a short screenplay about a thirteen-year-old boy who gets taken to a prostitute by his father on his birthday. Clark loved the plot idea but wanted something a little more original. Within three weeks, Korine wrote another script, and *KIDS* was born.

The two shopped it around Hollywood but there wasn't much interest until Cathy Konrad received a copy. Konrad worked for producer Cary Woods, who had just signed deals with Disney and Miramax to develop film projects. Woods had previously done several mainstream films including *Rudy*, the classic tale of an overachiever who goes to Notre Dame and walks onto the football team. But surprisingly, he liked the *KIDS* script and knew of two men, Michael Chambers and Patrick Panzarella, who might be interested in financing a small-budget film. When they signed on, *KIDS* became real.

There were only six weeks of preproduction and then six weeks to shoot the entire film. To add realism and save money, Clark and Korine decided to use amateurs for the cast. (Questions, never fully answered, have been raised as to whether underaged kids were used in the production.) The film stayed on schedule and budget, and just a few months later Woods took the project to Miramax. "When we saw the finished film," recalls Harvey Weinstein, "it was so stunning that there was no question that not only should we acquire it—we are the only company who should distribute *KIDS*."

Miramax paid $3.5 million for the film, a sizable amount for a project that probably would not produce much at the box office. The showing at the Sundance Film Festival erupted a firestorm of controversy, which is precisely what Miramax hoped for. As the company had done in the past with *Working Girls* and *Tie Me Up! Tie Me Down!*, Miramax figured controversy would bring more people into the theaters. "*KIDS* causes clamor," screamed *Daily Variety* in a headline, calling the film "a lurid and disturbing look at New York adolescents." It called *KIDS* "the most controversial American film made in the modern era or maybe ever."

But the Motion Picture Association of America (MPAA) gave *KIDS* an NC-17 rating, citing "explicit sex, language, drug use and violence involving children." Clark tried to appeal, claiming it was an R-rated production. But his efforts failed. So to distribute the film and get around Disney's "no NC-17 movie" rule, the Weinsteins created their own distribution company, Excalibur. "We expect Excalibur to be a one-shot deal," said Weinstein at the release. "We're not in the NC-17 business. But—with Disney's consent—we'll keep it going should another one arise."

Perhaps most shocking was Disney's position. Despite suggestions in the press that Disney was not happy with *KIDS*, people at Miramax don't remember it that way. Patrick McDurrah, who worked at Miramax and on the distribution of *KIDS*, says that Disney didn't care about the content of the film, only the rating. "They [Disney] have a policy: no movie with a harder rating than R, by its company or its subsidiary. They never raised any questions about the content of the film. Why would they? I ask you to look at Disney's other holdings and see what they are developing. It immediately becomes apparent

"Family entertainment is just a marketing package. People who think Disney is family entertainment are naive."

they don't give a s—- about anything but the bottom line. Family entertainment is just a marketing package. People who think Disney is family entertainment are naive." If *KIDS* had somehow been given an R rating, would Disney's Miramax have distributed the film? "You bet." Disney execs never publicly criticized the acquisition of *KIDS*.

The most disturbing thing about the film are the lurid sexual images of children, images that Professor Richard Mohr at the University of Illinois calls pedophilia. Mohr has written several books on sexuality and essays like "Knights, Young Men, Boys." He has also been active in the gay marriage movement and writes frequently about doing away with "traditional notions of marriage and sexuality." But when it comes to *KIDS*, Mohr notes that "Clark has carefully larded his film with kids' naughty doings in order to distract the critics' view from the cinemagraphic point of the movie which is to linger on naked boys—naked boys spritzing each other, naked boys relaxing in hustler poses, naked boys shooting the macho breeze." He correctly notes that the film's pseudodocumentary style is simply a vehicle to obscure the theme. "The documentary style makes the pretense of simply 'presenting the facts'—a would-be charitable and disinterested act," he writes. "But this posturing simply serves to insulate both director and viewer from taking responsibility for the movie's voyeurism, its visual lusting for kids."

It's a long way from the Mouseketeers.

CHAPTER FIFTEEN

Circus Miramax II

In early 1995 dozens of nicely inked invitations went out to Catholic leaders and priests in and around New York. Miramax was previewing a movie about a priest who was tempted to break the seal of confession, and the movie giant was soliciting comments from Catholic leaders. Almost twenty Catholic leaders showed up for the screening, including James Martin. "Finally, I thought, a movie about priests who weren't molesting children," he recalls. After a few minutes of introductory chatter and refreshments, the lights dimmed and the projector began to roll. For the next ninety minutes, the mostly Catholic audience was led through a twisted tale of sex and blasphemy, with no fewer than four scenes in which a priest engaged in sexual acts.

Priest is the story of Greg Pilkington, a priest who is a homosexual. When he isn't taking confession, he cruises gay bars, looking for anonymous trysts. But Greg is no more hypocritical than another character in the movie, a supposedly hard-line "conservative" priest who sleeps with his housekeeper. There is also a pathetic older priest who looks back on his life of celibacy as a colossal waste. For artistic "balance," there is a smug, theocratic bishop.

But these priests are more than sexually active; Greg is also blasphemous. He finds the body of the crucified Christ erotically enticing. "A naked man hanging there writhing in pain, utterly desirable!" he says. In a crucial scene he faces the crucifix, in tears, railing against Jesus's purity. "Don't just hang there. Do something, you smug, suffering [expletive]."

For those gathered at the screening, this was an unusual cinematic experience, to say the least. Miramax's invitation said the film was about "breaking the seal of confession." But *Priest* was really a thinly veiled assault on virtually all Catholic teachings.

For Miramax, the final credits were just the beginning of the show. The numbed audience was escorted into a nearby room where the media were waiting. "But Miramax clearly wanted to stir up controversy and started lobbing provocative questions our way," recalls James Martin. "I felt a bit bamboozled." For good measure, the company announced that it planned to release the film on Good Friday, one of the holiest Christian holidays. Catholic League President William Donohue lambasted the idea as "designed intentionally to insult the Catholic Church and Catholics nationwide." Just days later he was joined by New York's Cardinal John O'Connor, who rightfully called the film "viciously anti-Catholic." The outcry, in fact, became so great that Miramax eventually stepped back from the Good Friday release date.

But Miramax stuck by the film. "The priesthood is full of human beings, not saints," said Mark Gill, president of marketing for Miramax. He claimed the movie was a "real-world portrait" of the priesthood, an accurate depiction of church life.

The film's director, Antonia Bird, an intense, round Englishwoman with flyaway hair, described her reasons for making the film. "My intention in *Priest* was to expose religious hypocrisy, to expose the deep intolerance not only in the Catholic Church, but in society as a whole," she said, failing to note her extreme intolerance of the Catholic Church itself. "The script hit me in the gut—and I set out to achieve in directing the reaction I had when I read it."

Priest was released in April 1995. Despite its well-orchestrated controversy, *Priest* was a box office failure. Still, for the Weinsteins, the film was about more than making money. It was a statement. It demonstrated that Disney and Michael Eisner would not interfere with Miramax's most anti-traditional Disney movies. "We're not going to back off from edgy material," Harvey Weinstein promised shortly after *Priest* came out. "If I didn't do these things and deal with these issues, I couldn't be true to myself."

Even with the debacles of *KIDS* and *Priest,* Bob and Harvey Weinstein's desire to acquire and produce the most controversial films in America has not waned. Miramax is not simply about making money, the Weinsteins are fond of saying. They take seriously their self-defined role as serving as the incubator for young directors and writers. Director Kevin Smith says, "James Brown not withstanding, Harvey Weinstein is the hardest working man in show business—so much so that he'll do everything short of carrying people into the theater and nailing them to the seats to get them to watch our weird and stupid little movies." And the money from Mickey has allowed them to acquire plenty of that type of material.

One of the first things the Weinsteins did after Disney bought Miramax was sign a "first-look" deal with John Pierson, an independent film producer famous for launching young filmmakers with low-budget films. Pierson, a graduate of the New York University Film School, has been enmeshed in the

> **Priest** was really a thinly veiled assault on virtually all Catholic teachings.

independent movie scene since 1976. In 1986 he helped Spike Lee produce his breakthrough film *She's Gotta Have It,* and in 1989 he helped Michael Moore distribute his "sleeper," *Roger and Me.* Pierson had worked with Miramax before, closing the deals on *Working Girls* and *Clerks.* Miramax also penned "first-look" deals with Quentin Tarantino, Sean Penn, Robert Rodriguez, and other young filmmakers.

After *Priest,* Miramax distributed *Lie Down With Dogs,* a John Pierson film. The company advertised it as a "gay Gidget" and touted young director Wally White as a new success. *Dogs* takes place one summer in Provincetown, Massachusetts, which is dubbed in the film as "the ultimate gay resort." Tommie (played by director White) leaves his horrible life in Manhattan to pursue his friend Eddie's promise of "oodles of available men in P-town." Tommie has a variety of sexual escapades, and searches for a place to stay as a "houseboy." Even *The Advocate,* a major homosexual publication, trashed *Dogs* as "amateurish, self-conscious soft-core porn."

Undeterred by that film's failure, Miramax bought the distribution rights—for less than a million dollars because no other major entertainment company would touch it—to *Trainspotting. Trainspotting* is about heroin addicts in Scotland. The main character, Mark Renton, has chosen the life of what he calls a "sincere and truthful junk habit." Renton hangs around with fellow addicts, Begbie, a violent, alcoholic psycho; Spud, a hopeless heroin addict; and Sick Boy, who is "one sick individual." The narrative for the film preaches: "Choose life. Choose a job. Choose a career. Choose a family—but why would I want to do a thing like that?"

Early on in *Trainspotting*, Renton decides to kick his habit. After one last hit involving opium suppositories from a dirty toilet, he holes up in a rented room to sit through the agonies of withdrawal. And to take his mind off drugs, he goes with Sick Boy to the park to shoot dogs with an air rifle. When the Department of Health and Social Services arranges a job interview for him, Renton realizes he needs to make an effort at the interview or he'll lose his welfare money, but he doesn't want a job. When he discovers he decently flunked the interview, he is visibly relieved.

Renton then joins Spud and Begbie for a drink at a pub, where they start a fight. Later, he goes to a disco, where he meets Diane. She takes him home with her, and the next morning he discovers that the man and woman in the kitchen are not Diane's roommates but her parents. Diane heads out the door in her school uniform. Spud, meanwhile, tries to sleep with Gail, but she passes out before anything happens. And Tommy, another friend, doesn't get to have sex with Lizzy because he's lost their homemade porn video.

Now living a life without heroin, Renton is having trouble coping. Reality is too much for him, and after a few days of being drug free, he makes what he calls a "healthy, informed, conscious decision" to get back on drugs as soon as possible. His mates applaud his noble decision. Together they go on a spree of shoplifting and stealing to support their habits. Supposedly, heroin not only justifies crimes, it also kills conscience. When Allison discovers her baby has died, none of the addicts gathered to shoot heroin comment. Finally, Renton reaches for his heroin tools and says: "I'm cooking up."

But Renton and his mates do have ambitions, and even entrepreneurial spirit. They decide to become drug-dealers, as well as users.

As the movie ends, Renton runs off with the money, leaving his friends in a drug-induced fog.

When Miramax submitted *Trainspotting* to the Motion Picture Association of America (MPAA) it received an NC-17 rating for graphic sex and several explicit scenes involving characters shooting up. So, Miramax trimmed a few seconds from a sex scene involving the characters Renton and Diane, just barely pushing the film back into R-rating territory. As one member of the British production team put it, "All that's cut is a bit of undulating, nothing explicit really." The company was also forced to cut another scene in which Renton punctures his veins with a syringe just before he overdoses on heroin. Reluctantly, Miramax replaced the scene with a long, close-up shot of the character. Here, the Miramax formula worked. The film was disgusting, and it was a hit. The content of these movies never brought even a hint of concern from Disney execs. The Mouse was very positive. "These guys have been profitable and have a game plan that we believe in," said Joe Roth. "We like the films they make."

Miramax pins its hopes on young talent who push the limits of propriety. Another John Pierson discovery for Miramax was Kevin Smith. Operating out of Red Bank, New Jersey, Smith heads up View Askew Productions, a company whose mascot is a clown wearing a garter belt. Smith's first film for the Weinsteins was *Clerks*. After venturing to Universal to produce *Mallrats* (which bombed), he returned to Miramax for a multifilm deal.

The first film in the deal was *Chasing Amy*, the story of a man in love with a lesbian. Smith says he got the idea when he and producer Scott Mosler met lesbian writers Guinevere Turner and Rose Troime at the Sundance Film Festival in January 1994. The four of them spent time in a condo during the festival. Smith was there to promote *Clerks*, while Turner was pushing her film *Go Fish*. In Smith's words, they had a lot in common because they both made "grungy little black-and-white films that were very concerned with sex." The four shared what Turner calls "a cultural exchange." Smith wrote the script for *Chasing Amy* soon after.

The film was released in 1997 and begins with two best friends—

Holden (Ben Affleck) and Bank (Jason Lee)—signing copies of their popular comic book at a convention. Holden suddenly takes notice of a fellow artist named Alyssa (Joey Lauren Adams) and follows her to a bar, where he finds her making out with another woman. Although he's disappointed, a friendship blossoms through a series of pseudo-dates. They eventually become lovers, but Holden is taken aback when Alyssa tells him the details of her sexual past: promiscuity in high school and intercourse with two men at the same time. The film cost only $250,000 to make, but it grossed $12 million in 1997 alone.

Smith's next film will be *Dogma*—his look at Christian "mythology." He promises it "will piss a lot of people off—especially the Roman Catholic crowd."

Quentin Tarantino is another Miramax prodigy funded with Disney cash. A high-school dropout who used to work at a video store, Tarantino's manic and hyperactive personality mystifies even his friends. "When you work with Quentin, you can't try to rein him in," says Tarantino's friend and fellow director Alexandre Rockwell. "It'd be like trying to talk a crack addict out of robbing you. Basically you just listen to him for two hours." He's also semiliterate. He gave fellow director Allison Anders a poster for one of his films and signed it: "To Allison, from her oppsite [sic] number, love, hugs, and big wet, juciy [sic] kisses." And in a note to producer Jane Hamsher he praised her "leggs." His success comes from mixing violence and pop culture in a way that appeals to jaded baby boomers and Generation Xers.

Tarantino joined the Miramax circus in 1992 with his film *Reservoir Dogs*, the story of a violent gang. (*Reservoir Dogs* is so violent that video sales in Britain have been banned.) He wrote the film in three weeks, which was made easier because, allegedly, Tarantino borrowed scenes and dialogue from other movies, especially a 1987 Hong Kong action film, *City on Fire*. In 1995 Tarantino's critics produced a twelve-minute video entitled, "Who Do You Think You're Fooling?" that compared the two movies. They planned to show the video at the New York Underground Film Festival until it was abruptly and mysteriously withdrawn.

Next, Tarantino released *True Romance*. His favorite scene has

Patricia Arquette drilling a bad guy in the foot and back with a corkscrew. That episode, he said, made *True Romance* the perfect "date" movie. Whatever that tells us about Tarantino, the rating board didn't see it that way. To get an R rating, the gruesome scene had to be altered.

Tarantino struck gold in 1994 with the release of *Pulp Fiction*. The project had been developed by Tri-Star pictures, but the studio became queasy and dropped it. Harvey Weinstein, however, was all too glad to pick it up. Big-name talent—John Travolta, Bruce Willis, Samuel L. Jackson, and Uma Thurman—guaranteed it would be a hit.

If you watch *Pulp Fiction* or read the script you might understand why Tri-Star demurred. But you also wonder what Disney saw in it. The film is a menagerie of violence, multiple shootings, a man graphically and violently sodomized by two other men, copious cocaine use, and a heroin overdose. The shootings are particularly gut wrenching, with the victims often wounded in the groin, leg, or head, and their bodies convulsing in spasms while the gunmen watch them suffer.

The script includes dialogue like this:

Jules: Look, just because I wouldn't give no man foot massage, don't make it right for Marsellus to throw Antwan off a building into a glass motherf——- house, f——- up the way the n——r talks. That ain't right, man. Motherf——- do that to me, he better paralyze my a—, 'cause I'd kill the motherf——-.
Vincent: I'm not sayin' he was right, but you're sayin' a foot massage don't mean nothing, and I'm sayin' it does. I've given a million ladies a million foot massages and they all meant somethin'. We act like they don't but they do. That's what's so f——- cool about 'em. This sensual thing's goin' on that nobody's talkin' about, but you know it and she knows it, f——- Marsellus knew it, and Antwan knows it, f——- Marsellus knew it, and Antwan shoulda know f——- better. That's his f——- wife, man. He ain't gonna have a sense of humor about that s—.

Somehow Tarantino manages to work the word f—- into the script 171 times, and the word "n——r" 15 times. That feat obviously takes some sort of talent because he picked up an Oscar for best screenplay. And as far as Harvey Weinstein was concerned, Tarantino's language skills and violent imagination made him a talent unmatched in Hollywood. "Probably nobody out there is on his level," he told one reporter. "Even Spielberg doesn't act."

Tarantino, in fact, starred with George Clooney in Miramax's next film, *From Dusk Till Dawn*, a vampire western directed by Robert Rodriguez. Released in 1995 by Dimension Films, a subsidiary of Miramax, Clooney and Tarantino play two brothers on a mindless crime spree en route to Mexico. Clooney is Seth Gecko, a psychopath, and Tarantino plays Richie Gecko, identified in news bulletins throughout the movie as a "sex offender." He's basically a rapist with a foot fetish. Along the way, they take a female hostage. But after hearing voices, Richie rapes and murders her. From there the two brothers hijack a van and kidnap the family inside. They end up at a small-town watering hole, where it turns out that all the bar's topless dancing girls and bartenders are vampires. The house red wine is—naturally—blood. Suddenly the Geckos need to fight for their lives.

Dusk's formula was the same one used for *Pulp Fiction* and *Reservoir Dogs*—plenty of intense violence. The film's carnage and graphic scenes led film critic Joe Baltake to call it "the sickest, most perverted movie within memory." Its only match might be the movie Dimension Films released the next year—*The Crow: City of Angels*, the story of a mystical man brought back to life after he and his son are murdered by a gang. Ralph Novak in *People* magazine wrote, "Perverse violence, none of it interesting, and perverse sex, none of it sensual, fill this movie. It can hardly succeed on its merits, unless the sadomasochism crowd turns out en masse." Disney believes that these gore films represent the future. "An important part of Miramax's future growth will result from the Dimension Films label," said Chris McGurk, president of Disney's Motion Pictures Group, shortly after *The Crow* was released.

At the Mouse, everyone smiles at Miramax's success. In fact, in May 1996 Michael Eisner signed a new seven-year contract with the

Weinsteins. "The acquisition of Miramax Films three years ago proved beneficial to all," said Michael Eisner in a statement. "We are proud of Miramax's artistic achievements and financial results, and are especially pleased that the architects of these accomplishments, Bob and Harvey Weinstein, will continue their association with us."

After *From Dusk Till Dawn*, Tarantino produced *Curdled*, a thriller starring Billy Baldwin. *Curdled* is about a woman who mops up after murder scenes and becomes obsessed with murder. Gabriella (Angela Jones) is a Colombian-born resident of Miami who has been fascinated by gore since childhood. Murder and blood erotically arouse her, and at one crime scene, complete with blood-soaked floors, she performs a sensual dance. "It is not for the faint-hearted," noted the *Washington Post*. "In this movie there is more blood than scenery."

> The film *Priest* was about more than making money. It was a statement. It demonstrated that Disney and Michael Eisner would not interfere with Miramax's most anti-traditional Disney movies.

The most recent Tarantino/Miramax film is *Jackie Brown*. Jackie (played by Pam Grier) is a flight attendant who gets caught transporting drugs and money into the United States. With the help of bail bondsman Max Cherry (played by Robert Forster), she plans to heist $500,000 from her boss Ordell (played by Samuel L. Jackson). Robert DeNiro plays Ordell's loyal right-hand man, Michael Keaton is a federal officer, and Bridget Fonda stars as Ordell's oversexed and drugged-out girlfriend. Although the film offers less gore than *Pulp Fiction*, the language used caused controversy: the word "n——r" is used thirty-eight times. Director Spike Lee protested that "Quentin is infatuated with the word." Lee complained directly to Miramax Chairman Harvey Weinstein, telling him that Tarantino "uses it in all his pictures: *Pulp Fiction* and *Reservoir Dogs*. I want Quentin to know that all African-Americans do not think that word is trendy or slick." Weinstein seemed sympathetic, but stood by his director, prompting Lee to complain about a double standard. "If I had used the word 'kike' thirty-eight times in *Mo Better Blues*, it would have been my last picture."

Tarantino sometimes brings the violence of his films to real life. In October 1997 Harvey and Bob Weinstein were having a power lunch with the young director. They were sitting at a corner table in the hip Hollywood restaurant Ago when Tarantino spotted *Natural Born Killers* producer Don Murphy at a another table. Murphy had once been quoted calling Tarantino "a video geek—who thought he could act."

Tarantino approached Murphy. "Don," he said tapping him on the shoulder, "do you have something to say to me?"

"No," Murphy replied.

Tarantino then shoved him against the wall and began punching him in the head. Murphy, who is much larger and stronger than Tarantino, chose not to fight back. Although Harvey Weinstein intervened, someone called the police, who led Tarantino from the restaurant. As he blew kisses from the back seat of the police car, Weinstein talked Murphy out of pressing charges. Later, however, Murphy called his attacker "a barbarian."

"I really think I slapped some respect into the guy," Tarantino said.

Finding inexpensive independent films to distribute has grown increasingly difficult, so Miramax has used Mickey's money to produce its own films. By 1997 the studio was financing 60 percent of its movies, including high-brow movies like *Emma* and *The English Patient*.

The English Patient is Miramax's biggest critical success. It is the story of a romance between a mysterious count and a nurse during World War II, and won nine Oscars at the Academy Awards. But the Weinsteins' gruff and aggressive style caused problems, particularly when it came to creative control. Praised for its sensitivity and romance, *The English Patient* was at one point in danger of being transformed into something more explicit. Harvey Weinstein pressed director Anthony Minghella and producer Saul Zaentz to make the film more sensual and overtly sexual. But Minghella and Zaentz stood firm. "We had a little difference of opinion on *The English Patient* with Harvey Weinstein," says Zaentz, "but Anthony Minghella and I had final cut. You know all the Harvey and Bob stories." *The English Patient* made it through Harvey Weinstein unscathed, but not without some difficult moments. Zaentz describes working with Miramax as a positive experience, but says the Weinsteins "were angels— angels with claws."

The success of more mainstream films like *Emma, The English Patient,* and *Sling Blade* in 1996 and 1997 brought the company financial rewards and critical success. But bizarre films have remained the signature of the Weinsteins.

In January 1997 Harvey Weinstein was attending the Sundance Film Festival to acquire new films. He arranged for a private screening of one film in which he was particularly interested. *The House of Yes* was the directorial debut of Mark Waters. Although Weinstein didn't know Waters, he was familiar with the film's producers, Beau Flynn and Stefan Simchowitz. He had enjoyed their previous picture *johns*, a film about two street prostitutes, John and Donner. John's birthday is December 25, and he wants to spend Christmas in the luxurious Plaza Hotel. To help him raise the necessary $300, he enlists his best friend on the street, Donner, a naive Midwestern runaway. According to director Scott Silver (who was an executive producer of *The House of Yes*), John represents a subtle allegory of Christ, who must sacrifice himself for the sins of others. The movie's pivotal scene is when the manipulative John does his friend Donner a favor by taking a trick for him. Most film companies would shy away from a movie about a male prostitute who represents Christ, but Harvey Weinstein liked it. In the end, though, it was distributed by First Look Pictures.

Like *johns*, *The House of Yes* pushed the boundaries of propriety. Described by movie reviewer John Brodie as "a dark comedy about blue-blooded incest," the film is the story of a dysfunctional family with incestuous brother-and-sister twins. The brother tries to end the affair with his sister because he is getting married. But old habits prove hard to break. Even more bizarre, the brother and sister are aroused by reenacting the Kennedy assassination. (You figure it out.)

Incest is presented as a sensual alternative to more traditional relationships. As *Entertainment Weekly* put it, "*The House of Yes* is a
movie that dares to make sibling incest look sexy."

It must have worked for Harvey Weinstein. When he finished
watching, he immediately reached for his checkbook and committed
$2 million to buy the North American rights to the movie. "There was
a lot of interest from several distributors," said the film's producers,
"but we decided to go with Miramax after hearing how much they
loved the film and hearing their marketing concept for the movie."

That check was made possible by the Mouse, who made the
Weinsteins key players in the film business. "They would not even be
close to where they are today without that money from Disney,"
Patrick McDurrah, who worked at Miramax and whose Gotham
Entertainment Group signed a "first-look" deal with Miramax, told
us. "It helps all around. Your ability to get credit, to get advertising,
and servicing through studio operations. That really adds up. It all
came together for them with Disney."

It has all come together indeed, allowing a couple of guys from
Queens, who used to promote films about prostitutes inserting
diaphragms, to ride to the highest social circles in the nation. Harvey
and Bob are among President Clinton's biggest financial supporters.
They attended a private coffee hosted by President Clinton in the
Map Room of the White House in October 1995, and in late August
1997 Harvey was at the Farm Neck Golf Course on Martha's Vineyard,
Massachusetts, to celebrate his friend Vernon Jordan's birthday with
the president and first lady.

CHAPTER SIXTEEN

Victor Salva: Writer, Director, Child Molester

I t was supposed to be a night of celebration. In late October 1995 Disney's Hollywood Pictures was screening its new motion picture at the Galaxy Theater on Hollywood Boulevard. Disney had been touting the movie's director as its latest discovery, an unspoiled natural talent. Victor Salva was said to be blessed "with a gift for getting inside the heads of children."

Plenty of A-list Hollywood insiders were on hand for the event, including studio executives, actress Mary Steenburgen, actor Jeff Goldblum, and Disney Studios Chairman Joe Roth. After the screening, as all the glitterati made their way out of the theater, the mood abruptly changed. Disney Studios Chairman Roth was confronted by disturbing placards. "Victor Salva: Writer, Director, Child Molester," read one. "Support the Victim, not the Victimizer," read another. As the attendees continued making their way out, a twenty-year-old man with long, blond hair handed them leaflets that read in part: "Please don't spend your money on this movie. It would just go to line the pockets of this child molester."

The title of the new film was *Powder*, the story of a misunderstood albino teenager. Although Disney was busy heralding its new director, the Mouse failed to mention that he was also a five-time felon. The young blond man leading protesters that night was Nathan Winters, a one-time child actor who had been sexually abused by Victor Salva.

According to Rebecca Winters, Nathan's mother, the non-effect on Salva's career of such a shameful crime had left her son depressed and even suicidal. What was even worse was the source of Salva's redemption. As Nathan said, "I can't believe it's Disney. I'm not going to stand by. He should not be allowed to live his life as if nothing happened. I don't care what he does with his life, but he should never be around a child again."

Disney's involvement was ironic: It marked the first time a known child molester had directed a major Hollywood movie. But maybe even worse than releasing his film was how the Mouse dealt with Nathan's protests.

Victor Salva began his filmmaking career directing short amateur movies in the San Francisco area. He won a few prizes at film festivals, but movies were a part-time vocation. Salva kept himself busy working with children. He worked at a day-care center, was involved in Big Brothers programs, and even wrote children's books.

In 1983 he was living in Concord, California, and working in a day-care center when he met Rebecca Winters. "Victor was making this little movie called *Goblin's Gold*," she recalls. "He was talking about needing someone to sculpt the goblin's face, and I'm a sculptor. So we were introduced. Victor became our friend. He was a very good family friend. It wasn't that Nathan was ever an aspiring actor or anything. It was that Victor was our friend and was making these movies, and he starting telling us he was writing these scripts for Nathan and he wanted Nathan to act in them."

Nathan was only eight at the time, but Rebecca trusted Salva, who seemed to have an affinity for children. During the next four years, Salva made two films starring the boy. *Something in the Basement* was a predictable horror film in which young Nathan played a frightened little boy. The second film was *Clownhouse*, the story of a young boy terrorized by clowns.

While putting *Clownhouse* together, Salva attracted the attention of Francis Ford Coppola. Surprisingly, Coppola agreed to help finance the film. For all involved in the project, it looked as if they might now be part of something that could make it big.

But just as filming got under way, Rebecca Winters started to worry. "I just knew something was wrong. Victor stopped me going to the set, saying Nathan couldn't work if I was there. I had to hammer at Nathan that day to get him to tell me what was going on, but finally he did."

What Nathan told his mom was more horrifying than any movie.

The boy was being terrorized—not by fictitious clowns—but by Victor Salva. He told his mother that the two had touched each other in private places and had kissed. Horrified, Rebecca immediately pulled Nathan from the movie. Francis Ford Coppola, however, was not sympathetic. Coppola's company had a significant financial stake in the film, and according to Rebecca Winters, he threatened to sue her for breach of contract unless she returned Nathan to the set at once.

More worried for her son than about a possible lawsuit, Rebecca Winters contacted the police. Detectives interviewed Nathan, and, feeling they had sufficient probable cause, raided Salva's home. They found two explicit videos and an album of still photos. One video had extensive footage of Salva and Nathan engaging in oral sex. The other displayed young men taking showers. "We suspected there were other victims besides Nathan," says Sergeant Gary Primavera, who led the raid, "but we could never prove it."

Those who knew about convicted pedophile Salva were shocked when he resurfaced at, of all places, Disney.

Salva eventually pled guilty to oral sex with a minor, lewd and lascivious conduct, and procuring a child for pornography. According to Sergeant Primavera, "Victor has every characteristic of a pedophile that I know of, and I've worked with enough of them." Uncharacteristically, however, "[t]here was no remorse. The only sadness on Victor's part was that he got caught." In April 1988 Salva was found guilty on five felony counts.

Victor Salva served fifteen months of a three-year sentence in state prison. While sitting in his prison cell, Salva certainly had plenty of time to rethink what he had done. Instead, he began to formulate a movie plot about a misunderstood teenage boy. When he got out of jail, Salva sent a completed script to several studios, including Disney. Roger Birnbaum, the head of Caravan Pictures, which develops films for Disney, read it and was so impressed that he immediately bought the script and gave Salva the director's job. Disney even gave Salva $10 million to produce *Powder*.

Both Disney and Birnbaum claimed they had no knowledge of

Salva's criminal record, even though Francis Ford Coppola had worked with Disney on multiple projects and had firsthand knowledge of the Winters case. In addition, the case had been widely discussed in the Industry press. Shortly after Nathan's demonstration outside the Galaxy Theater, *Powder* coproducer Daniel Grodnik confessed that he had known all along about Salva's past. When the press asked him to comment on the protest, he said, "[T]he issue was already out and didn't have any heat." In other words, it was old news.

Powder is the story of an extraordinary boy born without hair or pigmentation after his pregnant mother is struck dead by lightning. Powder is rejected by his father, and raised by his grandparents. But when they die, he is discovered hiding in the basement of an old house by a local sheriff (actor Lance Henriksen) and a social worker (Mary Steenburgen). Powder is placed in a local state school where the lives of those who come into contact with him are changed forever.

Powder's milky-white appearance is only one facet of his uniqueness. Jeff Goldblum plays a science teacher who is fascinated with Powder. He is convinced that the boy is the next stage of human development. Powder has telekinetic powers and an "electric personality" that allows him to magnetize metal. Radios and televisions don't work around him, and during thunderstorms his body acts as a lightning rod. Then there are Powder's incredible intellectual gifts. He has memorized *Moby Dick* and hundreds of other books. He can read minds and feel other people's "hidden emotions." But even with all of these incredible talents, Powder is an awkward loner, something Salva thought all kids could relate to. As reviewer Ken Tucker put it in *Entertainment Weekly*, "The movie sucks up to teenagers by saying to them that just like Powder, you feel awkward because you're different, but you're also deeply wonderful."

Not so wonderful for Disney was the firestorm of controversy that erupted about Salva's past. The *Los Angeles Times, Daily Variety*, CNN, and the Associated Press all ran major stories. Those who knew about Salva were shocked when he resurfaced at, of all places, Disney. "It just blows me away," said Sergeant Primavera, who arrested Salva. "He had serious signs of being a pedophile."

William Dworin, head of the Los Angeles Police Department's unit for sexually exploited children, was also amazed, and immediately expressed concern for the safety of the children starring in the picture. He noted that pedophiles exhibit an extremely high tendency to repeat their crimes. "[Mr. Salva is] in a position of authority," said Dworin, "and as long as he's in a position to be around kids he's a threat to kids."

For his part, Salva tried to put it all behind him. "I paid for my mistakes dearly," he said. "Now, nearly ten years later, I am excited about my work as a filmmaker and look forward to continuing to make a positive contribution to our industry."

You would expect as much from Salva. But what about Disney? How would America's babysitter respond? The Mouse came down solidly on Salva's side. "He paid for his crime; he paid his debt to society," said Roger Birnbaum, expressing no regrets about Disney's relationship with a convicted child molester.

When Disney Spokesman John Dreyer was asked by an Associated Press reporter for comments, he said: "What's the point, other than you want to make headlines?"

Birnbaum, the head of Caravan Pictures, confessed he learned about Salva's criminal past about halfway through the filming of *Powder*. He says he confronted Salva who, in turn, admitted it was true. What makes this all the more amazing is that Disney has fired

> "Disney's... lack of response, is the most shocking of all. Not one Disney official has contacted our family to at least say they are sorry for our pain."

directors for failing to stay on schedule or keep under budget. Apparently, however, convicted pedophiles are allowed to keep working regardless of the risks to young actors. Birnbaum didn't even bother to tell anyone in the cast, including the younger performers or their parents. (Mary Steenburgen said she didn't know about the controversy until she saw the protests on opening night.) Birnbaum's solution was simple: "Key production people were told to keep an eye out for anything—just in case."

"To make the statement that they 'had people watch him' is not only absurd but dangerous," Nathan Winters and his mother said in a press release. "Disney's response, and in fact, lack of response, is the most shocking of all. Not one Disney official has contacted our family to at least say they are sorry for our pain."

Birnbaum also claims that he didn't tell the chairman of Walt Disney Motion Pictures, Joe Roth, about Salva's past. If true, that would be surprising, given that the two are inseparable friends. Birnbaum had worked as executive vice president at Twentieth Century Fox when Roth was head of the studio. There they labored side-by-side on numerous films like *Home Alone* and *Die Hard 2*. Together, they left Fox in 1993 to form Caravan Pictures. When Roth departed one year later to become chairman of Walt Disney Motion Pictures, he brokered a deal with Birnbaum to set up Caravan's operations on Disney property so they could continue to produce films together.

Despite the controversy, Disney continues to distribute *Powder*, which offers a pedophile's view of the world. While more subtle than films like Miramax's *KIDS* and *The House of Yes*, the imagery in *Powder* is unmistakable. "There are a lot of mean teenage boys who pick on Powder, and even in the midst of their cruelty, they always seem to be stripping off their shirts as Salva moves his camera in for a pan along their rippling musculature," says Ken Tucker of *Entertainment Weekly*. "You don't have to be aware that Salva was convicted of molesting a boy in 1988 to sense the film's barely latent homoeroticism."

Tom Maurstad, in his review for the *Dallas Morning News*, had the same reaction. He was particularly concerned about one scene in which Powder strays into the gym. "Powder briefly watches a group of boys playing basketball before looking through the bathroom doorway and spying a muscled young man standing before a sink. Powder (and the camera) takes a lingering look as the junior Atlas peels off his shirt and languidly splashes his torso with water—the film almost seems to go into slow motion. From there, the scene devolves into sexual taunting that backhandedly treats child molestation (incestuous, no less) as typical adolescent male banter. Before the scene is over, Powder has been stripped naked so the boys can exclaim over his hairlessness and watch his ever-so-white bum bob around in a mud puddle. You can't help but wonder what Disney executives were thinking as they sat in the screening room."

And it hasn't been just a few film critics raising questions about the film. Experts in pedophilia are equally disturbed by the imagery in *Powder*. Sandra Baker, executive director of the Child and Family Institute in Sacramento, California, says child molesters "think they are more perceptive and beautiful than other people. They feel misunderstood." The fact that Salva chose to create Powder as a pale, hairless, and sensitive outcast "fits what pedophiles can relate to," she adds. "They want their victims to be hairless visually. They don't want adult sex characteristics."

Certain scenes in the film also bother Los Angeles family therapist Lisa Hacker. At one point in the movie Jeff Goldblum, playing the teacher, tells Powder that he's "never had better sex" since being touched by him. Both that scene and another one later on, when the teacher strokes Powder's bald head, are "very intimate and inappropriate," says Hacker.

Disney either didn't see these elements in the film or chose to ignore them. When you read the promotional copy for the film, you wonder whether it's a description of the character Powder or Director Victor Salva describing himself. "Alienated from society, he tries to fit in but only finds intolerance. Despite the cruelty inflicted upon him, Powder's extraordinary compassion helps him to persist, and people begin to understand that their harsh judgment is more a reflection of their own ignorance and fear."

Those who know Salva say the film is really about him and his view of young males. "[Most] of Victor's films are about young boys who've been abused and misunderstood," says Candice Christie, who shared a home with Salva in the mid-1980s.

John Allred, cinematographer on two unreleased Salva films, says that "Victor's pain just oozes from this movie, as it does with every movie he's made." Such is the angst of this convicted pedophile.

But to Disney, none of this seems to matter. When the controversy first erupted, the conventional wisdom in Hollywood was that Caravan Pictures' Roger Birnbaum would receive the wrath of the Mouse. "Scuttlebutt in Tinseltown has Roger Birnbaum, the Caravan Pictures chief and co-producer of *Powder*, doing his producing thing elsewhere by year's end," said gossip columnist Mr. Show Biz. "Birnbaum is the guy who found out about writer-director Victor Salva's child-molestation conviction halfway through the filming of *Powder*, but made a decision to keep a lid on the explosive information. When Salva's story hit the papers, Birnbaum looked bad and Disney looked worse. Sources predict that Disney will encourage Birnbaum, quietly, of course, to step down as Caravan's chief." Naturally, nothing of the sort happened. Birnbaum's career with Disney, if anything, has flourished. Since *Powder*, he has produced such films for the company as *Rocketman*, *G.I. Jane*, and *Gone Fishin'*, among others.

To this day, Disney has never issued a statement of regret about employing Victor Salva or distributing *Powder*.

PART V
Disney's Other Faces

CHAPTER SEVENTEEN

Mr. Minnie Mouse

Every year millions see her wandering around Disney World. She approaches the guests with a bashful demeanor, flirtatiously tilting her head to the side in mock embarrassment. Her every move and gesture is choreographed. If she sees a shy child, she might beckon him, dance a little, or stoop to offer a hug. If the feminine mouse comes in contact with a man, she might snuggle or offer a fake kiss. If someone has a camera, she makes certain the moment is captured on film.

Minnie Mouse is one of the most popular characters at Disney World. But inside that costume is one of the Magic Kingdom's more bizarre secrets. At the new Disney, Minnie Mouse is often a man. "Because the costume is so small, the Mickey Mouse character is played by a girl since it usually only fits on a girl," says Spencer Craig, who worked at Disney World for almost twenty-five years. "But Minnie, on the other hand, is often played by a guy—and for an altogether different reason." That "different reason" is part of the gay subculture that is today blossoming at Disney. It seems that some gay male employees at Disney World enjoy playing the feminine mouse, flirting with and comically embarrassing male guests.

The Minnie Mouse stunt is but a part of the larger issue surrounding a clash between the old Disney and the new. Many current employees report that the company is divided into two camps—those who favor Disney's traditional way of entertainment and those who champion a new way that often infuses the Disney experience with gay themes, characters, and stories.

Garrett Hicks is an employee at the Disney film studio in Burbank. In his mid-thirties and sporting a blond, buzz haircut, Hicks is also a cochair of the Lesbian and Gay United Employees at the Walt Disney Company, the largest lesbian and gay employee organization in the entertainment industry. Hicks says, "There are hordes of gay and lesbian people at Disney."

While Hicks may have an incentive to exaggerate, you hear the same from others in the corporate office. "There are a lot of gay people here at every level," says Thomas Schumacher, vice president of Disney Animation. "It is a very supportive environment."

Senior Disney Publicist Richard Jordan agrees. "Someone in personnel," he says with a laugh, "must have a sweet tooth."

Elizabeth Birch, executive director of the gay-rights organization Human Rights Campaign, relates this conversation with Disney Chairman Michael Eisner: "I said to Michael Eisner, 'Thirty percent of your employees are gay,' and he said, 'You're wrong, Elizabeth. It's forty percent.'" While Michael Eisner disavows making the comment, there is little doubt that, in the words of *Buzz* magazine, "the happiest place on earth—as Disney likes to bill itself—is also one of the gayest."

And what is true for the corporate offices also seems to hold true at the theme parks. "Take away the gay workers," says Jeff Truesdell, a columnist for the *Orlando Weekly*, "and Disney World becomes the planet's largest self-service theme park."

Jimi Ziehr, a training coordinator at Disney's EPCOT, bluntly says that "gays outnumber the straights at Futureland operations, and there's nothing in the closet at Guest Relations." The sexual preference of Disney employees is such a common part of the company's lexicon that Disney World employees joke about it. Question: How many Disney straights does it take to screw in a lightbulb on Main Street? Answer: Both of them.

Gay employees fill a variety of roles at the company from lower echelon staff to the executive suite and the creative side of the business, including: Vice President of Hollywood Pictures Lauren Lloyd; Studio Producer Laurence Mark; Supervising Animator Andreas Deja; Senior Vice President of Disney's Interactive Division Steven Fields; Rick Leed, who heads the production company that produces Disney's TV show *Home Improvement;* and Senior Vice President of Animation Thomas Schumacher. This is not an entirely new development. There has always been a gay presence in the Magic Kingdom, particularly on the creative side of the company. Back in the 1930s, when one Disney animator was arrested on a charge of homosexuality, Walt stood by him. "Let's give him a chance," he told coworkers, "we all make mistakes." The animator returned and had a long career at the studio. He wasn't alone. But in the past homosexuality among Disney artists and employees never became a political issue.

The new development is how active and visible the gay community within Disney has become. "At the AIDS walk in Los Angeles, Disney always manages to have the largest teams carrying the biggest banners," says Todd White, director of creative detail at Disney. "I take my partner with me to Disney functions, and we're always treated with respect."

The gay activism began in earnest in 1990 when Sass Nielson, a forty-seven-year-old technical writer who also sat on the board of the Gay and Lesbian Alliance Against Defamation (GLAAD),

Gay male employees at Disney World enjoy playing Minnie Mouse, flirting with and embarrassing male guests.

tried to place a free notice in the company newsletter *Newsreel*. The notice was designed to solicit gay and lesbian employees to form a support group at the studio's Burbank lot. Employees at the newsletter initially refused to print the ad on the grounds that it was too "sexual" in nature. But Nielson persisted. Finally, with the aid of gay-rights organizations GLAAD and Hollywood Supports, she succeeded in convincing the company to run the ad. The response from the advertisement led Nielson to form Lesbian and Gay United Employees (LEAGUE).

One of LEAGUE's earliest projects was to revise Disney's employment policy so it would protect homosexuals from discrimination at the company. Disney employees belonging to the Hotel Employees and Restaurant Employees Union, Local 681, in southern California, joined the fight by demanding nondiscrimination protection from the company during contract negotiations. At first Disney was reportedly "hesitant" to make the policy change since sexual orientation–based discrimination was not prohibited by California or federal law. "So we made it clear to them that if they did not add sexual orientation, it was unlikely they would get a contract," says Jeff LeTourneau, a gay activist and then chief negotiator with Local 681. "And if they specifically refused to add sexual orientation, we let them know it could result in a nationwide boycott."

Disney relented, and in 1992 the policy changed. "We felt that this was in line with our written employment policy of not discriminating on any basis including sexual orientation," said a company spokesman at the time.

Success in changing the nondiscrimination policy led to a push for employee health benefits for the partners of gay employees. Since Disney company policy as of 1992 no longer allowed for discrimination based on sexual orientation, it would be inconsistent for the company to exclude gays and their partners from the health plan. LEAGUE fought hard for the change, but for the first several years the campaign was unsuccessful. The Mouse wasn't interested, largely for financial reasons. But when Disney acquired the ABC Television Network in 1995, the company faced a dilemma since ABC already offered the perk to its gay employees. "They couldn't very well have one part of the company getting benefits that the other wasn't being offered," says Richard Jennings, executive director of Hollywood Supports, the advocacy group that deals with gay-related issues in the entertainment industry.

Health benefits for the partners of gay employees at Disney came just months later in 1996, but not without controversy. Outside organizations criticized the move as an endorsement of the homosexual lifestyle from a company that had traditionally been family-oriented. And inside the company there were plenty of complaints that gay employees were receiving special treatment.

Disney said the policy was "nothing more than a commitment to provide good health care to our employees and their dependents." This was a surprising claim, given that the extension of benefits to gay partners came just as Disney was working to cut back the health care benefits of married employees at both the ABC Network and Walt Disney World.

John Clark, president of the National Association of Broadcast

Employees and Technicians, represents 2,700 employees at ABC. Clark says his employees began working without a contract on March 31, 1997, because the Mouse wanted to reduce their health benefits. In fact, Disney has already been stopped from lowering retiree health benefits because of a lawsuit brought by Disney employees.

Rich Siwica, a lawyer for the Walt Disney World and Service Trades Council, claims the policy change of including homosexual partners was discriminatory and violated the union contract. He complained that homosexual employees were now receiving benefits that heterosexual employees could not receive: The only "significant others" heterosexuals could put on their health insurance plan were their spouses. Disney's reply was that the company was simply helping out homosexual employees because they couldn't get married to their partners. But Siwica pointed out the company wasn't being consistent. The Disney employee contract also prohibits discrimination on the basis of marital status. Hence, unmarried heterosexuals should have the right to sign up their partners for benefits, too.

The growing gay activism at Disney extends beyond company employment policy. It also exerts a strong influence on the environment at the Magic Kingdom and on the sorts of projects Mickey and his friends are now taking on. And it goes beyond cross-dressing Minnie Mouse. Jane Kuenz is a member of the Project on Disney at Duke University, an organization of scholars and academics who research the Mouse. Kuenz has studied the working conditions at Disney World by interviewing hundreds of employees anonymously. She found evidence of the thriving gay subculture "everywhere:" a costumed Donald Duck seductively whispers "fag" as he walks by other Disney employees before he goes to flirt with the park's male guests; a female dancer lets a male musician perform in her stead and in her clothes; on the steps of Cinderella's Castle, a Christmas pageant is transformed into a drag show for knowing employees when male performers dress in women's costumes. RuPaul, the transvestite entertainer, has performed at Disney World.

Even the much-heralded Main Street Electric Parade, which for years proved to be the mainstay of the "Disney experience" at Walt

Disney World, was touched. On the main float, two of Cinderella's maids-in-waiting were men dressed in drag. "They had little wands and skirts," says one current employee. "We had to hang out by the gate and wait until the parade was finished to clean up, and they used to blow us kisses and stuff. They won't even hide it anymore."

Once a year in June things look altogether different at Disney World. Perhaps it's the man in a black, patent-leather miniskirt and pink-rhinestoned mouse ears strolling down Main Street. Or the two men in pink bodysuits parading around Fantasyland. Whatever the dress may be, the Mouse's world becomes a different sort of place when thousands flock to the annual Gay Day at the Magic Kingdom. In 1997 organizers estimated that sixty thousand gay patrons assembled at the park (others put the count lower).

Through group discounts, organizers plan a special day of festivities at Disney World for those interested in celebrating Gay and Lesbian Pride Month. Gay Day is not simply an organized visit to the Magic Kingdom, but a very public display of sexual identity. There is a lot of openly displayed affection during the event—holding hands, kissing, and the like. Men wear brightly colored boas, queen crowns, and princess hats. And there are plenty of interesting T-shirts with slogans even Goofy could understand: "You're a bad boy, now go to my room," "I can't even think straight," "Nobody Knows I'm Gay," and "So Be Gay."

The theme of the 1997 event was "A Day of Magic, A Night of Pleasure." There was an abundance of both public and private gay-themed parties, with signs pointing the way to "Lesbo-a-go-go"and "Muscle Beach." Before the 3:00 PM parade down Main Street, Gay Day organizers encouraged participants to join the traditional "gathering" for singing in front of Cinderella's Castle. Non–Gay Day families (who just happened to be in the park) heard them sing: "If you're gay and you know it clap your hands/If you're gay and you know it stomp your feet." Some cross-dressers even tried to hold their *own* parade down Main Street, but it never got fully organized.

After the "Day of Magic," the "Night of Pleasure" kicked off. Gay Day attendees flocked to Disney nightclubs, where transvestites, more perfectly primped than most of the real women in the room, giggled, tossed their coifs, and waved red fingernails while their partners slipped roving hands under their skirts.

Gay Day began in 1991 when a group of Orlando-area gay and lesbian computer enthusiasts decided to publicize on the Internet an informal gathering they had planned at the Magic Kingdom. It grew from a few hundred participants the first year to tens of thousands of attendees in 1997. Undoubtedly, Disney is happy about the money this generates. In 1995 participants spent an estimated $14 million on hotel rooms, tickets to the parks, meals, and the popular bright red Mickey T-shirts that have become the signature item of the event. As Kelly McQuain put it in the *Philadelphia Gay News*, "Disney has coopted the queers. In its voracious consumption of the American entertainment dollar, Disney has integrated us into its market."

Complaints by guests and some outside organizations, however, have prompted Disney to firmly deny that it has anything to do with Gay Day festivities. "We had no official dealings with members of this group and they were afforded no special privileges or considerations," says Ray Evans in an official Disney statement. Although Gay Day *is* an unofficial event at

On the main float, two of Cinderella's maids in waiting were men dressed in drag.

Disney, there is plenty of collusion going on. How far up the corporate ladder it goes is difficult to say. In a 1996 internal Disney memorandum, Clyde Min, the general manager at the Polynesian Resort, wrote to coworkers: "Each [Disney] resort has been asked to supply one Management Team Member to assist with the Gay Pride Day in the Magic Kingdom on June 1, 1996. I am looking for any volunteers who may be interested in helping with this event. Please let me know as soon as possible if you are interested as I need to respond with the name of our one volunteer very quickly."

Other actions taken by Disney indicate that it is actively involved in the event. In previous years the company has allowed six "official/unofficial greeters" to hand out Gay Day fliers and literature to park attendees, though Disney doesn't afford the same privilege to other groups. To accommodate the Gay Day crowd in 1997, officials at Disney's Pleasure Island nightclub took the special step of connecting the Mannequins and 8TRAX dance clubs for an after-hours mega-disco. Then there are the signs that occasionally pop up at the Magic Kingdom, like the double entendre at a Frontierland snackbar that shrieks, "Liberate Your Appetite!" At the Country/Western bar, cast members have been known to sprinkle gay comments throughout the shows. As far as Gay Day organizer Doug Swallow is concerned, "They [Disney] are doing whatever they can to maximize their return from the event."

Gay Day promotional literature shows Mickey and Donald holding hands. Officially these images are used without Disney's permission, but the normally litigious company has winked at the practice.

The Head Mouse, Michael Eisner, won't comment on Gay Day. But Disney did once try to head off problems by erecting signs at the ticket booths. They read: "Members of the gay community have chosen to visit the Magic Kingdom today in their recognition of Gay and Lesbian Pride Month. Disney does not discriminate against anyone's right to visit the Magic Kingdom." It seemed like a reasonable solution since it at least alerted unsuspecting guests to what they might see inside the gates. But the signs soon came down. Gay Day organizers thought they were offensive. But perhaps there was another reason: Their absence implies that Disney has no prior knowledge or control over Gay Day. They have never appeared again.

Even though Gay Day is not an official Disney event, there are things the company could do to temper the more peculiar aspects of the festivities. Most complaints from the guests are related to the sometime outrageous behavior that takes place—public same-sex kissing, flagrant costumes, confrontational T-shirts, and so forth. Disney already has rules that forbid guests from wearing clothes with overtly political or sexual messages. The annals of Disney are replete with examples of people booted from the park because they refused to cover up explicit T-shirts of heavy metal bands. Other visitors have been escorted out of the park for voicing political messages that might offend some park guests. And in extreme cases, Disney even reserves the right to banish people from "the happiest place on earth" for life.

Disney has also taken special precautions in the past to ensure that certain groups abide by park decorum. Complaints by guests and park employees about the behavior of Brazilian tour groups prompted Disney in 1996 to produce a Portuguese-language video for Brazilian tour operators explaining that groping Disney cast members, throwing coins inside tubas, and forcing people to join conga lines, among other things, are definite no-nos at Disney World. The company even hosted seminars for tour operators in Brazil to teach proper behavior. Disney won't say why the antics of Brazilians warrant special concern while those of Gay Day attendees don't.

The organizers of Gay Day expect it to be at Disney World well into the future, and have even suggested to company officials some tongue-in-cheek changes for the park:

"Cruising on the Jungle Cruise offers fashion queens a chance to show off their latest Banana Republic safari ensembles."

"Not forgetting the leather crowd, the Country Bear Jamboree would play host to the International Mr. Leather and Ms. Bullwhip contests. Imagine all those robot bears replaced with hairy-backed men in leather vests and nipple clips."

"Pirates of the Caribbean would be recast as a boat ride cum fashion show, with Disney's mannequin marauders replaced by International male models clad in lace-up silk pirate shirts and crotchless crocodile pants."

Disney's gay culture is flourishing beyond just the theme parks. It also influences the array of films and projects the company produces. Animated features now include "gay characters." And live-action feature films from both Miramax and Hollywood Pictures regularly address gay themes. As one gay Disney executive told *The Advocate*, "Old Walt would be spinning in his grave if he could see some of the stuff we're putting out today."

Lauren Lloyd is vice president of production for Disney's Hollywood Pictures,* and an open lesbian. During her first year with

---

* Hollywood Pictures is being phased out for commercial reasons.

the company, she had fifteen films in development. Of those films, fourteen have, in her words, "strong women's leads." Two are actually lesbian pictures, including *Story of Her Life* and *Chicks in White Satin*.

Lloyd says that at first it wasn't easy to get Disney's interest in producing "lesbian films" largely because company executives didn't think there was much money in them. She pitched them as romantic comedies. Lesbian movies, Lloyd says, have to offer "marketable subjects that are provocative to straight audiences" and must include "women that men really want to see."

On the small screen, Disney leads the way in producing and showing gay-themed programming. The ABC Network has more openly gay characters than any other television network. On the show *Relativity*, the network broke new ground with a passionate lesbian embrace, complete with caressing, nuzzling, and open-mouthed kissing. The popular Michael J. Fox sitcom *Spin City* features a character named Carter Heywood, who not only serves as an adviser to the mayor but is also a committed gay activist. The cop program *NYPD Blue* also features a gay male secretary.

But by far the biggest out-of-closet series was *Ellen*, where actress Ellen DeGeneres ignited a national debate by announcing her homosexuality on the show.

In a March 1997 *TV Guide* survey, 63 percent of those familiar with *Ellen* expressed little interest in watching the episode in which Ellen DeGeneres's character—Ellen Morgan—"came out," and 37 percent thought a gay lead in a prime-time sitcom was a bad idea. A meager 11 percent liked the concept. But Disney/ABC was aggressive about pushing the gay theme, hoping the controversy would boost *Ellen's* sagging ratings. When the first draft of the coming-out script was sent to Disney's Touchstone Television for review, it was sent back because it was deemed not gay enough. "The folks at Touchstone actually sent the first draft of the script back," says Executive Producer Mark Driscoll. "They said we had been too careful and hadn't dealt deeply enough with the core of the issue. Here we were, trying to be cautious with this sensitive topic, and they wanted more."

Fellow Executive Producer David Savel is equally proud of how

Disney handled the issue. "She [Ellen DeGeneres] came up with the idea of outing Ellen Morgan in the first place, and once Touchstone warmed to it, their main concern was where we could take the show in the long run. They were really very supportive, considering that they knew we would lose some sponsors and that the radicals would have a field day. But that was secondary to letting the character and the show grow."

Gay Day promotional literature shows Mickey and Donald holding hands. Officially these images are used without Disney permission, but the normally litigious company has winked at the practice.

The controversy generated by the coming-out episode did boost ratings for a while. But by the fall of 1997, they fell again, and *Ellen* sunk into the bottom third of network sitcoms before disappearing into oblivion in 1998.

Disney's slate of made-for-TV movies also championed some controversial gay themes. *Two Mothers for Zachary*, starring Valerie Bertinelli and Vanessa Redgrave, tells the true story of a mother who decides she is a lesbian, moves in with a female lover, and fights for custody of her child.

In 1995 Disney-affiliated Storyline Entertainment made *Serving in Silence: The Margarethe Cammermeyer Story*, the true story of a lesbian military officer who fights to stay in the army. It was a coproduction between openly gay producers Craig Zadan and Neil Meron, and Barbra Streisand's Barwood Films. Those involved in the project say the Mouse embraced it. "We've always found Disney more than willing to let us present gay stories," Meron says. "People get the company's traditional American family image mixed up with what in fact is a very inclusive, forward-thinking company."

Zadan says Disney also championed *What Makes a Family*, a made-for-TV movie about a lesbian couple raising a baby. "Disney knows it has to compete with cable, which built its audience on controversial programming. The networks are catching up with more progressive programming, and as usual Disney is leading the pack."

Why Disney is producing this programming is anybody's guess. The made-for-TV films on gay subjects have performed poorly. Some Disney insiders believe that reality will move the Mouse away from gay programming. "Disney is a bottom-line company," film producer Ralph Winter told us from the set of Disney's *Mighty Joe Young*. "There is a willingness to address controversial issues, but if it doesn't succeed, the company won't stick by it."

The fact, however, that Disney keeps trying to make gay projects succeed may be evidence of Disney's changing identity. "People see Disney as a squeaky-clean image of America," says Meron. "But in fact, the company has become a more realistic reflection of America, one that includes gays and lesbians. That's only fair, since so many of us are creating those images in the first place."

CHAPTER EIGHTEEN

Heigh Ho, Heigh Ho, It's Off to Work We Go

Disney loves a good cause, especially when it involves children. For years the Mouse has headed the United Nations International Children's Summit at Disneyland Paris (Euro-Disney), and Walt Disney Feature Animation was one of the earliest and most active members of UNICEF's International Animation Consortium for Children's Rights. Among those rights, according to Deborah Reber, an animation consultant with UNICEF, are "protection from sexual exploitation and child labor."

Lucky for Disney, UNICEF doesn't investigate hypocrisy.

On a hot, steamy August afternoon in 1995, federal agents raided sweatshops in Los Angeles and discovered two Disney licensees in violation of federal labor laws. The first, the Nathan J Company, employed kids as young as twelve to manufacture Disney apparel. The other was Too Cute, a company that owed hundreds of thousands of dollars in back wages to its employees. According to Scott Sutherland of the U.S. Department of Labor, most of the employees at Too Cute were Thai nationals working off debts to professional smugglers who had brought them to America.

Shortly after the raid Disney Vice President Tom Deegan claimed to be "shocked and angered that Disney merchandise was being manufactured in such a place." Yet those who track child labor sweatshops know the Mouse is a prime exploiter. The face of Disney the manufacturer is not a pretty one. All too often Disney clothes, toys, and trinkets are made by child laborers. Disney licensees have been caught using child labor on three continents. The National Labor Committee in New York, which tracks the activity of dozens of U.S. corporations to determine whether they use child and sweatshop labor, considers the Mouse one of the worst offenders. In fact, the council gives Disney the dubious distinction as being one of the "greediest sweatshop abusers" in the world.

Sweatshops became big news in 1996 when it was revealed that Kathie Lee Gifford's designer clothes company contracted with Honduran factories, using child labor at below-subsistence wages. Charles Kernaghan of the National Labor Committee first uncovered the problem and received considerable publicity for his efforts. At a Washington, D.C., press conference, a fifteen-year-old Honduran worker named Wendy Diaz told reporters that she made $21 a week and suffered abuse at the hands of her bosses. When Kathie Lee and husband Frank Gifford heard Wendy's story and saw further evidence that sweatshops were being used, they were clearly upset. The Giffords immediately became champions against child labor and endorsed third-party monitoring of garment factories and "a living wage that ensures work with dignity." Kathie Lee even helped organize the Apparel Industry Partnership with the U.S. Department of Labor to crack down on the use of child labor.

Wendy Diaz's plight, however, might have been worse. Had she been employed by a Disney licensee, she undoubtedly would have received even lower pay under more dangerous working conditions. Since uncovering the sweatshop conditions in Honduras, Charles Kernaghan has shifted his focus to Disney's labor practices and working conditions in Haiti. At four assembly factories owned by Disney suppliers, workers toil in tropical heat to meet production quotas for *Hunchback*, *Pocahontas*, Mickey Mouse, and *Lion King* garments. According to Kernaghan, the minimum wage in Haiti is 36 gourdes a day, or about $2.40. But these factory laborers rarely make the legal minimum wage. They are paid based on production quotas. And workers who don't produce enough are paid less. At the factory run by Disney contractor L.V. Myles, the daily piece-rate quota is set impossibly high. For example, in eight hours the workers must attach 1,600 collars on Disney T-shirts or close 1,600 shoulders—a ratio of more than three per minute. "The pressure to make the quota is great," says one worker. "If you even try to get up to use the bathroom they scream at you."

Even the most experienced workers fail to meet the quota. According to the National Labor Committee, which has examined the pay stubs, the average pay at the factory is about 12 cents an hour. "I work all day, I take a bus, I eat very little, and I have almost nothing to take home to my hungry family or to send my kids to school," one worker at the factory told Reuters News Agency.

At another factory in Haiti, workers produce "Mickey's for Kids" stuff and other children's clothing for a Disney licensee called Classic Apparel. There, the typical pay stub in April 1996 was about 28 cents per hour. The workers complain that the plant's lint-filled dust gives them headaches. Rats, reportedly, are "everywhere." The drinking water is right next to the toilet, and several women have complained of getting infections from the water. Kernaghan has visited these plants. "The workers are living in debt as indentured servants," he says. "People go to bed hungry. People who are making Disney shirts are living in utter misery."

The National Labor Committee, which tracks U.S. corporations to determine whether they use child and sweatshop labor, considers Disney one of the worst offenders.

As difficult as circumstances are in Haiti, these are some of the better facilities churning out Disney products around the globe. In the crumbling Lien Chieu district of Da Nang, Vietnam, sits a cavernous, poorly ventilated toy factory recently built by Keyhinge Toys, a Hong Kong–based company that produces Disney products. More than 90 percent of the 1,800 workers are teenage girls, says Thuyen Nguyen of Vietnam Labor Watch, a human rights organization based in Washington. Nearly all come from villages outside of Quang Nam-Da Nang Province and the take-home pay is 60 to 70 cents a day for a nine- or ten-hour shift. A seven-day workweek is often mandatory at the factory, and managers inflict corporal punishment, says the Asia Monitor Resource Center, a Hong Kong–based human rights group that has interviewed workers at the plant. Conditions are so bad that 772 workers reportedly resigned in less than a year.

Those who remained faced serious health problems. On February 21, 1997, according to the *Boston Globe*, dozens of workers at the factory collapsed. Several were admitted to the local hospital. A colorless liquid named acetone, used as a solvent in paints, had spread fumes through-out the factory, causing headaches, dizziness, nausea, and skin damage. In all, more than 220 workers fell ill from being poisoned. Several of the teenage girls saw their menstrual cycles affected by the high exposure.

The company's response was hardly sympathetic. Chen Wei Oing, deputy director of Keyhinge Toys, refused to pay any medical costs for the workers who were hospitalized. The day after the acetone poison-ing, he dismissed two hundred workers who expressed concern about the factory's safety. (The government intervened, and the workers were reinstated.)

Keyhinge has a ten-year contract to produce the Disney toys that eventually find their way into McDonald's Happy Meals. The Hong Kong–based firm manufactures Disney merchandise not only in Da Nang, but also on mainland China, where workers produce Disney toys in factories surrounded by prison-like walls and barbed wire. The toys pour out endlessly: Goofy squirt toys, Iago the Parrot push toys, purple sea horses from The Little Mermaid, Toy Story piggy banks, Mighty Ducks play figures, Minnie Mouse and Baby Mickey squeak toys, to name just a few. These factories employ children as young as fourteen. They also have safety problems. In January 1992, after whiff-ing toxic levels of benzene, twenty-three workers at the Chi Wah Toy Factory were hospitalized, and three later died.

China is an attractive place for less-scrupulous companies to manu-facture their products, says Simon Greenfield. Labor is plentiful and includes children. "It's an acceptable part of business practice in China," he says. "Any company manufacturing toys in China knows that."

Xiao Xie has worked for years in the spray paint department in the Sewco Toy factory in Zhonghsna, coloring various Disney toys for export to the west. The work is rigorous, and she smells paint chemi-cals all day. But Sewco does not provide adequate masks, so the sol-vents have worked their way into her throat and respiratory system. She has lost her voice from inhaling paint particles.

Xiao Zhou works in the sewing department of the Henggang Apollo Toy Factory, another Disney licensee. She, too, has respiratory problems from the particles she has inhaled. She says several of her coworkers have it even worse: they developed lung disease. But Apollo won't provide masks for employees.

Xiao Wang works at Sewco in the plastics department. For Wang the problem is not inhaling chemicals, but losing parts of limbs. He says workers often lose half of their right palms and all of their fingers when operating the dyeing machines at the factory. The machines are old and in ill-repair, he says, and Sewco provides little training, so injuries are common.

These factories require workers to labor seven days a week, with mandatory overtime until two or four in the morning. Factory employees regularly faint due to fatigue. And if they do pass out, they usually get fired, apparently for sleeping on the job.

Joe Allen is a former textile company executive who has been in the apparel business since 1948. He was CEO of a $50 million textile company that produced goods for Levi Straus, Stockton's, and others. Today he investigates sweatshops, including Disney's, and he doesn't like what he sees. "Mickey is no doubt one of the worst," he says. Recently Allen paid a visit to factories in China that produce Disney products. Posing as a prospective customer, he managed to get inside the factory walls with a hidden videocamera provided by NBC News. "It was horrible," he told us. "The conditions are just terrible. In some cases kids have their hands just being eaten away by chemical solvents. There are young girls operating machines that only a grown man has the strength to operate. The workers live in company quarters, sometimes sixteen to a room. This is no Disneyland."

Allen says using children to make Disney toys extends beyond Vietnam and China. In Indonesia, he found children producing stuffed animals for Disney, including dogs from *101 Dalmatians*, lions from *The Lion King*, and Winnie the Pooh. Posing again as a prospective customer, he visited a plant outside the capital city of Jakarta and videotaped children—as young as twelve—sewing for Mickey. "The owner of the place told me that they hired children and not their parents," says Allen, who caught the conversation on a hidden camera. "You have teenage girls working twelve-hour shifts with outdated equipment, exposed electrical wires, locked fire exits." Allen got the manager of one facility to tell him on camera that the key to his production success was using kids because that way "labor is easier to control, easier to manage, and the pricing is still cheaper. We have the advantage that way."

Disney licensees in other countries use child labor to cut costs. The Eden Group, a Disney licensee in Thailand that produces a whole line of Disney apparel called Mickey Mouse Americanwear, actually fired adult workers to bring on child laborers. Eden laid off a total of 1,145 women employees in March and August of 1996, according to the *Bangkok Post*. Most were between the ages of thirty and forty-five and had worked for the company for more than ten years. Srila Muangyos, a longtime employee, said that after she was locked out of the factory, she saw kids going in the factory doors. Jaruay Markchudy, head of the local women's union, thought Disney would never accept such an outrageous policy. So she contacted the Mouse and asked the company to revoke all its licensing agreements with Eden. The Mouse refused.

Disney maintains that it works hard to monitor the labor practices of its licensees. The company's Code of Conduct requires that "manufacturers will respect the right of employees to associate, organize and bargain collectively." It also stipulates that it expects manufacturers to "recognize that wages are essential to meeting employees' basic needs." Child labor is deemed unacceptable. But Disney licensees violate this code with impunity and maintain good relations with the Mouse.

The code used to mean something. During the late 1970s and early 1980s, accountant and auditor Joyce Cunningham often traveled to manufacturing facilities that produced Disney goods. "Sure," she told us, "there were industrial facilities that were busy and dirty, but there was never any hint that children were being used. I think it was pretty clear that it would not have been tolerated."

Spencer Craig joined Disney in 1971 and worked in merchandising for most of his twenty-four–year career, leaving in 1995. While with the company, he wrote the curriculum on merchandising for Disney University, the training facility for the Mouse's employees. He clearly remembers when and why Disney embraced unethical licenses.

"From a business standpoint it made sense to start using cheaper labor overseas and to rely on licensees who would use it," says Craig. "One of the decrees that came down beginning in 1984 [when Eisner came in] was that we were going to return twenty percent to shareholders. And we had to do that. That might be okay from a total corporate outlook, but when you look at merchandising in particular, that's pretty tough. It used to be that if you brought back a net 6 percent increase, you got promoted. That's the real world of merchandising. For them to come in and say, 'You're going to return twenty percent also,' it led us to use less scrupulous licensees and manufacturers. The profit motive drove it."

And that drive for profit has pushed the Mouse into the arms of some pretty unsavory company.

For years Disney licensees were manufacturing in a country few Americans could locate on a map. Burma—also known as Myanmar, the name given it by the ruling military junta—is a poverty-stricken nation wedged between India, China, and the lush mountains of Thailand. It is also an international pariah. The United Nations has condemned conditions in the country as "deplorable," and Secretary of State Madeline Albright has called the ruling military junta "Orwellian." Since 1988 Burma has been ruled by the State Law and Order Restoration Council (SLORC). Along with a brutal human rights record, the junta is best known in international diplomatic circles for its links with heroin traffickers. According to the State Department, 80 percent of the heroin entering the United States is produced in Burma.

"People who are making Disney shirts are living in utter misery."

Drug lords have a special status in Burma. They are protected by the government. In January 1996 the Burmese military reached a pact to garner profits with drug kingpin Khua Sa, who for several decades has served as Southeast Asia's chief heroin pusher, and who lives in open luxury. In 1989 he was indicted for drug trafficking, and U.S. authorities have offered $2 million for information leading to his arrest. Burma refuses to extradite him.

Sa is in good company. Drug lord Lo Hsing Han is also enjoying life in Burma, even though he is wanted on drug trafficking charges in Thailand. His ties to the government are so strong that in the spring of 1995 when his son Steven Law got married, seven government ministers were in attendance.

The *New York Times* recently editorialized: "For sheer nastiness few governments can compete with Burma's. It winks at heroin trafficking. It forces citizens to provide slave labor." In other words, it's a great place to make Mickey Mouse sweatshirts.

Two Disney contractors worked in Rangoon, Burma, for years. Mamiye Brothers/American Character Classics churned out thousands of "Mickey and Company" sweatshirts at a factory, while Victoria Garment Manufacturing Company Limited, a Hong Kong–based company, had four plants that spit out Mickey Mouse sweatshirts. These factories were certainly in a safe place—a military designated industrial zone outside Rangoon called Pyin-Ma-Bin. In July 1996 the facilities were upgraded by indentured servant construction crews that worked under army control.

Burma's attraction as a manufacturing site is obvious: ultracheap labor. The Disney licensee factories pay about six cents an hour, and workers routinely work sixty hours a week. Demands for better working conditions were answered with threats of imprisonment or execution, according to the *Boston Globe*. Children formed an active part of the labor pool.

Operating in Burma is not as easy as simply setting up shop. You need to form business partnerships with well-connected and powerful patrons. Mamiye Brothers/American Character Classics joined forces with the Union of Myanmar Economic Holdings (UMEH), a company 40 percent owned by Burma's Directorate of Defense Procurement, which imports military weaponry. The other 60 percent of UMEH is held by shareholders from the Burmese armed forces. The head of UMEH is not an MBA, but an active military officer named Colonel Aung Sann.

Drug money may also have been involved in this venture. Drug lords interested in diversifying their operations regularly throw money into legitimate businesses, especially clothing plants. The U.S. Embassy in Burma pointed out in a June 1996 Report on Foreign Economic Trends that a large number of the garment assembly firms in Burma are at least partly owned by "the opiates sector." Some analysts who track the drug trade in Burma believe it is essentially impossible to avoid contact with drug money. Francois Casanier is a research analyst with Geopolitical Drugwatch in Paris and tracks the narcotics business in the country. "All normal economic activities, if you can call anything in Burma normal, are instruments of drug money laundering," he says. "And no drug operation in Burma can be run without SLORC."

> **Eden Group, which produces a line of Disney apparel called Mickey Mouse Americanwear, fired adult workers to bring on child laborers.**

In order to get their products out of the country, Disney licensees had to strike a deal with an export firm. In Burma that usually means working with the company (owned by Steven Law, who is under a U.S. State Department ban for "suspicion of involvement in narcotics trafficking") that controls the wharf at Yangon Port. More than 90 percent of the cargo leaving Burma for the United States and other countries goes through that wharf.

When Larry Dohrs, a coordinator for the human rights organization Free Burma Campaign, found out in early 1996 that Disney was involved with Burma, he was truly stunned. "Disney is in with some unsavory company," he said bluntly.

When human rights groups and labor organizations first discovered that Disney had links to Burma, they immediately launched a protest campaign. The Free Burma Campaign, National Labor Committee, and other organizations made public Disney's involvement in Burma. At the same time, major news stories ran in the *Boston Globe*. Disney initially denied any contact with Burma. On November 18, 1996, Chuck Champlin, Disney's public relations director, issued a statement that read: "We wish to be perfectly clear on our company policy: Disney is not in Burma." Although he did admit that some subcontracting work was being done there, the company "decided five months ago to stop placing orders in that country."

But entire racks of Mickey and Company outfits made in Burma were in Macy's and other retailers throughout November and December 1996. So the organizers kept up their protests. Finally, by the end of 1996, Mamiye Brothers did pull production out of Burma. Chuck Mamiye, vice president of Mamiye Brothers, told the *Boston Globe* that the company pulled out for "strictly business reasons." Disney Vice President Tom Deegan said, "In the future, we will probably discourage our licensees from doing business in Burma."

Still, some Disney executives have not completely abandoned hopes for big profits in Burma. The *Asia Times* reported only months later, in early 1997, that the Israeli company Dor Energy had signed a memorandum of understanding with Myanmar Petrochemical Enterprises (MPCE), a venture run by the Burmese junta. Dor Energy is one-third owned by Shamrock Holdings, a company owned and run by Disney Vice Chairman Roy Disney and Disney Board Member Stanley Gold. For those involved, writes *Asia Times*, their "carefully-nurtured public image in the U.S. could be badly hurt by a financial partnership with SLORC's Myanmar—which is definitely no Disneyland."

Disney may have changed its ways concerning Burma after public protests, but it seems less than interested in tackling the child labor problem. Retailers and manufacturers have been asked by the U.S. Department of Labor to voluntarily pledge to monitor their contractors to make sure no child labor is being used. Dozens of well-known companies have joined, including Abercrombie and Fitch, Guess, Lands' End, Lerner New York, Levi Strauss, Liz Claiborne, Nordstrom, Patagonia, Victoria's Secret, the Limited, and others. Disney has not.

Disney remains active in UNICEF's International Animation Consortium for Child Rights, and pledges to use its creative talents to spread the message of children's rights. But before Disney preaches to the world, perhaps it should do more to protect children from its own rapacity.

CHAPTER NINETEEN

Mickey Mao

Disney films, television programs, and merchandise represent quintessential Americana, and can now be found in almost every country around the globe. That places unique demands on the company when it operates overseas. "Disney isn't a company as much as it is a nation-state," said Michael Ovitz, who resigned as the company's president in 1996. And like any other nation-state, the Mouse needs its own foreign policy to navigate the world's political intrigues.

In 1996, 18 percent of Disney's earnings came from overseas. But the Mouse expects most of its growth in the future to come from overseas sales, and is especially hopeful about its growth in the Chinese market. The prospect of selling 1.2 billion Chinese consumers videocassettes of *The Lion King*, Donald Duck comic books, and Mickey Mouse ears has Disney management salivating. But to achieve that goal, Michael Eisner and Disney senior management have gone to extraordinary lengths. Mickey's diplomatic face is not always a principled one.

Mickey Mouse trinkets were available in China as far back as the 1940s. But when Mao Zedong and the communists took power in 1949, Western cultural influences were banned, and several generations of Chinese youth were cut off from Mickey and his friends.

Disney executives started thinking about reentering the Chinese market in the early 1980s when the country started to liberalize under Deng Xiaoping. The company took small steps at first. Disney hired Nelson Ying, head of the China Group, a New York–based investment company with contacts in mainland China, to develop its China Pavilion at EPCOT in Orlando. It is one of the most successful pavilions at EPCOT. The buildings include a small-scale but beautifully replicated version of Beijing's Temple of Heaven. Even more impressive perhaps is *Wonders of China*—a film shown on a 360-degree screen. It includes spectacular views of the Shilin Stone Forest, the Gobi Desert, the Grand Canal, and, of course, the Great Wall of China. Filming *Wonders of China* was a massive undertaking. With the cooperation of the Chinese government, film producer Jeff Blyth spent months scouting locations. For a sequence on one-mile-high Huanghsna, one of the five sacred mountains of China, a Disney crew and 40 laborers carried the equipment—including the 300-pound Circle Vision camera rig—up 4,700 stone steps.

The results of these efforts were remarkable, as the pavilion brings the essence of China to central Florida. But it also puts money into the pockets of well-connected officials in Beijing. To this day Nelson Ying won't reveal the names of his investors; he will say only that they include individuals "from the mainland."

The links established through the China Pavilion at EPCOT were only the beginning of Disney's Mickey Mouse diplomacy with Beijing. Disney executives were not only interested in a pavilion at EPCOT; they also wanted to find a way to import films and merchandise directly into China. Breaking through the Great Wall of censorship into the Chinese film and television market for children was a high priority for Chairman Michael Eisner. So in 1985 the Mouse entered into serious negotiations with several Chinese media groups owned by the government to distribute its films and animated shorts. These government entities included Chinese Central Television (CCTV), which is run by the Chinese Communist Party. When it comes to children's programming, CCTV focuses particular attention on what it calls "the proper ideological upbringing of children," including loyalty to the Communist Party. Staff members at major news outlets are required by State Council regulation to "support Communist Party leadership, warmly love socialism, strive to study Marxism-Leninism-Mao Zedong Thought, and implement the Party's line, principles, and policies." Even as late as 1997, China's Minister of Propaganda Ding Guagen warned editors and film and television executives in the country to adhere to the party line and stress "politics at every level."

Negotiations did not begin well. While Chinese officials were interested in Disney's collection of high-quality animation, they had serious concerns about "cultural pollution" from the West. Disney was troubled by Beijing's strict limits on the profits that foreign companies could take out of the country. Even if Disney sold enormous quantities of goods, the vast majority of the profits would have to remain in China.

Perhaps because of these major differences, then–Disney President Frank Wells was entrusted to personally spearhead the campaign to bring Mickey to Beijing. In 1985 he met several times with Deputy Director of CCTV Hong Minsheng and senior members of the Communist Party. In the fall of that year, Wells made a visit to Beijing. "There are at least three generations of children in China who don't know who Mickey and Donald were," he said, and he was determined to rectify that.

The Chinese saw some utility in using Mickey. Hong offered Wells a deal. CCTV would run some Disney programs, but only if CCTV had complete editorial control. Chinese government editors and censors wanted to retain the rights to dub the programs and change the dialogue. It was an incredible demand, especially given Disney's long and well-established history of being a stickler for absolute creative control. Had this been any other potential market, Wells probably would have balked. But the lure of a billion potential customers was too much. Wells took the deal.

In early 1986 a delegation from CCTV met with Wells and Eisner in Burbank, where the historic agreement was signed. Chinese Party officials got pretty much everything they wanted. Disney would provide cartoons, including classics with Mickey Mouse and Donald Duck, at no cost. CCTV would be responsible for dubbing the programs into Chinese. But most important, CCTV would be allowed to make adjustments for "ideological content" and rework dialogue if necessary.

What Disney got out of the deal was first-time network access to a market Eisner described as "large to gigantic." The initial audience estimate was only 30 million, but CCTV expected that number to grow dramatically. At the time, about 60 percent of China's 1 billion people could receive television, and children's programming reached about 13 percent of the country's 300 million children.

When the first Disney programs aired in June 1986, everyone seemed pleased: Michael Eisner, millions of kids across China, and the Chinese Communist Party. "Chinese children need to absorb various kinds of good nourishment," said Hong at the first airing, "be it the Golden Monkey [a Communist Party cartoon], Donald Duck, or Mickey Mouse."

The hope at Disney was that these programs would serve as free advertising. Hundreds of millions of kids would see Disney's characters on TV and want to buy character-based products. "We guess that the consumers of China are ready for Mickey and Donald in their stores," said Frank Wells, "and we hope we can satisfy them."

But the Mouse was hoping for too much too soon. While Chinese authorities now had the rights to a whole collection of Disney cartoons that were destined to become popular with children, the huge markets for products failed to appear. Part of the problem was piracy. There was already a Donald Duck fast-food restaurant in Beijing. Mugs and T-shirts with characters resembling Mickey and Donald were available in places like Beijing's Friendship Store. These weren't Disney manufactures, but knockoff goods illegally copied without licensing from the Mouse. The government had not yet made a serious commitment to crack down on counterfeiters, and Disney was left with little immediate return for its Chinese diplomacy. By the end of the decade, the frustrated Mouse pulled out of China almost completely.

Even though its efforts had failed, Disney still appeared eager to fill the void made by Western companies reluctant to embrace China after the Tiananmen Square massacre. When the *Los Angeles Times* surveyed opinions from business leaders with investments in China, Disney's vice president for Corporate Communications, Erwin Okun, said, "Frankly, it's nothing to concern ourselves with." When it comes to diplomacy, Mickey believes in *realpolitik*.

Isolated by Western governments concerned about human rights, Beijing needed to bolster its image. It found an ally in Disney. In late

May 1990 Chinese Ambassador Zhu Quizhan and an entourage of dignitaries paid a highly publicized and choreographed visit to Disneyland. It was the first major public outing for the envoy since the massacre. Zhu Quizhan couldn't have asked for better imagery as the news cameras clicked away: The opportunity to be photographed shaking hands with Mickey Mouse was a nice contrast to the stark images of carnage less than a year earlier.

Two months later a delegation of five Chinese mayors made a pilgrimage to Disneyland. On a warm, sunny Sunday afternoon the mayors took photos of Disney characters and watched the Main Street Electrical Parade. "Our visit is not to convince anyone of our ideology," said Shanghai Mayor Zhu Rongji. "Many Americans don't understand the living conditions in China, don't understand the gap between Chinese and American culture."

Clearly Michael Eisner believes Chinese censorship and control can coexist with Disney commercial interests.

The Chinese government also looked to rehabilitate its image by presenting a sanitized version of China to Americans who couldn't or wouldn't visit China. In 1991 a Chinese government–owned agency called the China Travel Service (CTS) invested $100 million along with Chinese-American entrepreneur George Chen to develop an amusement park called Splendid China. The park is a Lilliputian village that features replicas of China's greatest sites on a thirty-one–hectare spot in Kissimmee, Florida, just down the road from Walt Disney World. CTS brought 120 artisans and craftsmen to Florida from Suzhou and Guangzhou to construct the buildings.

As you might expect, the story you get at Splendid China is essentially propaganda. The history and culture of Tibet, which China invaded in 1949 and began full occupation of in 1950, is presented as Chinese and the park includes replicas of buildings that were bombarded or destroyed by the Chinese Communist Army during its occupation of Tibet.

When construction began, there were public denials by Chen and others that the Chinese government was involved in the project. But once the attraction was completed in December 1993, complete ownership quickly transferred to the Chinese government. Four top officials from China's Communist Party attended the December 18, 1993, opening ceremonies. They were joined by several representatives from the Mouse.

Disney's bridge-building with Beijing began paying off with greater commercial opportunities. In early 1993 Beijing agreed to enforce copyright and licensing laws. That same year a Chinese-language Disney cartoon magazine was launched. Children's Fun Publishing Company was a licensee of the Walt Disney Company with exclusive publishing rights to the *Mickey Mouse Magazine* in China. It was the first publishing venture in China partly owned by a foreign company and approved by China's Press and Publications Administration, the Ministry of Post and Telecommunications, and the State Industry and Commerce Administration—in essence, all of the Chinese government. Within months the magazine was selling 150,000 copies monthly. When Chinese officials such as An Jinglin, executive deputy president of China National Radio (CNR), were asked about the Disney characters and how they might conflict with Chinese traditions, he said, "There is no contradiction."

Along with these comics, it also became easier for Disney to distribute movies in China. In 1995 *The Lion King* earned about 30 million yuan ($3.6 million) at the Chinese box office, and *Toy Story* was equally successful the following year. A program called *The China Disney Club* began airing on twelve television stations in 1995.

Disney's presence in China received another boost in 1996 when the company closed a deal with CNR. CNR is state-run and financed, and is controlled by the government's Ministry of Radio, Film, and Television. Every Saturday at 3:30 PM CNR broadcasts a half-hour program called *It's a Small World*. The program features Mickey, Minnie, Donald Duck, and the Lion King, with even an occasional appearance by Snow White and the Seven Dwarfs. It was another avenue to reach the Chinese market, but again there were limits: each program had to be approved by government censors. When the program was launched, An Jinglin said, "Children are the main force of the twenty-first century. They must master knowledge not only about China, but about the entire world. The program produced by our station in coop-eration with Disney is aimed at developing intelligence and inspiring curiosity, broadening their outlook and enriching their knowledge."

At the same time Mickey and friends filled China's airwaves, Disney was allowed to open "Mickey's Corner" stores, which featured a giant Mickey Mouse to lure customers inside. Mickey Mouse shoes, *Lion King* towels, and *Little Mermaid* T-shirts flooded the market. There were also fruitful discussions about building a Disney theme park in China. Chinese businessman Dr. Yiu Yat Hung, a committee member of the China Association of Enterprises with Foreign Investments, visited Orlando in September 1996 to meet with Disney officials. Yiu was pushing Shenzhen as a possible site. "We think our city would be the best place in China for a Disney park," he said.

By 1996 the Mouse had a cozy but secretive relationship with Beijing. "We've been very quiet about what we've built," said David Zucker, at the time senior vice president of Disney-owned ESPN International. "And China is a good example of that. We are the only foreign net-work distributed in China. We have very good relations with the gov-ernment and for obvious reasons, we've had to keep it very quiet."

Those "very good relations" had every reason to last, except for an important turn of events. In 1995 Michael Eisner brought Hollywood super agent Michael Ovitz on

Chinese Party officials got pretty much everything they wanted. Disney would pro-vide cartoons, including clas-sics with Mickey Mouse and Donald Duck, at no cost. Chinese Central Television would dub the programs and make adjustments for "ideo-logical content," reworking dialogue if necessary.

board as his new president to replace Frank Wells, who had passed away. Ovitz brought unrestrained energy, big-name talent, and, of course, a few pet projects to the job. And one of those pet projects would ultimately threaten to unhinge the Disney-Chinese partner-ship.

For years director Martin Scorsese was an Ovitz client and friend. Having grown up in the tough boroughs of New York City, Scorsese was attracted to the tranquil nature of the Dalai Lama and the pastoral beauty of Tibet. This passion was ignited after the director read a screenplay written by Melissa Mathison, who had penned the script for *ET* and who also happens to be the wife of actor Harrison Ford. While the film had originally been slated to be released by MCA, Ovitz decided to bring his client's project with him to Disney. Disney's Touchstone Pictures division agreed to partly fund the project, which eventually became known as *Kundun*.

Chinese officials from the Ministry of Radio, Film, and Television were not pleased when they first heard about *Kundun*. As the film began production in Morocco in late 1996, they sent the director of China's National Film Bureau, Liu Jianzhong, to Hollywood to warn Disney that its business interests in China would be at risk if the film proceeded. China also went public with its threats to Disney's lucrative Chinese enterprises. Yang Buting, vice director of the Ministry of Radio, Film, and Television, claimed that Disney "has indicated a lack of respect for Chinese sovereignty. Because of this, we are thinking over our business with Disney." It sent a chill throughout the Mouse, and indeed, the entire entertainment industry.

Michael Eisner, who had not known about the Scorsese project, was in a dilemma. He was not about to lose an opportunity to break into the enormous Chinese market. Yet if he were to drop the Scorsese film, there would be an uproar in Hollywood, where China's image was already none too good. Fifty-nine stars and directors, including Gregory Peck, Susan Sarandon, and Spike Lee, were pressing the Clinton administration to make human rights in China an issue at an upcoming meeting of the United Nations Commission on Human Rights. Disney had to stand firm in order to attract and keep major talent. "Disney's potential business in China is infinite," said Peter Dekom, a Los Angeles attorney who advises media companies operating in Asia. "But Disney has to decide whether it wants to facilitate business or stand for free speech." In the end, Disney decided to give the appearance of standing for free speech while appeasing Chinese demands as much as possible.

Disney's public stand to the Chinese threats appeared heroic enough. "We have an agreement to distribute *Kundun* domestically, and we intend to honor it," said Disney spokesman John Dreyer in December 1996. It was a public position that got the company plenty of good press. Richard Gere, a longtime supporter of the Tibetan spiritual movement, applauded Disney's stance. The *New York Times* ran an editorial entitled "The Mouse Makes a Stand" that lauded the decision. "By announcing yesterday that it would go ahead with a film about the Dalai Lama despite threats from China, the Walt Disney Company demonstrated that it would not accept censorship as the price of doing business in China or anywhere else."

Disney did not pull the plug on *Kundun,* but the Mouse did look for other ways to appease Beijing. Disney quietly sold off the foreign rights to the film. Marketing the movie in the United States was one thing, but distributing it in Asia was quite another. That would have been far too provocative to China. Disney also considered changing the *Wonders of China* film exhibit at EPCOT. For more than fifteen years, over sixty million tourists had gloried in the landscape of China by watching the film. "China is so vast that even within her borders there are distant lands," the film began. After visiting sites from the coastal region to the Gobi Desert, the airborne camera then dramatically circles the spiritual home of the Dalai Lama. The narrator then intones: "The Potala Palace dominates the city of Lhasa, the way Buddhism dominates Tibetan life."

Disney actually considered excising all references to Lhasa and Tibetan Buddhism from the film. As the *Asia Times* put it, executives viewed "the deletions as part of the logical rapprochement Disney must make if it is serious about building a number of theme parks in China."

Eisner also extended a hand of friendship in other ways. He made a highly public visit to the Chinese government–owned Splendid China park in Orlando. The *Orlando Business Journal* reported that Eisner was considering purchasing Splendid China from the government "at whatever price the Chinese want in order to ease relations with China." No sales plans have yet been announced.

Nelson Ying, the Chinese entrepreneur with the lucrative contract to run EPCOT's China Pavilion, even got into the act. Ying announced in early 1997 his plans to launch a scholarship program to train future Chinese diplomats at the University of Central Florida. Dick Nunis, chairman of Walt Disney Attractions, sits on the University's Foundation Board and offered to support the program. When the program was officially launched, Zeng Yi, deputy secretary of the Standing Committee of the People's Republic of China, came to Orlando for the ceremony. In the ceremony's most dramatic moment, Nelson Ying handed Zeng Yi a Chinese flag. Later, the Chinese visitor met with Disney executives.

But perhaps the biggest fallout from Chinese anger about *Kundun* was the fate of Michael Ovitz. He and Michael Eisner had experienced clashes ever since the super agent had strapped on his Mouse ears in 1995. His decision to bring *Kundun* to Disney was "the last straw" as far as Eisner was concerned. Ovitz resigned on December 11, 1996, with a hefty severance package in excess of $100 million. The move pleased Beijing; it backed off from its threats against Disney's Chinese enterprises.

Clearly Michael Eisner believes Disney can be a sophisticate in the world of commercial diplomacy. Chinese censorship and control can coexist with Disney commercial interests. A new cafe recently opened in the southern Chinese tourist town of Yangshuo and serves as an epiphany of sorts. The cafe's logo features a picture of Mao sporting a pair of Mickey Mouse ears. A sign in the window reads *Welcome to Mickey Mao's.*

CHAPTER TWENTY
Don't Know Much About History

O n November 18, 1993, Bill Clinton made a special appearance at the Magic Kingdom in Disney World. It was his day to be inducted into the popular Hall of Presidents attraction. Rising from a chair on stage, he slowly approached the lectern and proceeded to give a four-minute speech. Mind you, it was not the real Bill Clinton but an audio-animatron created by Disney's Imagineering Department. And it made Disney history. No sitting president had ever given a speech at the Hall of Presidents. Up to that point, the task had been reserved solely for Abe Lincoln (or his robot).

After the 1993 election, Michael Eisner, who contributed to the Clinton campaign and is active in the Democratic Party, wrote the newly inaugurated president an invitation to join the Pantheon of Presidents—and in a speaking role. Clinton eagerly accepted and even offered to tape his voice for the robot.

But adding the new president was not easy. Walt Disney Imagineering couldn't find a Clinton speech that was suitably "presidential." So in search of a solution, a new speech was commissioned for the robot. Lyricist Tim Rice, who had just won an Academy Award for his songs in the animated feature *Aladdin*, was tapped to write something officially inspiring.

The Hall of Presidents is a mainstay of the Magic Kingdom's Liberty Square, representing the "idea" of America on the eve of independence. While Walt Disney never pretended to be a historian, he did want an attraction that celebrated America. He saw the Hall of Presidents as an opportunity to bring visitors—especially children—into dramatic contact with American history.

Over the years, millions of schoolchildren and their parents have passed through the attraction. As the curtain rises, the audience is faced by extraordinary robotic likenesses of all the American presidents. Dressed in period costume, a spotlight shines on each leader as the roll is called. They sway back and forth, turn from side to side, nod, and fidget. The technical wizardry is fantastic. At the end of the presentation, Lincoln stands up and offers a dramatic call for national unity.

"At what point shall we expect the approach of danger? By what means shall we fortify against it? Shall we expect some transatlantic giant to step across the ocean and crush us with a blow? No. All the armies of Europe, Asia, and Africa combined could not by force take a drink from the Ohio, or make a track on the Blue Ridge. At what point, then, is the approach of danger to be expected? I answer: If it ever reach us, it must spring up among us. It cannot come from abroad. If destruction be our lot, we ourselves must be its author—and its finisher. As a nation of free men, we must live through all time or die by suicide."

At least for decades that is what Mr. Lincoln said. When President Clinton was added with his unprecented speaking part, Lincoln's speech was rewritten to offer a new version of American history.

Much of this change comes from the company's new consultant on history, Professor Eric Foner of Columbia University. Foner is the author of the prize-winning book *Reconstruction: 1863–1877* and numerous other works, including *Free Soil, Free Labor, Free Men*, a study of the ideology of Lincoln's Republican Party, and *Politics and Ideology in the Age of the Civil War*. Foner is a profound admirer of Howard Zinn, a self-described "radical" historian and author of *A People's History of the United States*, which Foner says "should be required reading for a new generation of students." He adds that "historians may well view it as a step toward a coherent new version of American history." *A People's History* is no ordinary history book. "Most histories understate revolt, overemphasize statesmanship, and thus encourage impotency among citizens," Zinn complained, and he was determined to not make the same mistake. In his book he writes, "One percent of the nation owns a third of the wealth. The rest of the wealth is distributed in such a way as to turn those in the 99 percent against one another." He hopes that the masses will come together to bring radical change in the country. "The more of the 99 percent that begin to see themselves as sharing needs, the more the guards and prisoners see their common interest, the more the Establishment becomes isolated, ineffectual. The elite's weapons, money, control of information would be useless in the face of a determined population. The servants of the system would begin using their time, their space—the very things given them by the system to keep them quiet—to dismantle that system while creating a new one."

For Foner this "new version" of history, or "new history" as he calls it, is intertwined with activism. In the introduction to the book *The New American History*, Foner writes: "In the course of the past twenty years, American history has been remade. Inspired initially by the social movements of the nineteen sixties and nineteen seventies— which shattered the 'consensus' vision that had dominated historical writing—and influenced by new methods borrowed from other disciplines, American historians redefined the very nature of historical study." To Foner, this is a good thing. "Once you incorporate the history of women or African Americans or other groups into that story, it's a different story then," he said on one television talk program. "That's the real challenge that the new history is posing, and that's why it is disturbing to some people."

Not content to simply toil away as a historian in the ivy-covered hall of academe, Foner is also a committed political activist, which helps explain the imprint he is undoubtedly putting on Disney's version of history. His activism is a family tradition. *The Nation*, a left-wing intellectual magazine, which counts Foner as a member of the editorial board, describes his family history this way: "He comes from a distinguished family of left-wing activists and scholars: Henry Foner and Moe Foner, his uncles, were leaders of progressive unions in New York City, and Philip Foner, another uncle, has been a prolific labor historian for decades. Jack Foner, Eric's father, lost his job in the City College of New York's history department in the first anti-communist purges of the forties."

Foner has remained true to his pedigree. Recently he organized a

series of "Labor Teach-Ins" on college campuses to "address the critical questions of economic, racial, and gender inequality, social injustice, and political powerlessness which trouble millions of Americans,"
according to the event's promotional literature. As chairman of the
event, Foner was joined by other activists like Cornel West and Betty
Friedan to encourage "progressive" activism by college students. "We
want to lend the support of a large number of academics and intellectuals to the revitalization of labor," Foner told the *New York Times*.
"From our point of view, there is no real hope for progressive social
change in this country without a strong labor movement, and without
a strong labor movement the conservative tendency of things is never
going to be reversed."

Robert Welsh, chief of staff of the AFL-CIO, which sponsored the
teach-in, called the event significant. "As part of our effort to rebuild
the progressive coalition in this country, it's important that progressive academics play a major role."

The issues touched on at the teach-in, particularly racial inequality
and social injustice, form the core of Foner's view of America.

He became involved with the Mouse after writing Disney a letter
complaining about Lincoln's speech at the Hall of Presidents. He felt
that Abe's emphasis on the internal strength of America smacked of
McCarthyism and represented "the Cold War era's interpretation of
Lincoln." (However, unlike the Clinton speech, which was manufactured by a Disney lyricist, Lincoln's remarks were actual—from an
1838 speech to the Young Men's Lyceum of Springfield, Illinois. Abe
was condemning a recent spate of racial lynchings in his home state.)
Foner wrote that he was "disturbed" as a historian that Lincoln "never
mentions slavery" in his speech. He claimed that the Lincoln speech
was picked "when blacks were simply ignored in presentations of
American history." Disney, Foner told the company, "has an obligation
to make its presentation as accurate and up-to-date in interpretation
as possible."

Of course the Hall of Presidents was never about addressing
national issues, but instead was intended to emphasize what
Americans held in common. Yet Foner's plea for "new history" obvi-

ously struck a sympathetic nerve in Burbank. Disney promptly hired him as a consultant and put him to work, first on the Hall of Presidents in Orlando.

Following his recommendations, the redesigned show shifted its focus from presidential leadership as the embodiment of democracy to exploring American racial and class history. It no longer emphasizes the freedom that we have as a result of the Constitution. Instead, the new introductory film tells us that freedom is "an unfinished agenda that challenges each generation of Americans, including our own." Freedom is relative, "an arena of conflict, carrying different meanings for different groups of people." The message of the attraction now is that not all Americans share a common freedom, and that

Lincoln's Hall of Presidents speech was rewritten to offer a new version of American history.

"our nation has had to struggle to expand the idea of freedom to encompass more and more Americans."

The remade Hall of Presidents has received high praise from people like Jon Wiener, another contributing editor of *The Nation* and a professor of history at the University of California, Irvine. He praises the new display as a "remarkably progressive program. The Lincoln speech has shifted from a vaguely McCarthyite warning against the 'danger within' to an acknowledgment of the centrality of race in American history; and the Hall of Presidents program has shifted from a vaguely fascistic celebration of presidential leadership to a challenge to visitors to consider the incompleteness of freedom in America today."

Look for Foner to play a leading role in future Disney projects that address historical issues. In 1994, when Disney announced its plans to build a Virginia-based theme park to be called Disney's American Adventure, Foner was an early consultant. According to Robert Weis, senior vice president of Imagineering, the park was going to "make you a Civil War soldier" and "make you feel what slavery was like during that time period, what it was like to escape on the Underground Railroad." Although the park was eventually cancelled because of strong local opposition, had it been completed, Foner's vision would have greatly shaped the guests' experiences.

Despite the cancellation of the Virginia theme park, the relationship between Disney and Foner continues to thrive. Already, work has been done revising "Great Moments with Mr. Lincoln" in Anaheim and other Magic Kingdom attractions.

Not all of Disney's retelling of history is done by auto-animatrons. Sometimes it happens on celluloid.

In June 1994 movie director Oliver Stone received approval from Disney's Hollywood Pictures for a controversial and secretive film project. Stone's last film had been *JFK*, which had been thoroughly denounced by critics as inaccurate and sensationalist. So much so that Stone's name was becoming synonymous with sensationalism and inventing "history." Nevertheless, Stone wanted to do another film about a national leader. "We had developed two consecutive projects about strong but fatally flawed political leaders—General Manuel Noriega and Eva Peron—which for one reason or another we decided not to proceed with," Stone recalls. "I was particularly interested in doing a character study of a powerful leader against a large historic backdrop, and Eric Hamburg—who had come to work with us from Indiana Representative Lee Hamilton's staff in Washington—suggested Richard Nixon. Eric met with Stephen Rivele and Christopher Wilkinson and asked them to submit a treatment. The idea appealed to me. I thought the time was right for a serious examination of this extraordinary man."

Oliver Stone had strong feelings about the former president. He recalled in a 1987 interview that during his student activist days he had encouraged the assassination of the president. "If you want to protest," he claimed he told fellow activists, "let's get a sniperscope and DO Nixon."

After Nixon's funeral in April 1994 Stone wrote a piece for *Harper's* in which he attempted to link Watergate to the Kennedy assassination. While some might have doubted Stone's sanity, Disney coughed up $43 million to back the project.

There was a tight lid on the script. So tight that when David Hyde

Pierce, the actor who plays Niles Crane on the sitcom *Frasier,* was invited to act in Stone's film, "His casting people called my agent and asked me to come in. But they wouldn't tell us what for, what the character was or what the movie was." To lend credibility to the project, Stone traveled the country and met with former Nixon aides and confidants, including former White House Counsel Leonard Garment and Press Secretary Ronald Ziegler. Although Stone and Disney publicized these meetings as "fact-finding" efforts, most of those who met with Stone said he was largely passive and uninterested. "Stone did ask me if the President had smelled funny," one recalled.

The early film script that emerged from the pens of Stone, Rivele, and Wilkinson was filled with so many untruths that it had to be revised for fears of litigation. For example, the May 1995 shooting script contains a coarse scene in which Nixon's friend Bebe Rebozo attempts to persuade Nixon to commit adultery with a young woman. In real life, however, the scene never took place, and when Disney attorneys discovered that Rebozo was still alive, they raised a fuss. So rather than face litigation on charges of slander, the Bebe character was changed to a fictional Cuban-American named "Trini." When you read the annotated script it says: "Trini is a composite character. Richard Nixon had a number of male friends who were successful businessmen and with whom he spent time."

The script also invented stories about former CIA Director Richard Helms. Inconveniently for Stone and Disney, Helms managed to get an advance copy of the script, and Stone received a letter from Helms's lawyers. The Disney Legal Department once again got nervous and had Stone cut the Helms character out entirely.

A fear of lawsuits hung over the film. "I was a little bit concerned playing a living person," recalls David Hyde Pierce, who played John Dean, "and having read Oliver's script and not knowing how much of it was fact, how much of it was fiction, how much of it was slander and [I thought] we're all going to jail."

No one was in jail on opening night, but Stone began the movie with a prologue on a black screen: "This film is an attempt to understand the truth of Richard Nixon. It is based on numerous public sources and on an incomplete historical record. In consideration of length, events and characters have been condensed and some scenes among protagonists have been conjectured."

It was Stone's attempt to mask what was actually in the film. As historian Stephen Ambrose puts it, "That last sentence hides a multitude of lies."

In the film, Stone presented a Nixon few would recognize. He had Nixon drinking heavily throughout, though aides said such occurrences were rare. The annotated script cited Nixon biographies by Stephen Ambrose and Tom Wicker as sources about the president's drinking. But Wicker wrote that he found only one authentic case of Nixon being drunk, when he was in Moscow in 1959 as vice president. And Ambrose wrote in his biography: "Whatever Nixon's problems in life, and Lord knows there were many, alcohol was not one of them."

Stone has Nixon swearing throughout the film. But Nixon rarely used foul language. Most of the "expletive deleted" words on the Nixon tapes are "hell" and "damn," according to Nixon biographer Stephen Ambrose, who listened through more than sixty hours of them. Stone shows Richard and Pat Nixon as a couple living in an asexual marriage, only one misstep ahead of divorce. This, too, is an invention—and a painful one for the Nixon children.

More bizarre is Stone's transference of his own conspiracy theories to Nixon. In scene 117, for example, we see a dejected Nixon alone in his sitting room with the door closed. He downs a handful of pills with a glass of Scotch. "[T]hese guys went after Castro," he says. "Seven times, ten times. What do you think—people like that, they just give up? They just walk away? Whoever killed Kennedy came from this— this *thing* we created. This beast. That's why we can't let this thing go any further." This was the main thrust of the movie, that a cabal was really running things, serving as the puppet masters for every significant event that occurred in American life. According to Wilkinson, "The beast became a metaphor for the darkest organic forces in American Cold War politics: The anti-communist crusade, secret intelligence, the defense industry, organized crime, big business."

"The beast" killed JFK and controlled Nixon, according to the film. In one scene a voter tells Nixon during a TV debate: "You're just a mouthpiece for an agenda that is hidden from us." This nicely sums up the movie's theme.

In scene 124 Nixon is in the Lincoln Sitting Room with General Alexander Haig and Henry Kissinger. The Supreme Court has just ruled that the Nixon White House must release the Watergate tapes.

Nixon: Can we get around this, Al?
Haig: It's the Supreme Court, sir; you don't get around it.
(Nixon, silenced, looks down at the paper in his hands and sighs.)
Haig: If you resign, you can keep your tapes as a private citizen.
    You can fight them for years.
Nixon: And if I stay?
(There's a long pause.)
Haig: You have the army.
(Nixon looks up at Haig, then over at Kissinger.)
Nixon: The army?
Haig: Lincoln used it.
Nixon: That was civil war.
Haig: How do you see this?

This is all pure fantasy. Nixon never believed in any sort of "beast," nor did Haig and Nixon ever discuss putting the army in the streets to stay in power. Oliver Stone's fantasy version of events offended not only historians like Stephen Ambrose, but also Nixon critics like journalist Daniel Schorr, who made Nixon's famed enemies list. "A lot of people undoubtedly will accept *Nixon* as historical truth, which it is only partly. But the part that is not historical truth would be called libelous," Schorr said, "if there were somebody alive to sue for libel."

Had Disney presented *Nixon* simply as an entertaining film it would have been easier to dismiss the inaccuracies. But both Oliver Stone and the Mouse clung to the line that this was history. The press kit distributed by Hollywood Pictures assured journalists and reviewers that this film was based on truth. "The writers of Nixon have gone to great pains to insure the film's veracity, to the fullest extent possible," it read.

To buttress that claim, Disney released through its Hyperion Books Division a "scholarly" book entitled *Nixon: An Oliver Stone Film*. The tome includes essays about the Nixon years, an annotated screenplay, and Watergate documents. The script is dressed up with what looks like scholarly footnotes, designed to lend credence to the Stone version of events—but actually they don't. Several key scenes are falsely attributed to Nixon's own writings, when in fact they are Stone's inventions. "I am quoted in about a third of the footnotes in the book that he's put out," says historian Stephen Ambrose, "and he very often quotes me [saying] the opposite of what I said."

Disney even had the gall to push the film as an educational tool. *Nixon*, Disney said, would allow high school students an opportunity to "better understand" the former president. A study guide was distributed to thousands of high schools around the country. Brett Dicker, senior vice president of Disney's Hollywood Pictures, even penned an introduction.

"Dear educator," his introduction begins. "Oliver Stone's *Nixon* is a dramatized attempt to understand the man behind the tarnished presidential seal, who, to paraphrase his own words, scaled life's greatest heights and plunged into its deepest valleys. The film offers scholars, educators, and students everywhere the opportunity to draw their own lessons from this film biography of one of the most influential leaders of modern U.S. history. The purpose of this study guide is to help you deepen your students' understanding of the film and enhance their appreciation of the significance of the historical Nixon." The guide never makes mention of the invented facts and conspiracies that make up the subtext of the film. Indeed, the guide assures the teacher that "everything is accurate and documented."

Everything, that is, except the facts.

CONCLUSION

When we started working on this book, we set out in search of what Disney and the Magic Kingdom were really all about. And what we found behind the mask of the Mouse is something not even Walt himself would believe. If you are having difficulty recognizing the new Disney, don't worry—it's not you. Today's Mouse is markedly different from what it was even fifteen or twenty years ago. While the old Disney was a quality entertainment company you could trust with your kids, it's difficult to say the same today. Kids that plug in Disney's new animation videos will be watching programs that purposely include adult content. At Disney World, unnecessary risks will be taken with their safety, either by covering up crimes or operating the rides in a potentially unsafe manner. And Disney's Hollywood Records and Mammoth Records will offer America's youth songs about rape, killing, and sex with demons, while at the same time glorifying drug use by their bands.

In 1994 Michael Eisner told shareholders, "Whether we like it or not, because we are Disney, we are held to a higher standard. But that is appropriate." Yet even if you hold

> **Keeping the myth of Disney innocence alive is crucial for the Mouse's financial success.**

the new Disney to a normal standard, the Mouse comes out looking like a rat. Disney has become a company that seems all too willing to take amazing risks with its customers, employees, and reputation.

How should we judge Disney? The reasonable way would be to apply the "Eisner standard." In chapter one, we described a speech the Disney chairman gave to the American Society of Newspaper Editors on April 3, 1998. In that address, Eisner argued for a higher standard in entertainment, one in which "good judgment and common sense" would be used by Hollywood in the images and values that it projected.

He said films and entertainment should not "debase" the culture. "Short-term profits—maybe even long-term profits," he noted, "do not excuse clearly unethical decisions."

It's hard to see even by this standard how the Mouse measures up. When you underscore the variety of recent Disney projects, whether it is a film intended to make incest "look sexy" or distributing soft-core porn, it's easy to see how the company has embraced projects that debase the culture.

That speech, however sincere Michael Eisner might have been in giving it, highlights the yawning gap between the myth and reality of today's Disney. The new company wants very much to maintain the image of the old Disney: the responsible entertainment company that you can trust. The Mouse wants to encourage the belief that the company is the same one today's adults grew up with. If we've changed at all, is the Disney line, it's only in terms of size and scope. As Professor Janet Wasko, who studies Disney at the University of Oregon, points out, "Disney so deliberately promotes itself as family values and good entertainment. Disney is just taken for granted—you just assume it's going to be wholesome and good."

That squeaky-clean image is the essence of what gives Disney the most powerful brand name in entertainment. "The special appeal of Disneyland, Disney films, and products—family entertainment—comes from the contagious appeal of innocence," is what Michael Eisner told *New Perspectives Quarterly*. Without it, Disney ceases to be Disney.

The Mouse will go to extraordinary lengths to perpetuate this myth. The reason crimes are covered up at Disney World is to maintain the myth that bad things don't happen in the Magic Kingdom. As we've seen, it's the same reason the company is unwilling to cooperate in efforts to nab child molesters working at Disney World. And it also explains why Disney doesn't apprehend and fire voyeurs who peep on guests and fellow employees. Taking action means admitting there is a problem. Keeping the myth of Disney innocence alive is crucial for the Mouse's financial success.

This image of Disney innocence and the spectacular management abilities of Michael Eisner have helped to make the Mouse a roaring financial success. Since 1984 the company has averaged an annual return of more than 20 percent. As we've seen, much of that success emanates not so much from new ventures like Hollywood Records or Miramax, but instead from the tried and true: animation and theme parks. But in recent years the true rate of Disney's profitability has been called into question. According to Abraham Briloff, an accounting professor at Binghampton University writing in the prestigious financial publication *Barron's,* Disney has inflated its profits in recent years. Briloff says the Mouse created an unreported $2.5 billion reserve that inflated Disney's earning since 1996. Using standard account principles, Briloff says, Disney is not nearly as profitable as it seems. "Indeed the 25 percent earnings surge Disney reported in fiscal '97 would have come to 10 percent," he says, "without benefit of the accounting device. And far from an 18 percent earnings increase in the December quarter, net would have been flat."

Making a profit is, of course, what business is all about. But the singular pursuit of money is something new at Disney. Walt Disney was like so many other successful titans of business—Bill Gates, Sam Walton, etc.—in that he concentrated on creating quality products and knew that if he succeeded the money would come later. "Money is something I understand only vaguely and think about only when I don't have enough to finance my current enthusiasm, whatever it may be," Walt once said. "All I know about money is that I have to have it to do things."

But things at the new Disney company are entirely different. As *Brandweek,* the hard-nosed advertising industry bible, described the change at Disney: "Great brand names emerge after their makers discover a better mousetrap for a needy market, managing to suffuse the product with a halo of quality and concern for the customer. Then fossilization sets in, markets change, and quality gets rolled over by the almighty lust for quarterly returns. Mickey's squeaky-clean image no longer counts most. Revenues do."

Look behind just about any of the company's irresponsible acts and you will find a money motive. Why produce music with outrageous lyrics while promoting the drug culture? Because there is potential money to be made. Why does safety seem to "come last," as one employee put it? Because as Disney World employees describe it, management has determined that it is more profitable to operate the park in a relatively unsafe manner than to make safety changes. Why is Mickey involved in the distribution of skin flicks? Because if someone is going to take a peek, the company figures it might as well get its cut. Why avoid pressing licensees on child labor? Because it's cheaper to produce goods employing kids instead of adults.

This intense pursuit of a few extra dollars sometimes reaches even absurd proportions in the new Magic Kingdom. Workers at Disney World told us that several years ago the refrigeration system for drinking fountains was turned off. So on a hot day, when you dash around the park, a visit to the drinking fountain will mean plenty of warm, caustic water. The scheme is quite deliberate: the new Disney would rather have patrons buy cold water at $2.50 a bottle than drink it free from the fountain. The company is looking to save on anything. Recently employees in the Disney World janitorial service were reprimanded by supervisors. The reason? They were changing the toilet paper rolls in the park too soon. For a company that prides itself on "guest service," it was a strange move. But park management figured that each leftover sheet apparently threatened to "wipe away" profits.

And yet there is more to the change at Disney than simply protecting its image and making money. Disney is more than a company, it's a value system. Professor Benjamin Barber of Rutgers University, author of *Jihad vs. McWorld: How the Planet is Both Falling Apart and Coming Together*, is right when he says, "Disney is buying much more than our leisure time. It has a purchase on our values, on how we feel and think and what we think about." There has also been a shift in what sort of themes the company embeds in its children's programming. As we've seen, the film *Pocahontas* includes environmental and spiritual messages designed to not simply entertain, but influence. The company's rewriting of history at the theme parks and the movie house is not done to boost profits. But it is hoped that these changes will get us to think about historical events in a particular way.

The Walt Disney Company is doing very well financially. But money alone is not enough to drive a company. Over the long term a company has to be about something. Maytag is about reliability. American Express is about service. Wal-mart is about low prices. But what is the new Disney about?

It is certainly no longer about the "contagious appeal of innocence." Disney has lost its innocence. Mickey Mouse, the innocent fun-loving everyman, has been betrayed.

APPENDIX A
Disney's Pedophile Problem

Orange County Sheriff's Office $N \mathcal{C}$ *Orlando, Florida*
Investigative Report   *Case Number 97-281247*

Investigator

Matthew J. Irwin
Orange County Sheriff's Office
Major Case Bureau
Sex Crimes Unit
2450 W. 33rd Street
Orlando, Florida 32839
Telephone: (407) 836-4020

Offense Information

Original Offense(s):

Attempted Lewd Act Upon a Child
F.S.S. 800.04

Computer Pornography
F.S.S. 847.0135(3)

Address of Occurrence:

Pine Shadow Condominium Complex
Kirkman Rd., Orlando, Florida 32811

Date and Time of Occurrence:

07/14/97 @ 1230 hours

Victim Information:

State of Florida

Suspect Information:

Laber, Christopher J.
W/M/36; **DOB:** 11/14/60
4737 Emerald Forrest Way, #1801
Orlando, Florida 32811
Telephone: (407) 841-1387

This August 1997 Orange County, Florida, Sheriff's Office report describes the investigation against Disney employee Christopher Laber, a hard-core pedophile who used his employee card for discounts on toys to seduce his victims. He was arrested and pled guilty to engaging in sex acts with a thirteen-year-old boy named "Matt."

Orange County Sheriff's Office   *Orlando, Florida*
Investigative Report   *Case Number 97-281247*

Employer Information.
Walt Disney World
Transportation Supervisor
Lake Buena Vista, Florida

Physical Description:
Height: 5'11" *Weight:* 195 lbs. *Hair:* Brown *Eyes:* Hazel
SSN: 075-40-1216 *Florida D/L:* L160-110-60-414-0
FDLE #: None Located *FBI #:* None Located
Orange County Jacket #:

Synopsis of Testimony: Mr. Laber admitted to attempting to meet the ficticious 13 yr.
old boy. Mr. Laber admitted that he would have engaged in sex
acts with the 13 yr. old boy if the boy was consensual. Mr.
Laber admitted to engaging in sex acts with another 13 yr. old
boy named "Matt."

Witness Information

#1

Payne, Victor
Deputy Sheriff / Agent
Orange County Sheriff's Office
Felony Squad
2400 W. 33rd St.
Orlando, Florida 32839

Synopsis of Testimony: Agent Payne placed an "under cover" telephone call to Mr. Laber,
pretending to be a 13 year old male. This conversation was audio tape
recorded

●   ●

Orange County Sheriff's Office   *Orlando, Florida*
Investigative Report   *Case Number 97-281247*

#8

Binks, John
Detective
Orange County Sheriff's Office
Major Case Bureau
Sex Crimes Unit
2450 W. 33rd St.
Orlando, Florida 32839
Telephone: (407) 836-4020

Synopsis of Testimony: Assisted with the surveillance and arrest of Mr. Laber.

#9

Fusco, Steve
Detective
Orange County Sheriff's Office
Major Case Bureau
Sex Crimes Unit
2450 W. 33rd St.
Orlando, Florida 32839
Telephone: (407) 836-4020

Synopsis of Testimony: Assisted with the surveillance and arrest of Mr. Laber.

#10

Brooks, Lori Ann
W/F/35; **DOB:** 01/20/62
2232 Venetian Ave.
Orlando, Florida 32809
Telephone: (407) 222-4795

Synopsis of Testimony: Ms. Brooks reported that her son may have been sexually assaulted by
a man named "Chris." Ms. Brooks said that her son met "Chris" via
America Online.

5

Orange County Sheriff's Office   *Orlando, Florida*
Investigative Report   *Case Number 97-281247*

#11

Synopsis of Testimony: ▮▮▮ met Mr. Laber while using AOL ▮▮▮ engaged in various
sexual acts with Mr. Laber ▮▮▮ picked Mr. Laber out of a
photo-line-up.

Narrative

On 05/07/97, Ms. Lori A. Brooks reported that her son, who is ▮ years old, may have been
seduced by an adult male whom her son met by using the computer online service America
Online, hereafter referred to as "AOL." Ms. Brooks provided enough information, including the
suspect's screen name, and the first name of "Chris", that I was able to leave the suspect E-mail,
introducing myself as a 13 year old boy. I informed the suspect, who used the AOL screen name
"Iso men," that I had been in contact with another boy, online, whom he knew. I told "Iso men"
that this other boy told me to contact him.

On 07/08/97, I received E-mail from "Iso men" which acknowledged my e-mail and
informed me of the times he would be online. "Iso men" also signed the name "Chris" at the
bottom of the e-mail. This corresponded to the information provided by Ms. Brooks.

On 07/11/97, without further contact with "Iso men," I received e-mail from "Iso men" that
contained a graphic image file which he alleged to be a photograph of himself.

On 07/12/97, while utilizing AOL, I met "Iso men" online. I made initial contact with "Iso
men" simply stating "Hi." "Iso men" replied and a conversation ensued. With the exception of
my initial contact with "Iso men," this conversation was saved and printed out. My impression of
our conversation was that "Iso men" remained intentionally vague with regard to any explicit
sexually oriented conversation although he did clearly attempt to elicit sexually explicit
conversation from me. "Iso men" also arranged to have me call him so that we could meet within
the next few days. "Iso men" gave me his home telephone number (407-841-1387) and his pager
number (407-980-9207) and asked that I call him on the following Monday morning (07/14/97).

Orange County Sheriff's Office   *Orlando, Florida*
Investigative Report   *Case Number 97-281247*

On 07/13/97, without any contact with "Iso men," I received another e-mail from him. This e-mail basically was his attempt to remind me that I was supposed to call him on 07/14/97. "Iso men," again gave his home telephone number and signed the name "Chris."

On 07/14/97, prior to making contact with "Chris," Detective Gergenti was able to identify the person and the location of the residence which had the unique telephone number (407) 841-1387 assigned. This telephone number was assigned to a person named Christopher Laber who lives at 4737 Emerald Forrest Way, #1801, Orlando, Florida 32811.

On 07/14/97, I arranged to have Agent Victor Payne of the Orange County Sheriff's Office place a controlled telephone call to "Iso men"/ "Chris." Agent Payne posed as a 13 year old boy named "Joe." This telephone conversation was audio tape recorded. On our first attempt to call "Iso men" / "Chris" at home, there was no answer. I then paged "Iso men" / "Chris" and waited for him to return the call. A few minutes later a male returned the page and identified himself as "Chris." During this conversation, "Chris" made several remarkable statements. "Chris" told Agent Payne that he was a "pleaser." "Chris" defined a "pleaser" as someone who will do whatever they can to make a person happy. Agent Payne portrayed a boy who was sexually inexperienced and confused with regard to his sexuality. "Chris" told Agent Payne that he had "to start somewhere" and "When you do something for the first time it's always new." "Chris" expressed to Agent Payne that he did not like pain and was not into painful sexual acts.

"Chris" then began discussing his encounter with a boy he described as being under eighteen years old named "Matt." "Chris" described how he was scared when it came to getting involved with boys under the age of eighteen years. When asked what he and "Matt" did, "Chris" said "Well, we did...we did just about everything. I mean, I met him a few times, and ah...we fooled around a little bit and..." "Chris" explained the use of different lubricants such as K-Y Gel and Crisco cooking grease. "Chris" explained that these products assist in relieving pain during intercourse but that neither of the products "taste good." "Chris" made several other remarkable statements regarding the same topic, please refer to the attached transcript for further details. It was then arranged that "Chris" would come to a residence that Agent Payne described in order to meet the fictitious 13 year old boy.

Within minutes, members of the Orange County Sheriff's Office Sex Crimes Unit watched as a white male driving a brick red Pontiac Grand Prix, matching the description that "Chris" had given, drive past the residence described by Agent Payne. This person never stopped and was lost by the surveillance team for a few minutes. The vehicle was then located outside the residence located at 4737 Emerald Forrest Way, #1801, Orlando, Florida 32811.

Orange County Sheriff's Office   *Orlando, Florida*
Investigative Report   *Case Number 97-281247*

A short while later, a white male exited 4737 Emerald Forrest Way, #1801, Orlando, Florida 32811 and was approached by Detectives Moch and Webb. This person was identified as Christopher Laber. I informed Mr. Laber of the case we had been working and that I would require him to come to the Orange County Sheriff's Office for an interview.

Mr. Laber requested that he be allowed to re-enter his apartment to get shoes and other personal items such as his wallet and keys. I allowed him to re-enter the apartment as long as I could go with him to ensure he would not obtain any weapons or attempt to lock himself in the apartment. Mr. Laber agreed to let me enter the apartment with him. Immediately upon entering the apartment I noticed a computer system in the living room area of the apartment. I seized the computer system as evidence in this case. A property form was completed and given to Mr. Laber describing the articles of property that were seized. Photograph's of Mr. Laber's apartment were taken including photograph's of Mr. Laber's pager and cellular telephone displaying the telephone number from which the controlled telephone call was made.

Once the computer system was dismantled, Mr. Laber was taken to the Orange County Sheriff's Office Investigations Building for an interview. Prior to arriving at the OCSO Investigations Building, no questions relevant to this investigation were asked. Once we arrived at the OCSO Investigations Building, Mr. Laber was given his Miranda Rights, which he waived. Mr. Laber made several remarkable statements during this interview. Mr. Laber admitted being the person with whom I made contact via the computer service AOL. Mr. Laber admitted that he was intending on having a sexual relationship with the boy he knew as "Joe," if "Joe" was a willing participant. Mr. Laber also said that he was simply looking for a friend with whom to spend time. Mr. Laber also acknowledged that the person he believed to be "Joe" was supposed to be a 13 year old boy. Mr. Laber said that he was homosexual but did not feel that he was sexually attracted to juvenile boys. Mr. Laber said that he had only had a sexual relationship with one juvenile boy whom he knew as "Matt."

On 07-30-97, Ms. Brooks brought her son██████████████████████, to the Orange County Sheriff's Office Investigation's Building for an interview regarding this case.████ gave sworn testimony that he engaged in oral and anal sex with Mr. Laber.████ picked Mr. Laber out of a photoline-up as the person he engaged in the sexual acts with.████ said that he met Mr. Laber while utilizing AOL.████ said that he never gave Mr. Laber his real name but instead used the name "Matt."████ statement was audio tape recorded, please refer to the statement for further details of the interview. Mr. Laber is being charged for this crime under OCSO case number 97-182101.

8

Records

Orange County Sheriff's Office   *Orlando, Florida*
Investigative Report   *Case Number 97-138338*

Investigator: Matthew J. Irwin

Offense(s):   1.   Attempted Lewd Act Upon a Child
                                       F.S.S. 800.04
                                       (Orange County)

                                 2.   Computer Pornography
                                       F.S.S. 847.0135(3)
                                       (Orange County)

                                 3.   Possession of Child Pornography
                                       F.S.S. 827.071(5)
                                       (Osceola County)

Address of Occurrence: 4675 S. Kirkman Rd., Orlando, Fl. 32811
                                                        &
                                        2810 Frontier Dr., Kissimmee, Fl.   34744

Date and Time of Occurrence: 04-07-97 @ Approximately 1750 Hrs.

Date of Assignment: 04-06-97

Victim Information:

State of Florida

Suspect Information:

		W/M/29	
H:	Bradley, Christopher 2810 Frontier Dr. Kissimmee, Florida 34744		**DOB**: 07-16-67 **PH**: (407) 344-3899
W:	Walt Disney World Animation Section Lake Buena Vista, Florida		**PH**: (407) 560-1617

1

This April 1997 Orange County, Florida, Sheriff's Office report on Disney animator Christopher Bradley describes his arrest on charges of an attempted lewd act upon a child and 120 counts of possession of child pornography. He pled guilty.

Orange County Sheriff's Office   *Orlando, Florida*
Investigative Report   *Case Number 97-138338*

Physical Description.
Height: 6' 01"   *Weight*: 195 lbs.   *Hair*: Brown   *Eyes*: Brown
SSN: 591-39-4072   *Florida D/L*: Unknown
FDLE #:   None Known   *FBI #*: None Known
Orange County Jacket #: None Known

Testimony:
       In an audio tape recorded statement, Mr. Bradley admits have a conversation via computer with a person he believed to be a 13 year old female named "Nikki." Mr. Bradley admits that he engaged in conversation with "Nikki" where he indicated his desire to have a sexual relationship with "Nikki."

Witness Information:

Webb, Elaine - Detective, Orange County Sheriff's Office
#1:   2450 W. 33rd St.
Orlando, Florida 32839   *PH*: 836-4020

Testimony:
       Detective Webb assisted in the interview of Mr. Bradley and also assisted in recovering Mr. Bradley's Computer.

Blackmon, Julia - Detective, Orange County Sheriff's Office
#2:   2450 W. 33rd St.
Orlando, Florida 32839   *PH*: 836-4020

Testimony:
       Detective Blackmon made three undercover telephone calls as the thirteen year old female, to Mr. Bradley and engaged him in sexually oriented conversation. Mr. Bradley told Detective Blackmon that he would engage her in sexual intercourse upon their meeting on 04/07/97. Detective Blackmon also assisted in the interview of Mr. Bradley.

Caldwell, Dave - Corporal, Orange County Sheriff's Office
#3:   2450 W. 33rd St.
Orlando, Florida 32839   *PH*: 836-4020

2

Orange County Sheriff's Office   *Orlando, Florida*
Investigative Report   *Case Number 97-138338*

Testimony:
        Corporal Caldwell read Mr. Bradley his Miranda Warning and obtained the audio
tape recorded statement from Mr. Bradley.

Dr. Matthew Seibel, Pediatrician
#4: 300 N. Lake Destiny Dr.
Maitland, Florida   *PH*: 381-7364

Testimony:
        Dr. Seibel reviewed approximately 156 graphic images and confirmed that 120 of
those images were that of nude children under the age of 18 engaged in sexual activity
and/or poses.

Narrative:

On 04-06-97 during the evening hours, I was utilizing the computer service America
Online, hereafter referred to as AOL. My screen name while utilizing this service was "Niki012".
AOL allows individuals to create an "Online Profile" for each screen name. These "Online
Profiles" may or may not be truthful and/or accurate. With my screen name of "Niki012", I
profiled myself to be a twelve year old female. Along with a profile, each screen name is offered
an opportunity to write a "Personal Quote". These personal quotes appear when ever someone
chooses to review an "Online Profile". My "Personal Quote" under the screen name of
"Niki012" was "Looking for something more."

While using AOL on 04-06-97, I was in a "Chat Room" entitled "Orlando". A "Chat
Room" is a location within AOL where individuals from across the nation and in Canada,
depending on service availability, can converse with each other in real time via their computer.
"Chat Rooms" are created and titled by the subscriber's of AOL. The title's of these "Chat
Rooms" typically indicate the topic of discussion taking place in that particular room. Generally,
AOL allow's up to twenty three people in any given "Chat Room", although this may vary.
While conversing in a "Chat Room", one may communicate to all other's in their particular
"Chat Room" or one may select another subscriber in their particular "Chat Room" and send that
individual an "Instant Message". An "Instant Message" is a communication between two
subscriber's which is completely private.

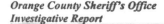

While in this "Chat Room" entitled "Orlando" on 04-06-97, I received an "Instant Message" from another subscriber using the screen name "NSWRFL". The very first thing that "NSWRFL" asked me was "*Looking for something more??????? What more is there?*", this indicated to me that this person had already checked my AOL "Online Profile" prior to contacting me through an "Instant Message."

This person then introduced himself as "Chris" and sent me a graphic image of himself. "Chris" also told me that he was from Australia. "Chris" asked me my age. I replied that I was thirteen years old. "Chris" also asked me where I lived. I replied "*kirkman / conroy area*" "Chris" then said "*I live out by the airport*" "Chris" then, indirectly, asked me if I had ever had sex. I told him that I had never gone all the way. "Chris" then said "I'd love to meet you, but I know I'd wind up getting in big trouble." "Chris" then began explaining that any relationship between he and I would have to remain a secret or he could end up in jail. "Chris" then asked "how could I meet you?? I mean would we have a chance to be together? If we dated?" He then asked me "Do you want to meet me sometime?" "Chris" then gave me a telephone number where I could call him and suggested that I call him between 1530 hours and 1600 hours. This number is (407) 560-1617. The next portion of conversation was in regards to any potential sexual relationship. "Chris" explained that we would have to be very discreet in public. Refer to the attached transcript for further details. I then informed "Chris" that I needed to sign off of AOL. "Chris" reminded me to call him on 04-07-97. I then said goodnight. However, I did not sign off of AOL.

Approximately fifteen minutes later, "Chris" sent me another "Instant Message" reminding me to call him and ensuring that I had his telephone number. He then wanted to stay online and chat for a while longer, which I declined. "Chris" then said "That's ok, I'm probably going to dream about you tonight." We then said goodnight again and ended the conversation. I then checked the AOL profile for the screen name "NSWRFL" and found that there was none.

On 04/07/97 at approximately 1600 hours, Detective Blackmon placed an undercover telephone call, posing as "Nikki" to the telephone number (407) 560-1617 and asked for "Chris." The person who answered the telephone identified himself as "Chris" and also had what appeared to be a foreign accent possibly from Australia. "Chris" wanted to meet with "Nikki" (Detective Blackmon) on that date. Detective Blackmon advised "Chris" that she would need to call her mother to get permission to go out. The telephone call was terminated with the understanding that "Nikki" (Detective Blackmon) would call "Chris" right back when she received an answer from her mother. While off the telephone, I informed Detective Blackmon that I wanted her to tell "Chris" that she would be unable to meet with him on this date and that she may meet with him tomorrow (04/08/97).

Orange County Sheriff's Office   *Orlando, Florida*
Investigative Report   *Case Number 97-138338*

During the next telephone call, "Nikki" (Detective Blackmon) told "Chris" that she could not meet him on that day (04/07/97). "Chris" began an attempt to convince "Nikki" (Detective Blackmon) that she should allow him to come over regardless of her mothers decision stating that since "Nikki's" mother was at work she would never find out. "Chris" pursued this attempt relentlessly causing Detective Blackmon to tell "Chris" that she would call him right back. While off the telephone I decided again not to meet with "Chris".

Detective Blackmon called "Chris back and restated her desire to meet with him on another day. Again "Chris" attempted to convince "Nikki" (Detective Blackmon) to meet him on 04/07/97. "Chris" made statements that he didn't know if he would be able to meet with her on any other day other than 04/07/97. In the middle of this telephone conversation I decided to tell Detective Blackmon to arrange to meet with "Chris" on 04/07/97.

After the first conversation, it was realized that the audio tape recording did not work. Since it was imperative to the investigation to return the telephone calls expeditiously they were completed without any recording device. Detective Blackmon completed a supplemental report detailing the extent of their conversations.

"Chris" had already informed Detective Blackmon that he worked for Walt Disney World and was presently at his work station. Detective Blackmon gave "Chris" directions to the NationsBank located at 4675 S. Kirkman Rd., Orlando, Florida 32811 and informed him that she would meet him there as soon as he arrived. "Chris" told Detective Blackmon that he would be driving a red and silver pickup truck and would have a red ball cap on. "Chris" then said that he would be there in approximately twenty minutes.

Members of the Orange County Sheriff's Office Felony Squad immediately set up a surveillance of the NationsBank parking lot. At approximately 1750 hours, a red and silver Dodge Ram pickup truck pulled in the NationsBank parking lot and parked where Detective Blackmon had informed "Chris" to park. The members of the Felony Squad approached the lone male driver of the vehicle and identified him as Christopher Bradley and also noticed that Mr. Bradley had an Australian accent.

I approached Mr. Bradley and identified myself. Mr. Bradley was then handcuffed and taken to the Orange County Sheriff's Office Investigation's Building.

After speaking with Mr. Bradley for a short period of time, Detective Blackmon and I turned the interview process over to Detective Webb and Corporal Caldwell. Corporal Caldwell read Mr. Bradley his Miranda Warning which Mr. Bradley waived. Mr. Bradley gave an audio tape recorded statement to Corporal Caldwell which was transcribed and attached to this report. During this statement, Mr. Bradley admitted that he was aware that the person he expected to meet was a thirteen year old female named "Nikki."

5

Mr. Bradley also admitted that he had agreed to engage in sexual intercourse with this person he thought to be "Nikki." (See transcript for further details of the statement).

Mr. Bradley then gave consent for me to go to his residence and seize his computer as evidence in this case. I also informed Mr. Bradley that I would be inventorying the files in this account for evidentiary purposes. Mr. Bradley gave his consent. Mr. Bradley said that he no longer wanted the computer and wanted me to have the computer.
Mr. Bradley also said that I could do whatever I wanted to with the computer. I informed Mr. Bradley that the computer was being seized as evidence in this case and that he could not simply give me the computer. Detective Webb and I dismantled the computer at Mr. Bradley's residence and placed the components in my OCSO assigned vehicle. We then left Mr. Bradley's residence.

On 04/08/97 while inventorying the files in Mr. Bradley's America Online computer directory, I found approximately 286 graphic image files. Most of these files were pornographic in nature. Most of the pornographic images appeared to be that of children under the age of 18 engaged in various sexual acts or poses.

I selected 156 of the 286 graphic images to present before Dr. Matthew Seibel, a pediatrician for the Child Protection Team. Of the 156 graphic images, Dr. Seibel confirmed that no less than 120 of the graphic image files depicted nude children under the age of 18 years engaged in sexual acts or poses.

Composite floppy disks containing these images have been attached to this report in a sealed envelope. The names of these graphic image files are cited below:

!!!!!!#.jpg	!!!!!!11.jpg	!!!13luv.jpg	!!3_kids.jpg
!!!!!13f.jpg	!!!!12g.jpg	!!10suck.jpg	!05mommy.jpg
!!!!!15.jpg	!!!!kids.jpg	!!11fukn.jpg	!!!!skny.jpg
!!!!10bj.jpg	!!!!ygbn.jpg	!!12&mom.jpg	!08teddy.jpg
!!!!0suk.jpg	!!!11dau.jpg	!!12bnna.jpg	!09cowga.jpg
!!!7jerk.jpg	!!!go4go.jpg	!!12indi.jpg	!10eaty.jpg
!!09read.jpg	!!10cute.jpg	!!12tami.jpg	!10grl.jpg
!10stuff.jpg	!10suck.jpg	!!coke.jpg	!13bra.jpg
!8sitfk.jpg	!8spre2.jpg	!9&13.jpg	!9doggie.jpg
!boy&sis.jpg	!india3.jpg	!jew_bj.jpg	!lilsis.jpg
!lolipop.jpg	&14sauna.jpg	___2.jpg	___11g.jpg
___k8.jpg	_cory.jpg	_06cumm.jpg	_07tast.jpg
_family.jpg	_loli03.jpg	_loli86.jpg	_11yrfuk.jpg
_9fuksis.jpg	04spre_1.jpg	06plugd.jpg	07sucky.jpg
08&10spa.jpg	08clit.jpg	10&13.jpg	10boysis.jpg

Orange County Sheriff's Office   *Orlando, Florida*
Investigative Report   *Case Number 97-138338*

10g&mom0.jpg	11-12&13.jpg	11cards.jpg	11cind.jpg
11doggy.jpg	11doself.jpg	11fing.jpg	11spread.jpg
11suk12.jpg	11x2kiss.jpg	12pool.jpg	12pubes.jpg
12suck.jpg	13bra&~1.jpg	13yrbutt.jpg	14float.jpg
14play.jpg	4yrsold.jpg	5sucky.jpg	5suk.jpg
7jerk.jpg	7pose.jpg	8plus8y.jpg	8yr&mom.gif
9&dad.jpg	asiayng.jpg	beth&dad.jpg	bigsistr.jpg
breann08.jpg	bro&sis.jpg	cindy.jpg	cindy01.jpg
cindy05.jpg	cubasuck.jpg	cutepuss.jpg	fam3.jpg
fkkk28.jpg	fm-vybyg.jpg	ll-cl-08.jpg	ll-cl-14.jpg
ll-cl-16.jpg	ll-n2fl1.jpg	meg&cuz.jpg	mom_kids.jpg
mom~daug.jpg	momhair.jpg	nud34.jpg	schild15.jpg
teenbath.jpg	tn-11x11.jpg	veryyoun.jpg	wholefam.jpg
wtrski.jpg	wwfbio7.jpg	y10&aunt.jpg	y10orgie.jpg
y11.jpg	yf-13j~1.jpg	yngfrnds.jpg	Zp-beach.jpg

With the information described above, I believe that probable cause does exist to believe that Christopher Bradley did violate Florida State Statutes 800.04, 847.0135(3) and 827.071(5) regarding Attempted Lewd Act Upon a Child, Computer Pornography and Possession of Child Pornography, respectively.

On 04-16-97, the above information was presented before the Honorable Michael F. Cycmanick, Circuit Judge in and for the Ninth Judicial Circuit, in the form of an affidavit for arrest warrant. Judge Cycmanick issued an arrest warrant for Mr. Bradley regarding the violation of Florida State Statutes 800.04 and 847.0135(3) pertaining to Attempted Lewd Act Upon a Child and Computer Pornography, respectively.

On 04-17-97, the above information was presented before the Honorable Margaret Waller, Osceola County Judge. Judge Waller issued an arrest warrant for Mr. Bradley for violating Florida State Statute 827.071(5) regarding the Unlawful Possession of Child Pornography.

On 04-17-97, Mr. Bradley was located by the Osceola County Sheriff's Office at his residence. Mr. Bradley was then arrested without incident and placed in the Osceola County Jail.

⭐	**Orange County Sheriff's Office**			**Investigative Report**	

Deputy initiating original report:	*M. IRWIN*	Date of Offense:	*4-7-97*	Case Number:	*97-138538*
Victim: Last, First, Middle	*STATE of Florida*			Other Agency Case Number:	*NA*

Victim Address (#, Street, City, State)	

Offense(s):	*ATT. LEWD ACT / POSS. CHILD PORN*	Offense Changed to:	*COMPUTER PORNOGRAPHY*
Value of Property Stolen:	*NA*	Recovered:	*NA*

Suspect Name: Last, First, Middle	*Bradley Christopher*	DOB: *7-16-67*	Race: *W*	Sex: *M*

CBA:	✓	The perpetrator in this case was arrested by Deputy/Officer: Name: *IRWIN*　　　Of　*OCSO*　　　On: *4-17-97* 　　　Agency:　　　　　　　Month/Day/Year
FSAO:		A Charging Affidavit was filed with the State Attorney on _____. 　　　　　　　　　　　　　　　　　　　　　　Month/Day/Year
INAC:		A follow-up investigation was made on this case and 　1. No suspects were identified 　2. Victim declines to assist agency with investigation.
EC:		The office of the State Attorney was contacted in reference to this case and prosecution was declined on _____ per _____.　**L MOORE** 　　　　Month/Day/Year　　Name:
EC:		The victim in this case declines to assist further in this investigation even though the perpetrator could be prosecuted.
EC:		This case has been referred to Health and Rehabilitative Services for the purpose of maintaining supervision as prosecution is neither possible nor practical.
UNF:		No criminal violation exists.
Closed:		This case was turned over to _____ for further investigation. 　　　　　　　　　　Agency Name:

Remarks:	*SEE REPORT*

[signature]	*[signature]*	*4/28/97*
Investigator	Supervisor Approving	Date of Report

White - Records　**Yellow** - Investigations　**Pink** - Crime Analysis　**Gold** - Deputy Initiating Original Report
10-1295 (11/89)

Disney World employee John Mushacke is arrested on charges of lewd and lascivious acts on a child, possession of child pornography, and promotion of child pornography.

SAO Sex Crimes Unit   Fax:1-407-836-2376   May 20 '98   12:20   P.02/03

OFFICE OF THE STATE ATTORNEY \
NINTH JUDICIAL CIRCUIT OF FLORIDA

FINAL DISPOSITION REPORT FORM

May 20, 1998

COURT CASE NO: CR95-3120
RE: STATE VS. JOHN R. MUSHACKE   AGENCY NO: FDLE
OR-95-20-002

DATE OF OFFENSE: 08/01/93

CHARGES: LEWD,LASCIVIOUS ASSAULT OR ACT ON CHILD
          POSS. MAT. DEPICTING SEXUAL PERF. BY CHILD
          PROMOTE SEX PERFORMANCE/CHILD
          LEWD ACT IN THE PRESENCE OF A CHILD
          LEWD ACT IN THE PRESENCE OF A CHILD
          USE OF A CHILD IN A SEXUAL PERFORMANCE
          SEXUAL PERFORMANCE BY A CHILD
          GRAND THEFT 2ND DEGREE - (>$300,<$20000)
          GRAND THEFT 2ND DEGREE - (>$300,<$20000)
          GRAND THEFT 2ND DEGREE - (>$300,<$20000)

The above-referenced case was disposed of on **February 16, 1996** as follows:

     LEWD,LASCIVIOUS ASSAULT OR ACT ON CHILD - Pled Guilty
     POSS. MAT. DEPICTING SEXUAL PERF. BY CHILD - Pled Guilty
     PROMOTE SEX PERFORMANCE/CHILD - Pled Guilty
     LEWD ACT IN THE PRESENCE OF A CHILD - Pled Guilty
     LEWD ACT IN THE PRESENCE OF A CHILD - Pled Guilty
     USE OF A CHILD IN A SEXUAL PERFORMANCE - Dismissed By State
     SEXUAL PERFORMANCE BY A CHILD - Dismissed By State
     GRAND THEFT 2ND DEGREE - (>$300,<$20000) - Dismissed By State
     GRAND THEFT 2ND DEGREE - (>$300,<$20000) - Dismissed By State
     GRAND THEFT 2ND DEGREE - (>$300,<$20000) - Dismissed By State
The Defendant was sentenced on February 20, 1996 as follows:

     Ct. 1 - Adjudicated Guilty
             279 Days Orange County Jail Credit For Time Served
             2 Years Community Control Level I Followed by
             10 Years Supervised Probation
             Psychiatric Evaluation & Counseling.
             HIV Testing
             Submit to Blood Draw for DNA
             No Contact With Victim Or Victim's Family.
             Waived PSI
             No Unsupervised Contact With Minors
             No Employment With Business Catering To
             Children Or Amusement Parks.
             To Fonfeit Disney Equipment.
             Restitution Ordered For Victim's Counseling
             Reserve To Set Amount.
     Ct. 2 - Adjudicated Guilty

Disney World employee John Mushacke pled guilty to molesting a thirteen-year-old girl. He used Disney videocameras to film his abuse of the girl.

279 Days Orange County Jail Credit For Time Served
2 Years Community Control Level I Followed by
10 Years Supervised Probation
Psychiatric Evaluation & Counseling.
HIV Testing
Submit to Blood Draw for DNA
No Contact With Victim Or Victim's Family.
Waived PSI
No Unsupervised Contact With Minors
No Employment With Business Catering To
Children Or Amusement Parks.
To Fonfeit Disney Equipment.
Restitution Ordered For Victim's Counseling
Reserve To Set Amount.

Ct. 3 - Adjudicated Guilty
279 Days Orange County Jail Credit For Time Served
2 Years Community Control Level I Followed by
10 Years Supervised Probation
Psychiatric Evaluation & Counseling.
HIV Testing
Submit to Blood Draw for DNA
No Contact With Victim Or Victim's Family.
Waived PSI
No Unsupervised Contact With Minors
No Employment With Business Catering To
Children Or Amusement Parks.
To Fonfeit Disney Equipment.
Restitution Ordered For Victim's Counseling
Reserve To Set Amount.

Ct. 4 - Adjudicated Guilty
279 Days Orange County Jail Credit For Time Served
2 Years Community Control Level I Followed by
10 Years Supervised Probation
Psychiatric Evaluation & Counseling.
HIV Testing
Submit to Blood Draw for DNA
No Contact With Victim Or Victim's Family.
Waived PSI
No Unsupervised Contact With Minors
No Employment With Business Catering To
Children Or Amusement Parks.
To Fonfeit Disney Equipment.
Restitution Ordered For Victim's Counseling
Reserve To Set Amount.

Ct. 5 - Adjudicated Guilty
279 Days Orange County Jail Credit For Time Served
2 Years Community Control Level I Followed by
10 Years Supervised Probation
Psychiatric Evaluation & Counseling.
HIV Testing
Submit to Blood Draw for DNA
No Contact With Victim Or Victim's Family.
Waived PSI
No Unsupervised Contact With Minors
No Employment With Business Catering To
Children Or Amusement Parks.
To Fonfeit Disney Equipment.
Restitution Ordered For Victim's Counseling
Reserve To Set Amount.

APPENDIX B
Peeping Toms

WALT DISNEY WORLD COMPANY
P.O. Box 10,000
Lake Buena Vista, Florida 32830-1000

STATEMENT OF WITNESS/SUBJECT

Person Giving Statement		
Name: James Hertogs	Place:	Investigations
Dept 56M Investigations	Date:	1-8-92
	Time:	1600
	Days Off:	

On 1-8-92 I interviewed John Giangrossi, Dept 89E Costume. I was assisted by Investigator

Charlie Moran and Giangrossi refused a shop steward. The interview began at approximately

1122 hours and ended at approximately 1230 hours when O.C.S.O. Sgt. Mike Colfield began his

interview of Giangrossi. During the interview with Giangrossi he related the following

events. In August of 1991 he first accidentaly observed the dancers in the Penthouse

without clothing when he entered believing they were gone during the course of his work.

...as embarrassed and departed the area. He allowed this to work on his mind and during

September of 1991 he heard a rumor of a dumb waiter elevator inside the Penthouse. He

entered the Penthouse and finally found the cover on the inside wall pulled off allowing

entrance to the maintenance shaft. It was dark so he dropped a coin to see how deep the

hole was and found that it had a solid floor. This all happened during the early morning

hours after the park closed.

Approximately 3 weeks later he first entered the shaft without a camera to observe the

dancers. He entered the Penthouse before the last show was over and then gain entry into

the shaft. He recalled this as a Thursday as he came to pick-up his pay check this day.

He related that he was inside the shaft for 15 to 20 minutes and was able to observe partial

nudity of the dancer by looking through the opening in the wall for a control knob of the

speaker system which was loose and left out against the wall. He could see the room and

the opposite side wall mirrior which then would allow him to see nearly the entire room.

... 14 days later he again on a Thursday entered the Penthouse prior to the last show

ending and entered the shaft. Again he did not bring a camera but was able to observe

SIGNATURE: C. n. ...	PERSON TAKING STATEMENT:

This internal Disney security report describes the investigation into Peeping Toms who secretly videotaped employees changing their clothes and then showed the videotapes to coworkers. Disney eventually caught employee John Giangrossi in the act but didn't bring law enforcement into the investigation of this felony.

CONTINUATION

Related Reports:

DATE
DA   YR
1 8 92

☐ CRIME REPORT   ☒ STATEMENT   ☐ OCCURRENCE REPORT   ☐ S.I.

full and partial nudity of the dancers during his 15 to 20 minute stay inside the shaft.

His third trip into the shaft was again on his day off and this time at approximately 1200 hours. He brought a black drop cloth with him to cover a vent in the rear of the shaft so that the sunlight would not come into the shaft and give away his position. He also brough into the shaft a wardrobe smock to cover him and a video camera which he rented from Rent-a-Cam on I-drive. He filmed approximately 5 minutes of film while remaining inside the shaft for 30 minutes. He observed and filmed partial nudity at this time.

On the next day a Thursday he returned again with the same camera and this time filmed approximately 10 to 15 minutes of full and partial nudity while observing the same. This taping was done on a second video tape and the first tape remained at his home.

3   4 days later he went to a party which was attended by three other cast members from Stage Tech. He remembered two of the cast members as Mark Schnallinger and Nick Buzzik. He showed the first video (five minutes) to the group and was asked if he had any others which he replied "No". They also asked him how he had gotten the video and he replied that he was "not saying". When asked why he brought and showed the video he related that the techs always were talking about the dancers and how they would like to take them out etc. and he felt they would like the video. This video (#1) was then damaged while at home by spilling soda on the tape and he threw the tape into the garbage.

In November 1991 he talked to a custodial host named Victor who said that you could see th dancers by going into the Penthouse Radio Room. John stated that he ignored this remarks and did not give Victor information on the mechanical shaft.

After talking to Victor he again went to the Penthouse and entered the shaft on his day off. He brought a camera he borrowed from cast member Robert Rivera. He brought the se- nd tape with him and added another 5 minutes of taping of full and partial nudity. He remained inside the shaft for 30 minutes.

the Penthouse after everyone had left and installed an extension

CONTINUATION   PAGE_____OF_____

Related Reports:

DATE
MO / DA / YR
1 8 92

☐ CRIME REPORT   ☒ STATEMENT   ☐ OCCURRENCE REPORT   ☐ S.I.

into the outlet and the other inside the shaft. He returned 2 to 3 days later with the

Rivera camera but the camera malfunctioned and he obtained no new film and observed

nothing as one of the dancers placed the speaker knob plate back into the wall.

He insisted that he did not return until today 1-8-92 and that he entered the shaft at

approximately 0940 hours and remained inside until he left at 1105 hours. He related that

he observed full and partial nudity and that he also filmed full and partial nudity. This

was done on a third tape which we now had in our possession. He related that the second

tape was stolen from his home and that he had no knowledge of its whereabouts. He admitt

to masturbating while watching the dancers undressed. He gave permission to search his

locker, vehicle, and home for the missing tapes.

VERNON DONALDSON   Custodial

On 3/3/91, Vernon Donaldson was caught in the ladies
restroom in an employee break area. He was observed looking
over the top of the stall while a female employee used the
facility.

Donaldson's record card showed a similar incident and he had
received a verbal reprimand.

On 3/27/91, another employee complained of Donaldson looking
over the stall.

Donaldson received a written reprimand and was removed from
interior details.

*This summary and the report that follows are from Disney World security files, and outline how the
company handles employees who repeatedly peep on others: with a written reprimand.*

MENT — INCIDENT REPORT

REPORT NUMBER
IS-14-04-91

CLASSIFICATION
Confidential

DATE
April 4, 1991

_st and Final

Sexual Harassment

This investigation was initiated on 3/9/91 when I was contacted by Wayne Marshal, Supervisor, Custodial, MAGIC KINGDOM, in reference to employee Vernon Donaldson, Dept. 489, HD 2/1/91, DOB 4/12/58. Marshal explained that he had been contacted by Assistant Supervisor David Petersen, Monorails, that the female hostesses were having a problem with Donaldson while in the ladies restroom. Petersen had a copy of a written statement by Monorail hostess Diane Stidham who stated that as she attempted to use the ladies restroom in the break area, she had observed Donaldson looking over the top of the stall. Stidman stated that Donaldson was not visible when she entered the restroom and had made no sound to advised her that he was there.

Marshal and I reviewed Donaldson's record card which revealed that he had received a verbal reprimand from Assistant Supervisor Johnny Petersen for a similar incident.

On 3/30/91 I interviewed Donaldson after he declined a shop steward. Donaldson stated that he was in the restroom cleaning when Stidman entered the restroom. Donaldson stated that he did announce himself and in no way attempted to view Stidman. Donaldson executed a written statement and was released to Marshal.

On 3/31/91 I was-contacted by Petersen who advised that he had an additional employee who had the same problem with Donaldson. I interviewe Monorail hostess Nicole Botsford who stated that on 3/27/91, she was using the ladies restroom in the same location when she observed a Custodial hos looking over the top of the stall. Botsford stated that the host made no

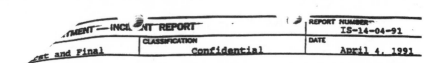

announcement that he was in the restroom nor was he visible when she entered.

On 4/3/91, I advised Marshal of the incident. Marshal requested a copy of Botsford's statement for review by Custodial Manager Charles Everett. Marshal advised that Donaldson received a written reprimand for his actions and would be removed from all interior details.

All documents pertaining to this investigation are retained in the files of this office.

Investigation closed.

Glenn Hester
Security Investigations

cc: Bob Matheison
    Phil Smith
    Bill Sullivan
    Greg Weeks
/lh

FLORIDA DEPARTMENT OF LAW ENFORCEMENT

Pursuant to federal r   on (28 CFR 20) this record may be used only for the ;   purpose for which it
has requested. Charge   ud dispositions as coded herein reflect standardized unir   fense and disposition
classifications for computerized criminal history records. More detailed and specific information may be available
from contributors. The department does not warrant that these records are comprehensive or accurate, only that
this record contains all information on the subject that the department has received and is presently authorized
by law to disseminate.

POST OFFICE B
TALLAHASSEE, FLA
PHONE 9

REPORT FOR STATE INFORMATION BUREAU   BATCH 19941017001

THE FOLLOWING RECORD IS ASSOCIATED WITH TRANSACTION: 2
CONTROL NBR: M   NAME: FELICIANO, ESSENE

SID NBR: 3193625   PURPOSE CODE:P   PAGE NBR: 1

BECAUSE ADDITIONS OR DELETIONS MAY BE MADE AT ANY TIME,
A NEW COPY SHOULD BE REQUESTED WHEN NEEDED FOR FUTURE USE

              - FLORIDA   CRIMINAL   HISTORY -

NAME   STATE ID NO.   FBI NO.   DATE REQUESTED
FELICIANO, ESSENE   FL-03193625   10/18/94

SEX RACE BIRTH DATE HEIGHT WEIGHT EYES HAIR BIRTH PLACE   SKIN
M   W   01/26/72   6'02'' 200   BRO   BLK   NY

FINGERPRINT CLASS   SOCIAL SECURITY NO.   MISCELLANEOUS NO.   SCR/MRK/TAT
09 TT 03 05 03
12 54 05 06 02

   IN AFIS - 2

OCCUPATION   ADDRESS   CITY/STATE
DISHWASHER   5041 FREDRICK AVE   W MELBOURNE, FL

AKA   DOB   SOC   SCR/MRK/TAT
                                        089-50-8879

ARREST- 1   12/24/90   OBTS NO.-0002493387
    ARREST AGENCY-SARASOTA POLICE DEPARTMENT   (FL0580100)
       AGENCY CASE-96483   OFFENSE DATE-
       CHARGE 001-SHOPLIFTING-
              STATUTE/ORDINANCE FL812-015   LEVEL-
              DISP-TURNED OVER TO ANOTHER AGENCY
                  FL0580000

ARREST- 2   03/09/91   OBTS NO.-0001953250
    ARREST AGENCY-SARASOTA COUNTY SHERIFF'S OFFICE   (FL0580000)
       AGENCY CASE-86369   OFFENSE DATE-03/09/91
       CHARGE 001-RESISTING LEO-WO VIOL
              STATUTE/ORDINANCE FL843-02   LEVEL-MISDEMEANOR
       CHARGE 002-LARC-PETTY
              STATUTE/ORDINANCE FL812-014   LEVEL-MISDEMEANOR

Disney employee Essene Feliciano was caught peeping on women changing their clothes. Despite his actions and this extensive criminal record, he kept his job.

FLORIDA DEPARTMENT OF LAW ENFORCEMENT

Pursuant to federal re...on (28 CFR 20) this record may be used only for the s... purpose for which it was requested. Charge...nd dispositions as coded herein reflect standardized uniform...rfense and disposition classifications for computerized criminal history records. More detailed and specific information may be available from contributors. The department does not warrant that these records are comprehensive or accurate, only that this record contains all information on the subject that the department has received and is presently authorized by law to disseminate.

POST OFFICE B
TALLAHASSEE F
PHONE 90...

SID NBR: 3193625   PURPOSE CODE:P   PAGE NBR: 2

```
ARREST-   3    04/03/91     OBTS NO.-0001953739
    ARREST AGENCY-SARASOTA COUNTY SHERIFF'S OFFICE                    (FL0580000)
    AGENCY CASE-00086369                    OFFENSE DATE-04/03/91
    CHARGE 001-VEH THEFT-AUTO
              STATUTE/ORDINANCE FL812-014        LEVEL-FELONY
JUDICIAL-
    AGENCY-12TH CIRCUIT COURT - SARASOTA                    (FL058015J)
    CHARGE 001 -COURT SEQ                    COURT NO.-91000937FA
       SUPPLEMENTAL ARREST DATA-
    PROSC DATA-SAME AS ABOVE
              DISP DATE-05/02/91               DISP-FILED
       COURT-DATA-SAME AS ABOVE
              DISP DATE-01/07/93               DISP-GUILTY/CONVICTED
              COUNSEL-PUBLIC     TRIAL-NONE    PLEA-NOLO-CONTENDRE
              SENT DATE-01/07/93
                        888
              PROBATION- 1Y                    COMM CONTROL-
```

```
ARREST-   4    07/01/92     OBTS NO.-0005027872
    ARREST AGENCY-ORLANDO POLICE DEPARTMENT                    (FL0480400)
    AGENCY CASE-169421                    OFFENSE DATE-07/01/92
    CHARGE 001-BATTERY-LEO-
              STATUTE/ORDINANCE FL784-01        LEVEL-FELONY
    CHARGE 002-RESISTING LEO-W VIOL
              STATUTE/ORDINANCE FL843-01        LEVEL-FELONY
    CHARGE 003-LOITER AND PROWL-
              STATUTE/ORDINANCE FL856-021       LEVEL-MISDEMEANOR
JUDICIAL-
    AGENCY-9TH CIRCUIT COURT - ORLANDO                    (FL048015J)
    CHARGE 002 -COURT SEQ                    COURT NO.-CRO920006892A
       SUPPLEMENTAL ARREST DATA-
              STATUS-                          LEVEL-        3RD DEG
    PROSC DATA-AMENDED      ,RESISTING LEO-RESISTING OFFICER
              STATUTE/ORDINANCE-FL843-02        LEVEL-MISDEMEANOR,1ST DEG
              DISP DATE-08/21/92               DISP-FILED
       COURT-DATA-SAME AS ABOVE
              DISP DATE-03/02/93               DISP-GUILTY/CONVICTED
              COUNSEL-PUBLIC     TRIAL-NONE    PLEA-NOLO-CONTENDRE
              SENT DATE-03/02/93
              CONFINEMENT-               6M   ,JAIL
                        002       ,CRO920006892A  363
              SUSPENDED SENT-                   CREDITED TIME-       1D
```

```
ARREST-   5    08/25/92     OBTS NO.-0000482407
    ARREST AGENCY-LAKE COUNTY SHERIFF'S OFFICE                    (FL0350000)
    AGENCY CASE-46795                    OFFENSE DATE-08/25/92
    CHARGE 001-PROB VIOLATION-REF GRAND THEFT AUTO
              STATUTE/ORDINANCE FL948-06        LEVEL-
```

FLORIDA DEPARTMENT OF LAW ENFORCEMENT

Pursuant to Section... in 28 CFR 201 this record may be used only for the specific purpose for which it was requested. Charges and dispositions as coded herein reflect standardized uniform charge and disposition classifications for computerized criminal history records. More detailed and specific information may be available from contributors. The department does not warrant that these records are comprehensive or accurate, only that this record contains all information on the subject that the department has received and is presently authorized by law to disseminate.

POST OFFICE BOX
TALLAHASSEE, FLA
PHONE 904-4...

SID NBR: 3193625   PURPOSE CODE:P   PAGE NBR: 3

            DISP-HELD
                FL0580000

ARREST- 6   04/11/94   OBTS NO.-0006058912
    ARREST AGENCY-ORANGE COUNTY SHERIFF'S OFFICE   (FL0480000)
    AGENCY CASE-52911   OFFENSE DATE-04/11/94
    CHARGE 001-BURG-
            STATUTE/ORDINANCE FL810-02   LEVEL-FELONY
    CHARGE 002-INDECENT EXPOSURE-
            STATUTE/ORDINANCE FL800-03   LEVEL-MISDEMEANOR

ARREST- 7   05/30/94   OBTS NO.-0003034988
    ARREST AGENCY-WEST MELBOURNE POLICE DEPARTMENT   (FL0051600)
    AGENCY CASE-940504050   OFFENSE DATE-05/30/94
    CHARGE 001-BATTERY-DOM
            STATUTE/ORDINANCE FL784-03   LEVEL-MISDEMEANOR
            DISP-TURNED OVER TO ANOTHER AGENCY
            FL0050000 NO 168410

WHEN EXPLANATION OF A CHARGE OR DISPOSITION IS NEEDED, COMMUNICATE
DIRECTLY WITH THE AGENCY THAT CONTRIBUTED THE RECORDS.
THIS CONTAINS FLORIDA RECORD ONLY.
UNKNOWN AS TO NATIONAL RECORD STATUS.
THE USE OF THIS RECORD IS CONTROLLED BY STATE AND FEDERAL REGULATIONS.
IT IS PROVIDED FOR OFFICIAL USE ONLY AND MAY BE USED ONLY FOR THE
PURPOSE REQUESTED. THIS RECORD MAY BE USED FOR CRIMINAL JUSTICE PURPOSES
AS DEFINED BY THE NCIC ADVISORY POLICY BOARD AND CODE OF FEDERAL REGULATIONS.
END OF RECORD

ESSENE FELICIANO   EPCOT Center Custodial

On 8/27/92, Feliciano was observed peering into the Morocco
Entertainment trailer by a dancer. Feliciano denied looking
in the window
No action was taken.

400009

This summary and report concerning Essene Feliciano peeping on a fellow employee indicate "no action was taken."

SUPPLEMENTAL REPORT ☒ INITIAL REPORT CONTINUED ☐		PAGE 1 OF 2

INCIDENT LOITERING & PROWLING	RELATED REPORT NUMBER	REPORT NUMBER

TIME RECEIVED 2109	TIME DISPATCHED 2109	TIME ARRIVED 2115	TIME IN-SERVICE 2300		DATE: AUG 27 1992

Subject: NAME (Last, First, Middle) FELICIANO, ESSKNR   Age 20   DOB 1-26-92   Race HISPANIC   Sex M

ADDRESS Res. 38811 MCKINNON RD. LADY LAKE FL   Zip   Phone 753-8639

Bus.   Zip   Phone

Height 6-2   Weight 195   Hair BRN   Eyes BRN   Complexion DARK   Occupation CUSTODIAL

Shirt CUSTODIAL   Pants   Shoes COSTUME   Dress — WHITE   Oddities

Quan.	Brand Name	Description - Serial No.	Value Stolen	Value Recovered	Value Demanded
			$	$	$

AT 2115 HRS, AUG. 27, 1992, I RESPONDED TO THE MOROCCAN ENTERTAINMENT TRAILER, LOCATED IN THE REAR OF THE MOROCCAN PAVILION TO ASSIST MOTOR 11 HOSTESS, STACY GREGER, WHO WAS DISPATCHED TO INVESTIGATE A REPORTED PROWLER PEERING INTO THE TRAILER WINDOWS.

UPON ARRIVAL I WAS MET BY HOUDA KAMARI AND ABDELALI AJRAOUI, MOROCCAN CAST MEMBERS WHO REPORTED OBSERVING CUSTODIAL HOST, ESSANE FELICIANO, TAKER, LOITERING BEHIND THE ENTERTAINMENT TRAILER AND PEERING THROUGH THE REAR WINDOW AT KAMARI WHO WAS REPORTEDLY CHANGING CLOTHES.

FURTHER INVESTIGATION REVEALED FELICIANO WAS OBSERVED, BY KAMARI, STANDING OUTSIDE THE TRAILER WINDOW WHEN SHE OBSERVED THE CURTAIN MOVE AND SHE WENT TO THE WINDOW AND PULLED BACK THE CURTAINS, AS REPORTED IN HER ATTACHED STATEMENT.

ADDITIONAL INFORMATION REPORTED BY ABDELALI AJRAOUI ALLEGED THAT HE OBSERVED FELICIANO RUNNING FROM BEHIND THE TRAILER AFTER KAMARI ADVISED HIM OF SEEING FELICIANO AT THE WINDOW, AS REPORTED IN HIS ATTACHED STATEMENT.

AT 2125 HRS FELICIANO ACCOMPANIED ME TO EPCOT CENTER SECURITY INVESTIGATIONS OFFICE. AT 2130 HRS EPCOT CENTER CUSTODIAL SUPERVISION WAS NOTIFIED. CUSTODIAL REST. SUPERVISOR ROBERT SIMANSKI, DEPT 5W1, EPCOT CENTER WAS CONTACTED AND RESPONDED TO EPCOT CENTER INVESTIGATIONS WHERE HE WAS APPRISED OF THE INCIDENT. FELICIANO DENIED THE ALLEGATIONS AND FREELY GAVE A WRITTEN STATEMENT REGARDING HIS PRESENCE THERE AND ACTIONS, AFTER DECLINING A UNION REPRESENTATIVE. FELICIANO'S STATEMENT IS ATTACHED WITH THIS REPORT.

Security Hostess Name (Print) I.D. Number LISENBY, KEITH #922	Reviewed by Signature	Date	Total	404072
Referred To:	Month	Day	Year Property Recovered	

CONTINUATION 3582 PAGE 2 OF 2

Related Report: LOITERING + PROWLING

DATE MO 8 DA 27 YR 92

☐ CRIME REPORT   ☐ STATEMENT   ☒ OCCURRENCE REPORT   ☐ S.I.

FELICIANO WAS RELEASED TO ASST. SUPERVISOR ROBERT SIMANSKI WHO INSTRUCTED FELICIANO TO DEPART FOR HOME.

SIMANSKI REPORTED NO FURTHER ACTION WOULD BE TAKEN REGARDING FELICIANO AT THIS TIME AND THAT FELICIANO WOULD RETURN TO WORK AS SCHEDULED.

AT APPROXIMATELY 2000 HRS, DATE, ASST. SUPERVISOR OF MOROCCO, NAIMA S'MIRI WAS CONTACTED AND APPRISED OF THE INCIDENT.

Signature: Keith Simmby #9928   Report No: 404073

INVESTIGATIVE SUMMARY		REPORT NUMBER: IS-14-08-9
First and Final	CLASSIFICATION Confidential	DATE Sept. 25,

SUBJECT Voyeurism

This investigation was initiated on 8/15/92 at 1730 hours when D[
village Marketplace Merchandise Host Harvey Cooper, Dept. 509, Captai[
Tower, HD 3/14/91, DOB 3/29/67, advised that on 8/11/92 he had observ[
Maintenance Host looking into the top of the fitting rooms during ope[
hours. Cooper observed the host in the stockroom of the Captain's To[
on a ladder, looking over the top of the fitting rooms. The fitting [
do not have ceilings, but do have plastic grates.

The subject was subsequently identified as Vincent Amato, Dept.
Marketplace Maintenance, HD 7/1/91, DOB 1/19/59. Cooper stated that
fitting rooms were occupied with two female guests approximately fif[
sixteen years old.. Cooper watched Amato for two to three minutes bef[
saying anything. When Amato realized he was being watched he climbed
the ladder and opened an electrical box that was approximately four a
half feet off the floor. Cooper had noticed that Amato frequents the
and is constantly in and out of the stockroom.

On 8/16/92 at 1745 hours Donald (Chip) Koepke, Dept. 509, Mercha[
Captain's Tower, HD 12/15/91, was interviewed and stated he had witn[
Amato looking into occupied fitting rooms. Koepke stated that on 8/1[
he observed Amato looking directly into an occupied fitting room fro[
stockroom. Koepke further stated that Amato was in and out of the
Captain's Tower stockroom throughout the evening on 8/12/92.

On 8/16/92 Tracey Moskala, Dept. 509, also witnessed Amato look.
into occupied fitting rooms at the Captain's Tower. Moskala stated
8/7/92 or 8/8/92 she entered the stockroom and had observed Amato on
ladder by the fitting rooms. Moskala further stated that Amato had

Three Disney employees report seeing Disney janitor Vincent Amato secretly peeping on female guests—including young teenagers—as they tried on clothes in a Magic Kingdom changing room. As the security report makes clear, Disney did not contact the police or even fire Amato for these offenses.

INVESTIGATIVE SUMMARY			REPORT NUMBER IS-14-08-
First and Final	CLASSIFICATION Confidential		DATE Sept. 25,
SUBJECT Voyeurism			Page two

left hand on the fluorescent light above the fitting rooms. Moskala

that Amato's torso was twisted, facing the fitting rooms with his ri

hand on the grating. Moskala stated that Amato is at the Captain's '

three times a week and in the Captain's Tower three to four times a '

On 8/18/92 at approximately 1510 hours Investigator Ed Vercamen

interviewed Amato after he declined a shop steward. Amato denied lo

into occupied fitting rooms and any wrongdoing. Amato was released

Dickerson, Maintenance Supervisor, who placed him on suspension.

On 8/27/92 I was advised by Mike Davis, Employee Relations that

was given a written record and transferred to Dept. 516, Team Disney

Building Maintenance.

All documents pertaining to this investigation are retained in

files of this office.

Investigation closed.

Frank Ragiacorte
Security Investigations

cc: Art Levitt
    Phil Smith
/lh

400018

CONFIDENTIAL

ATOR ASSIGNED:			DATE:	SUSPENSE DATE:

(handwritten form — Disney security report)

Date: 12-31-90 — *SEELY*

Classification: Suspicious Circumstance

Date of Occurrence: 12-31-90

Date of Complaint: 12-31-9?

SUMMARY OF INVESTIGATION

Information contained in this file is confidential. *M. [initials]*

12-31-90 / Investigators Michael Catins and Diane Heller observed subject seated on bench at board walk between Aruba and Barbados at 2105 hours. Subject departed the area immediately after Heller + I passed. Subject was followed thru Aruba to his vehicle, which was parked in the North end of Aruba by woods. Subject identified as Seeley, Richard F. Dept 3AS, H.Q. 5-21-88, D.O.B 7-17-49. Seeley was entering a Dark Blue Pontiac 600 4dr, with Florida Temporary Tag E-458964. Seeley stated he had been jogging around the lake and stopped on the bench to rest. Seeley was advised of W.D.W Policy regarding loitering on property after working hours. Seeley departed the area. It was obvious that Seeley had not been running. He was wearing blue jeans, a grey T-Shirt and tennis shoes with no socks. Subject was not perspiring as he would be if he was running. Additional. I observed Seeley at the Grand Floridian Beach Resort on 8-17-90 at 2215 hours. Subject was walking behind building #8 and appeared to be looking in the area on of the sliding windows in the rooms. Seeley stated he was just out for a walk. Seeley advised of

CLOSED	☐ UNFOUNDED	☐ RECOVERY	☐ OTHER		CLOSED TO IS #

400050

In this initial Disney security report, company investigators had a positive ID from a guest that Disney employee Richard Seeley was exposing himself to guests in the park. The report notes that Seeley had been caught before peeping into guest bedrooms at night. Despite this evidence and Seeley's long criminal record on similar charges, Disney did nothing.

CONTINUATION PAGE 2 OF 2

Related Report: Suspicious Circumstance

DATE MO DA YR: 7 23 90

☐ CRIME REPORT ☐ STATEMENT ☑ OCCURRENCE REPORT ☐ S.I.

Aruba Village parking Area. The subject was identified as: Richard P. Seeley Dept 345, Contemporary Florist, H.D 5-21-8. D.O.B 7-17-49. Seeley stated that he had been jogging around the lagoon at the Caribbean Beach Resort. Seeley was wearing blue jeans, a army T-Shirt and Tennis Shoes (Non running type). Nor was Seeley perspiring, indicating that he had not been jogging. Seeley was advised of W.D.W policy as it pertains to off Duty Employees loitering in guest areas.

Additionally, on 8-17-90, this writer discovered Seeley walking behind building number eight, Grand Floridian Beach Resort at 2230 hours. Seeley claimed at that time that he was just out for a walk. Seeley was also advised of W.D.W Policy by this writer at that time. Seeley was parked at the Polynesian Village Resort when he was contacted at the Grand Floridian. Security Asst Supervisor Andy Yevchak notified. Caribbean Beach Resort Duty Manager notified.

400051

Signature: Michael Shaw I-12 9064

Report No:

This Disney Security Occurrence Report from the company's security files describes the first known flashing case involving Disney employee Richard Seeley. Disney fired Seeley more than a year later, after numerous other instances in which he flashed guests.

CONTINUATION PAGE 2 OF____

Related Report: Seeley, Richard E-

DATE MO DA YR: 1 3 91

☐ CRIME REPORT   ☐ STATEMENT   ☐ OCCURRENCE REPORT   ☒ S.I.

Policy and departed towards the Polynesian Resort where I-believe his vehicle was parked. On 12-30-90, A guest of the Caribbean Beach Resort alledged that a w/m subject, 6'2" Redish hair exposed himself on the boardwalk between Aruba and Barbados. When the guest walked up to the boardwalk, the subject was seated on the same bench where Seeley was found on 12-31-90. Seeley matches the description except for the hair color. The boardwalk area is poorly lighted and the guest was not positive of the description. Investigations Supervisor notified. O.C.S.O detective Dave Clark notified and stated he would verify if Seeley had a previous criminal history on file for similar offenses.

1-3-91 / OCSO Det Clark counsel subject Seeley does have previous arrest records on lewd conduct charges, Indecent exposure, Loitering & Prowling, Resisting arrest w/o violence and wearing a mask while committing an offense. Subject currently employed by W.D.W company. Carl Booth notified.

400052

Signature:____   Report No:

CHANGE CO.
RECORDS
CLERK OF COURT
886-2392

1459

REPORTED 2300	SECURITY DEPT. — OCCURRENCE REPORT		PAGE 1 OF 1	
COMPLETED 0020	LOCATION POLYNESIAN RESORT — SOUTH BEACH		DATE 1 23 92	
NAME SEELEY RICHARD . W/M 7-11-49 DOH 5/21/88		AGE	PHONE NO. 354-4500	
ADDRESS SSN 288-48-4942 DEPT 3AY MAIN FLORIST SHOP — SANDLAKE Rd,				
NAME			AGE	PHONE NO.
ADDRESS				
NAME			AGE	PHONE NO.
ADDRESS				
NAME			AGE	PHONE NO.
ADDRESS				

OFFENSE SUSPICIOUS CIRCUMSTANCE	ACTION Contact made	RESULTS Documented.

REMARKS Above subject called in as suspicious by Poly engineering; and, has been called in on numerous previous occasions with no contact made. Tonight he was contacted on the south beach dressed in black ski cap, black jacket, dark blue jogging pants and black combat boots. He said he came to watch the light show on the lake. He was advised of company policy - further investigation to continue. Subject was driving Black Dodge 600 HX2 51C, Rd D50338,

ATTENTION Ann Parsell	SUPERVISOR APPROVAL Kim Manna	OFFICER F. Wilcoxson #9217

29768 0588   SEE REVERSE SIDE FOR LEGEND CODE   (NO CARBON REQUIRED)   WOW Printing Dept

In this Disney Security Occurrence Report, Disney employees report seeing employee Richard Seeley on numerous instances peeping on Disney World guests in their bedrooms.

t.d. 6 12 89
DoB 4-6-57
SSN
Dept 630

WALT DISNEY WORLD COMPANY
P.O. Box 10,000
Lake Buena Vista, Florida 32830-1000

STATEMENT OF WITNESS/SUBJECT

Person Giving Statement			
Name: Kim E. Yates Poly Engineering	Place:	Poly Hotel	
	Date:	1-26-92	
	Time:	6:40 PM	
	Days Off:		

On Thursday 1-23-92 I observed an
Individual walking From The North Side of
Poly Building #10, (Moorea) Toward The Beach on
The north Side of Building #5 (Tonga). I followed
The individual For a Few minutes as he walked.
I have Seen This person many Times in These
same areas, always dressed in The same
manner, (Dark Shirt, Dark pants or shorts
and Black shoes). He has been seen by
me as many as 30 Times over The past
2 years. At least 4-6 Times I informed
either a Supervisor or Duty Manager, or
A security person. This person is always
in a Dark area, never Have I seen Him
In any other area. A description of This
person would be Tall, Dark Hair, Thin.
I Have Seen This person Along The north
Side of Poly Hotel Along The Beaches, From
one end of Hotel To The other. On Thursday
1-23-92 I contacted Security about This individual

SIGNATURE: K. E. Yates

PERSON TAKING STATEMENT:
#9218

WITNESS:

400056

RICHARD SEELEY   Florist Division Office

Seeley was observed on 1/23/92 wandering behind guest rooms.
He had been seen in the same area many times by Kim Yeats of
Maintenance. He claimed to be there to watch a water
pageant. A criminal records check determined Seeley had
been arrested for indecent exposure and was convicted on
4/10/89. Seeley admitted to 4 other arrests for indecent
exposure and loitering and prowling.

On 1/28/92, he was terminated for violation of Company
policy/misconduct detrimental to the Company.

400044

*This Disney Security Summary and Incident Report concerning the Richard Seeley case describes
Seeley's repeated offenses against guests. Despite Seeley's admission of these crimes, his extensive
sex crimes arrest record, and his admission that "he had a problem and needed to seek professional help," Disney never contacted the police.*

SECURITY DEPARTMENT — INCIDENT REPORT		REPORT NUMBER —02-92
STATUS First and Final	CLASSIFICATION Confidential	DATE Jan. 29, 1992
SUBJECT Indecent Exposure		

This investigation was initiated on 1/23/92 at approximately 2300 hours when Investigator Fred Wilcoxson made contact with a W/M subject wearing dark clothing, and wandering around behind guest rooms at Building 10 of the Polynesian Village Resort. The subject was reported by Kim Yates, Dept. 830, Poly Maintenance, HD 6/19/82, DOB 4/6/57. Yates claimed to have observed the same individual on numerous occasions in the same area, always wearing dark clothing.

The subject was identified as Richard Seeley, Dept. 3A4, Florist Division Office, HD 5/21/88, DOB 7/17/49. Seeley explained to Wilcoxson that he had come to the Poly Beach to watch the Water Pageant. Wilcoxson advised Seeley that he was not authorized to be in the guest area and to depart.

Further investigation revealed that Seeley had been arrested in the past for Indecent Exposure, Committing a Crime While Wearing a Mask and Resisting an Officer Without Violence. Public records of the Orange County Courts revealed that on 4/10/89 Seeley was convicted for the above charges and sentenced to six months in the Orange County Jail. The jail time was suspended on the condition that Seeley complete six months of supervised probation, forty hours of community service, attend mental health counseling and pay $242.50 in fees. According to the court records, Seeley satisfied all the conditions of the suspension.

I contacted Emmitt Holtzclaw, WDW Florist Manager, Cathy Chamberlain and Michael Giallella, Employee Relations and apprised them of the case.

On 1/28/92, Investigator Gus Collins and I interviewed Seeley after declining a shop steward. Seeley freely admitted that for approximately two years he has frequented the WDW Resorts with the intent to expose his

APPROVAL

400045

SECURITY DEPARTMENT — INCIDENT REPORT		REPORT NO. SBCM-02-92
STATUS First and Final	CLASSIFICATION Confidential	DATE Jan. 29, 1992
SUBJECT Indecent Exposure		Page two

genitals to guests and on many occasions had in fact exposed himself.
Seeley further admitted to having been arrested on four other occasions for
Loitering and Prowling and/or Indecent Exposure. Seeley stated he was
aware that he had a problem and needed to seek professional help. He
admitted he knew he was violating Company policy and the law, but the
problem had escalated to the point that he could not control it by himself.
Seeley executed a written statement and was released to Floral Assistant
Manager Frank Delia who placed him on suspension.

On 1/28/92 Employee Relations Representative Fredricka Howard advised
me that Seeley would be terminated for Violation of Company
Policy/Misconduct Detrimental to the Company.

All documents pertaining to this investigation are retained in the
files of this office.

Investigation closed.

Randy Watts
Security Investigations

cc: Lauren James
     Vince Sikora
     Phil Smith
     Bob Wacker
/lh

400046

FLORIDA DEPARTMENT OF LAW ENFORCEMENT

Pursuant to federal regul... (28 CFR 20) this record may be used only for the stated purpose for which it was requested. Charges and dispositions as coded herein reflect standardized uniform offense and disposition classifications for computerized criminal history records. More detailed and specific information may be available from contributors. The department does not warrant that these records are comprehensive or accurate, only that this record contains all information on the subject that the department has received and is presently authorized by law to disseminate.

POST OFFICE BOX 1
TALLAHASSEE, FLA. 3
PHONE 904-488-7

REPORT FOR STATE INFORMATION BUREAU   BATCH 19941017001

THE FOLLOWING RECORD IS ASSOCIATED WITH TRANSACTION: 6
CONTROL NBR: M   NAME: SEELEY, RICHARD EUGENE

SID NBR: 1033342   PURPOSE CODE:P   PAGE NBR: 1

BECAUSE ADDITIONS OR DELETIONS MAY BE MADE AT ANY TIME,
A NEW COPY SHOULD BE REQUESTED WHEN NEEDED FOR FUTURE USE

— FLORIDA   CRIMINAL   HISTORY —

NAME	STATE ID NO.	FBI NO.	DATE REQUESTED
SEELEY, RICHARD EUGENE	FL-01033342		10/18/94

SEX	RACE	BIRTH DATE	HEIGHT	WEIGHT	EYES	HAIR	BIRTH PLACE	SKIN
M	W	07/17/49	6'00''	165	BLU	BRO	PA	MED

FINGERPRINT CLASS	SOCIAL SECURITY NO.	MISCELLANEOUS NO.	SCR/MRK/TAT
06 04 02 SR 14	288-48-8942		SC R FGR
04 03 TT 05 18			

OCCUPATION	ADDRESS	CITY/STATE
FIREMAN	22745 CURLE RD	ORLANDO, FL

ARREST-   1   03/12/75   OBTS NO.-
   ARREST AGENCY-ORLANDO POLICE DEPARTMENT   (FL0480400)
      AGENCY CASE-59812   OFFENSE DATE-03/12/75
      CHARGE 001-LOITERING-AND PROWLING
             STATUTE/ORDINANCE FL856-021   LEVEL-MISDEMEANOR

ARREST-   2   04/27/85   OBTS NO.-
   ARREST AGENCY-ORANGE COUNTY SHERIFF'S OFFICE   (FL0480000)
      AGENCY CASE-150908   OFFENSE DATE-04/26/85
      CHARGE 001-INDECENT EXPOSURE-
             STATUTE/ORDINANCE FL800-03   LEVEL-MISDEMEANOR
   JUDICIAL-
      AGENCY-ORANGE COUNTY SHERIFF'S OFFICE   (FL0480000)
      CHARGE 001 -COURT SEQ   COURT NO.-MO853338
         COURT DATA-DISORD CONDUCT-
             STATUTE/ORDINANCE-FL800-03   LEVEL-MISDEMEANOR
             DISP DATE-05/13/86   DISP-CHARGE DISMISSED

Disney employee Richard Seeley's arrest record.

FLORIDA ~~~PARTMENT OF LAW ENFC ~EMENT
Pursuant to federal reg. .n (28 CFR 20) this record may be used only for the state. purpose for which it
was requested. Charges and dispositions as coded herein reflect standardized uniform offense and disposition
classifications for computerized criminal history records. More detailed and specific information may be available
from contributors. The department does not warrant that these records are comprehensive or accurate, only that
this record contains all information on the subject that the department has received and is presently authorized
by law to disseminate.

POST OFFICE BOX 148
TALLAHASSEE, FLA. 323(
PHONE 904-488-7651

SID NBR: 1033342   PURPOSE CODE:P   PAGE NBR: 2

ARREST-   3   02/05/86   OBTS NO.-
    ARREST AGENCY-ORANGE COUNTY SHERIFF'S OFFICE   (FL0480000)
      AGENCY CASE-150908   OFFENSE DATE-02/05/86
      CHARGE 001-INDECENT EXPOSURE-
              005 CNTS,
              STATUTE/ORDINANCE FL800-03   LEVEL-MISDEMEANOR

ARREST-   4   10/09/89   OBTS NO.-0001903125
    ARREST AGENCY-ORANGE COUNTY SHERIFF'S OFFICE   (FL0480000)
      AGENCY CASE-150908   OFFENSE DATE-10/09/89
      CHARGE 001-INDECENT EXPOSURE-
              STATUTE/ORDINANCE FL800-03   LEVEL-MISDEMEANOR
      CHARGE 002-RESISTING LEO-WO VIOL
              STATUTE/ORDINANCE FL843-02   LEVEL-MISDEMEANOR
      CHARGE 003-WEAR MASK WHL COMMIT OFF
              STATUTE/ORDINANCE FL775-0845   LEVEL-

WHEN EXPLANATION OF A CHARGE OR DISPOSITION IS NEEDED, COMMUNICATE
DIRECTLY WITH THE AGENCY THAT CONTRIBUTED THE RECORDS.
THIS CONTAINS FLORIDA RECORD ONLY.
UNKNOWN AS TO NATIONAL RECORD STATUS.
THE USE OF THIS RECORD IS CONTROLLED BY STATE AND FEDERAL REGULATIONS.
IT IS PROVIDED FOR OFFICIAL USE ONLY AND MAY BE USED ONLY FOR THE
PURPOSE REQUESTED. THIS RECORD MAY BE USED FOR CRIMINAL JUSTICE PURPOSES
AS DEFINED BY THE NCIC ADVISORY POLICY BOARD AND CODE OF FEDERAL REGULATIONS.
END OF RECORD

APPENDIX C

Mickey's Firehouse

IN THE UNITED STATES DISTRICT COURT
FOR THE MIDDLE DISTRICT OF FLORIDA
ORLANDO DIVISION

ERNEST JAY PHILLIPS and
BELINDA PHILLIPS, his wife,

    Plaintiffs,

vs.   CASE NO: 96-560-CIV-ORL-18

REEDY CREEK IMPROVEMENT
DISTRICT, WALT DISNEY
WORLD CO., a foreign
corporation, JOHN BEST, in his
individual and official capacity
as Manager of Reedy Creek
Fire Services, GENE RIVERS,
in his individual and official capacity
as former District Manager of Operations
for Reedy Creek Fire Services,
JOHN HOWE, in his individual and
official capacity as former district
Manager of Training for Reedy Creek
Fire Services and LT. BRUCE JOHNSON,
individually and in his official capacity,

    Defendants.

_____/

AFFIDAVIT

STATE OF FLORIDA:

COUNTY OF LAKE:

    BEFORE ME, the undersigned authority, this day personally appeared VIRGIL

KENDRICK, to me personally known or who has produced _FL DL K536-85 -_

_41-221-00_____ as identification, who first being duly sworn, deposes and says:

Paramedic Virgil Kendrick, who worked at a Disney firehouse in the shadow of Cinderella's Castle, describes in this July 29, 1997, sworn affidavit the sexual attacks he witnessed. He also mentions that the attacks were announced beforehand over the public address system.

1. That I am over the age of eighteen (18) years and have personal knowledge of the matters contained herein.

2. I was employed as a paramedic by REEDY CREEK IMPROVEMENT DISTRICT and WALT DISNEY WORLD CO. from approximately May of 1970 to April of 1984.

3. For part of the time I was employed as a paramedic, I worked on the same shift and at the same station as ERNEST JAY PHILLIPS.

4. I witnessed ERNEST JAY PHILLIPS being harassed by BRUCE JOHNSON and Ralph Smith on several occasions in the bathroom at the Reedy Creek Fire Station. On several occasions, MR. PHILLIPS had completed taking a shower, but had only a towel wrapped around him when his towel was pulled off and he was thrown to the ground by BRUCE JOHNSON and Ralph Smith. On one separate occasion, when MR. PHILLIPS' towel had been pulled off and he was thrown to the ground, BRUCE JOHNSON threatened to anally penetrate MR. PHILLIPS with a hot dog.

5. On numerous occasions, I heard BRUCE JOHNSON announce over the public address system at the Reedy Creek Fire Department that a sphincter viewing or viewing would be occurring. This announcement was made on a regular and continuous basis during the last year or two of my employment.

2

6.   While working at the Reedy Creek Fire Station, I heard MR. PHILLIPS complaining about and talking to Bill Campbell about the harassment and abuse of MR. PHILLIPS by BRUCE JOHNSON. Mr. Campbell stated that MR. PHILLIPS would have to handle the situation himself.

FURTHER AFFIANT SAITH NOT.

_____
VIRGIL KENDRICK

SWORN TO AND SUBSCRIBED before me this 29 day of _____July_____,
1997.

Margo L Glasgow
My Commission CC620039
Expires February 9, 2001

_____
NOTARY PUBLIC
STATE OF FLORIDA AT LARGE
PRINT NAME: _Margo L Glasgow_
COMMISSION NO: _CC620039_
COMMISSION EXPIRES: _2|9|2001_

IN THE UNITED STATES DISTRICT COURT
FOR THE MIDDLE DISTRICT OF FLORIDA
ORLANDO DIVISION

ERNEST JAY PHILLIPS and
BELINDA PHILLIPS, his wife,

    Plaintiffs,

vs.   CASE NO: 96-560-CIV-ORL-18

REEDY CREEK IMPROVEMENT
DISTRICT, WALT DISNEY
WORLD CO., a foreign
corporation, et. al.,

    Defendants.
_____/

AFFIDAVIT

STATE OF FLORIDA:

COUNTY OF ___DADE___ :

    BEFORE ME, the undersigned authority, this day personally appeared

LAWRENCE E. JESSUP, JR. to me personally known or who has produced _____

___Fla Drivers Lic___ as identification, who first being duly sworn,

deposes and says:

1

Lawrence Jessup, a labor negotiator for the firefighters that work at Disney World, describes in this August 14, 1997, sworn affidavit how he brought the firehouse sexual attacks to the attention of senior Disney and Reedy Creek officials on numerous occasions. Disney did nothing to fix the problem.

1.   That I am over the age of eighteen (18) years, and I have personal knowledge of the matters contained in this Affidavit.

2.   In both 1989 and 1992, I was hired by The Reedy Creek Firefighters' Association, Local No. 2117, to assist in negotiating a labor agreement with Reedy Creek Improvement District. I attended the negotiations for the firefighters' labor agreements that went into effect in 1989 and 1992. The negotiations were also attended by Jerry Montgomery, an employee of Walt Disney World Company, who acted as a labor negotiator for Reedy Creek Improvement District in 1989 and the lead negotiator for Reedy Creek Improvement District in 1992.

3.   In addition, James Puterbaugh, President of The Reedy Creek Firefighters' Association, Local No. 2117, attended the contract negotiations

4.   In addition, many of the firefighter members of The Reedy Creek Firefighters' Association attended the negotiations.

5.   During negotiations for the 1992 labor contract, I brought up the subjects of sphincter viewing, fullering and using harassment as a means to test character, as all of those were practices which I understood were occurring at the fire stations. I specifically discussed the subjects with Mr. Montgomery, Mr. Puterbaugh and Don Helenthall and expressed the need for the conduct to be eliminated.

2

FURTHER AFFIANT SAITH NOT.

_____
LAWRENCE E. JESSUP, JR.

SWORN TO AND SUBSCRIBED before me this _14_ day of August, 1997.

_____
NOTARY PUBLIC
STATE OF FLORIDA AT LARGE
PRINT NAME: _VALERIE D. WOLIVER_
COMMISSION NO: _CC524262_
COMMISSION EXPIRES: _Jan 21, 2000_

```
NOTARY SEAL
VALERIE D WOLIVER
NOTARY PUBLIC STATE OF FLORIDA
COMMISSION NO. CC524262
MY COMMISSION EXP. JAN. 21,2000
```

3

1 sphincter viewing; is that correct?

2   A.   That is correct.

3   Q.   I am asking you a fairly broad question.

4 I will probably come back and ask you some specifics

5 later because I'm taking notes and I may come back

6 and ask you some specifics, but I would like for you

7 to describe to me what occurred on the day when you

8 believe you were sphincter-viewed.

9   A.   They cleared the couches in the dayroom,

10 moved the couches back, because the couches were in

11 the middle of the room there, and they restrained me

12 and put their arms around me. And I couldn't move

13 or go or, you know, walk or, you know. I'm going:

14 What the heck is going on? What are you doing. Get

15 away from me, you know, leave me alone.

16   And they put me out in the middle of the

17 floor of the dayroom. They handcuffed me. They put

18 handcuffs on me. They undid my pants, took down my

19 pants and my underwear, and they forced me to bend

20 over. Vince Byrd --

21   Q.   Who?

22   A.   Vince Byrd, Gerry Vincent Byrd, had a

23 medical gown on, a white lab coat and latex gloves

24 and a surgical mask and all that kind of stuff, and

25 they were all wearing gloves, and they exposed my

Firefighter John Conway, in a March 19, 1997, sworn deposition, describes how he was attacked at the Magic Kingdom firehouse. Conway sued Disney, claiming the attacks violated his civil rights. Disney quietly settled with him in July 1998.

1 anus to everybody in the room.

2   Everybody was laughing, carrying on. They

3 took a pencil, I believe it was a pencil, the eraser

4 end of a pencil, and they forced -- they pushed it

5 around in my butt.

6   Q.   In your anus?

7   A.   Yes.

8   Q.   Now, during this time --

9   MR. REID: Move to strike his narrative.

10   Q.   During this time you indicated that your

11 hands were handcuffed. Were they handcuffed

12 together? Were they handcuffed to something else?

13 Describe for me how you were handcuffed.

14   A.   My hands were handcuffed behind my back.

15   Q.   And you've referred throughout that they

16 physically forced you and they all were wearing

17 gloves. Can you describe for me specifically,

18 giving me the names of who they were?

19   A.   Yes.

20   Q.   Who is that?

21   A.   Dennis New. Gerry Vincent Byrd. David --

22 God, I can't think of his last name. How horrible.

23 Gary Armstrong. Greg Lang.

24   MS. SIGMAN: Is that Lane or Lang?

25   THE WITNESS: Lang, L-a-n-g.

29

1   A.   Not David Grifis. Not David Grifis. I

2 can't think of his name right off. How could I

3 forget his name?

4   Q.   Okay. But another individual also?

5   A.   Yeah.

6   Q.   If the name comes to you during the course

7 of the deposition, if you'll just let us know, I'd

8 appreciate it.

9   Anybody else?

10   A.   No.

11   Q.   Now, the names of the individuals that

12 you've just given us, are those the individuals who

13 actually participated in either physically

14 restraining you or sticking a pencil, eraser end of

15 a pencil, into your anus?

16   A.   Yes.

17   Q.   Were there other individuals in the

18 room --

19   A.   Yes.

20   Q.   -- when this occurred?

21   A.   Yes.

22   Q.   Can you give me the names specifically of

23 those individuals, the ones that you recall?

24   A.   All I can recall, Butch Dougherty and

25 Jimmy Puterbaugh. And the others, I can't even

30

1 remember. I was shocked.

2   Q.   Had you been warned that this was going to

3 happen to you?

4   A.   No.

5   Q.   Had you heard that it might happen to you

6 because you were a new man on the job out there?

7   A.   Yes.

8   MR. REID: Objection, leading.

9   Q.   Who had you heard that from?

10   A.   I can't remember individual names at this

11 time. I was not the only one sphincter-viewed that

12 day. They took another individual.

13   Q.   Okay. Wait just a minute and we'll get to

14 that. I'm going to ask you a specific question

15 about that.

16   Well, do you know which individual of the

17 ones that you named was the one who stuck the eraser

18 end of a pencil into your anus?

19   A.   No, I can't. I don't. At that point I

20 was in shock.

21   Q.   After this occurred, what happened next?

22   A.   They forced me to walk around the station

23 with the handcuffs on, my pants down around my

24 ankles, and my underwear down around my ankles.

25 They led me back to the -- there was two little

31

1 rooms in the back of the bunk room.   One was a

2 laundry room and the other room was a bunk room.

3   The laundry room, they put me and the

4 other individual in, and they handcuffed us to the

5 laundry racks that were in the room.   These were

6 metal laundry racks that they hung the uniforms on.

7 As a matter of fact, the laundry racks are still out

8 at the station at this time, or they still use those

9 same laundry racks.

10   They closed the door, turned the lights

11 off.

12   Q.   Now, let me stop you there for a minute.

13 When you say "they", are you talking about the same

14 individuals that you identified earlier?

15   A.   Yes.   However, in the laundry room, it was

16 Gerry Vincent Byrd and Dennis New.

17   Q.   Just those two?

18   A.   That I can recall.

19   Q.   I mean, do you believe that there were

20 more individuals that you can't recall specifically

21 their name or do you simply recall there only being

22 two other people doing this to you, Vincent and

23 Byrd?   I mean Byrd and New?

24   A.   Right.

25   Q.   After they closed the door and turned the

32

1 lights off, what happened then?

2   A.   Naturally we yelled and screamed and

3 hollered and, you know, hey, let us out of here, you

4 know. You know, we didn't know what the heck was

5 going to go on. I didn't know what was happening.

6 The door was locked. The lights were off, and, you

7 know, I didn't know when they were going to let us

8 out. We were hollering and screaming, and we

9 carried on and hollered and hollered and hollered,

10 let us out, let us out, let us out.

11   Q.   How long were you in there?

12   A.   A good 20 minutes.

13   Q.   And approximately 20 minutes after you had

14 been handcuffed in the laundry room, what happened

15 next?

16   A.   They came in and turned the lights on and

17 let us go.

18   Q.   When you say "they", are you talking again

19 about Byrd and New?

20   A.   Yes, ma'am.

21   Q.   Were there any other individuals that you

22 can recall that came back?

23   A.   No.

24   Q.   You said that there was a -- you were not

25 the only one handcuffed in the laundry room at that

33

1   time.   Who was the other individual?

2   A.   Michael Tucker.   What they did with

3   Michael Tucker before I was sphincter-viewed is --

4   Q.   Well, let me ask you a specific question.

5   On the same day that you were

6   sphincter-viewed, as you've described it, did you

7   witness anyone else being sphincter-viewed?

8   A.   Yes.

9   Q.   Who?

10   A.   Michael Tucker.

11   Q.   And did that occur before or after you

12   were viewed?

13   A.   Before I was viewed.

14   Q.   And where did that occur?

15   A.   In the dayroom.

16   Q.   Same location where it occurred to you?

17   A.   Yes.

18   Q.   Can you describe for me what you saw occur

19   with Michael Tucker?

20   A.   They did the same thing, handcuffs,

21   restrained him, the lab coat with all the gloves and

22   everything.   They forced him to bend over, and they

23   went like they were going into his anus with their

24   hands, and from what I saw, they would come up like

25   this with their fingers.

34

1 Q.   When you say "come up like this" --

2 A.   Where they'd go --

3 Q.   You're moving from the bottom to the top?

4 A.   Right, as they were coming up from your

5 butt with their fingers and lifting up into the

6 air -- it was either chocolate syrup or beans that

7 was on his fingertip.

8 Q.   There was a dark substance on his

9 fingertip?

10 A.   (Nods head)

11 Q.   Is that a yes?

12 A.   Yes.

13 Q.   Would it be correct that you don't know

14 what the dark substance was?

15 A.   Correct.

16   MR. REID: Objection, leading.

17 A.   I did not know what the dark substance

18 was.

19 Q.   What else did you witness occurring with

20 Michael Tucker in the dayroom that day?

21 A.   That was it.

22 Q.   Who --

23 A.   They did the same thing with Michael with

24 his pants down around his ankles and his underwear.

25 They paraded him around with me at the same time.

James Mix   5/21/97

55

1   MR. REID: You'd rather get it over with?

2   THE WITNESS: Yes.

3   MR. REID: Do you need to make a phone

4   call to anybody to let them know --

5   THE WITNESS: No, not yet.

6   MR. REID: Okay.

7   BY MS. BURKE:

8   Q.   Mr. Mix, are you aware of any occasion

9   where Bruce Johnson attempted to get Jay Phillips to

10   come out of a room by using ammonia-soaked rags?

11   A.   Yes.

12   Q.   Tell me about that, please.

13   A.   Jay was in a linen closet, storage closet,

14   and Bruce had us get some towels. He poured ammonia

15   on them and put them at the base of the door. And

16   when the towel was initially put down there, Jay

17   pulled it out, pulled it under the door, and I

18   assume when he smelled the ammonia, he tried to push

19   it back, and Bruce wouldn't allow him to push it

20   back out from under the door.

21   Q.   So you participated in that by getting

22   towels for Mr. Johnson?

23   A.   Yes.

24   Q.   What was the purpose of trying to get

25   Mr. Phillips out of the linen closet?

LIBBY LESTER REPORTING SERVICES
ORLANDO, FLORIDA (407) 425-6543 or (800) 525-3994

Firefighter James Mix, in a May 21, 1997, sworn deposition, describes the sexual attacks he witnessed and how they were announced on the public address system.

```
 1        A.    It was horseplay, fun, you know,

 2   harassment.

 3        Q.    Nobody stopped -- nobody tried to

 4   intervene?

 5        A.    Not generally, no.

 6        Q.    ` And it's your perception that nobody tried

 7   to intervene because they simply thought it was fun

 8   and horseplay and harassment?

 9        A.    My personal perception was either you

10   participated or you became a victim.

11        Q.    Is that why you participated?

12        A.    Yes.

13        Q.    Was it your perception that any of the

14   management personnel out at Reedy Creek knew this

15   was going on?

16        A.    Yes.

17        Q.    What leads you to believe that?

18        A.    It was openly talked about.  When it was

19   said over the PA at times that there was, you know,

20   going to be a viewing, the lieutenant and commander

21   would -- if they were in the dayroom or whenever

22   anything started happening, they would get up and

23   leave.

24        Q.    By lieutenant and commander, who are you

25   referring to?
```

Dep. of James Mix   29

5/21/97

1   Q.   Even what year?

2   A.   Not really.

3   Q.   And where did this occur in the station?

4   A.   This occurred in the dayroom.

5   Q.   And what happened?

6   A.   Several people were chasing Danny Akers to

7   sphincter view him because he was new. I remember

8   Jim Barkhau, Charlie Forsyth and Danny Anderson

9   grabbed him, bent him over the back of the couch.

10   And Jim Barkhau was sitting on his head and pushing

11   his chest into the couch.

12   Danny Anderson and Charlie Forsyth pulled

13   his pants down, and Charlie Forsyth had a

14   laryngoscope and was getting ready to penetrate him

15   with the laryngoscope, and he was stopped by someone

16   else.

17   Q.   Who?

18   A.   Scott Lyons stopped him from doing that.

19   Q.   Where were you while this was going on?

20   A.   I was in the dayroom.

21   Q.   Who else was in the dayroom that you can

22   recall?

23   A.   Scott Lyons. Let's see. You know, it's

24   hard to recall who all else was there.

25   Q.   Do you recall anyone else that was there?

Firefighter James Mix, in a May 21, 1997, sworn deposition, describes the attack he witnessed on fellow firefighter Danny Akers.

SELECTED SOURCE NOTES

PART I: NEW FRONTIERS

Chapter 1: The New Disney

Information concerning Michael Eisner's arrival at Disney, his background, and the early changes at Disney come from Joe Flower, *Prince of the Magic Kingdom* (New York: John Wiley and Sons, 1991); John Taylor, *Storming the Magic Kingdom: Wall Street, The Raiders and the Battle for Disney* (New York: Ballantine Books, 1991); and Aljean Harmetz, "The Man Re-Animating Disney," *New York Times Magazine*, December 29, 1985.

The Jiminy Cricket story and Fred Mayer quote is from Fred Gebhart, "Poison Prevention Month Returning without Jiminy's Help," *Drug Topics*, February 18, 1991. Comments from Spencer Craig, Philip Hawley, and Ken Wales are from their interviews with the authors.

Text of Michael Eisner's April 3, 1998, speech before the American Society of Newspaper Editors (ASNE) was obtained from the ASNE.

Chapter 2: Mickey Rocks: Sex, Drugs, and Satan

Joe Roth's quote is taken from James Bates and Claudia Eller, "How'd Disney Ringmasters Let It Happen?" *Los Angeles Times*, June 27, 1997. Ricky Vodka's visit to Disney Studios is described in the interview Vodka did for "This week's special roast: Humble Gods," *MuCoMo Coffee Break*, April 9, 1997. Information on his friendship with John Wayne Gacy is from the Hollywood Records website www.hollywoodrec.com. Information on Gacy is from "All appeals fail; Gacy is executed," *Chicago Tribune*, May

10, 1994. Biographical information and promotional quotes from Hollywood Records are taken from the Hollywood Records website, as is the Doug Carrion quote. Disney's pulling of the album *Insane Clown Posse* is detailed in "Disney withdrew obscenity-laced rock album," Reuters, June 26, 1997.

Information about the launch of Hollywood Records comes from Melinda Newman, "Hollywood Shows Diversity," *Billboard*, September 29, 1990. Information concerning Prince Akeem is mentioned in Jon Paleles's, "Show time on the stomp," *New York Times*, June 11, 1995. The Lifers Group information came from "H'wood Records Offers Fresh Approach," *Billboard*, February 2, 1991. Hollywood Records marketing schemes, including the distribution of bongs and the nude cyclists, are mentioned in Robert Sam Anson's, "Geffen Ungloved," *Los Angeles Magazine*, July 1995, 49. That article also discusses the Hollywood Records deal with Queen. Sacred Reich's involvement in the drug legalization movement is from the interview Sacred Reich gave with *Metal Rules*, January 1996. Their lyrics are from the album *Heal*. The financial misfortunes at Hollywood Records and the suggestion that it is "the Titanic captained by the Three Stooges," comes from Michael Lev, "Can all those upstart record labels survive?" *New York Times*, January 5, 1992.

The resignation of Peter Paterno is highlighted in "Paterno to Leave Hollywood After Contract Is Up," *Billboard*, September 11, 1993. The case of Mark Hudson comes from information in Danelle Brisebois's interview with *Seconds Magazine*, April 1995. *See also* "A Smashing Time," *Rolling Stone*, May 4, 1995; and Chuck Philips's, "Hollywood Records executive fired amid harassment complaints," *Los Angeles Times*, March 17, 1995. The transition from Paterno to Pfeifer is based on "Hollywood Faces Future with Clean Slate," *Billboard*, June 24, 1995, 16. Michael Eisner and Joe Roth's attendance at Hollywood Records' weekly staff meetings and moving of office to the Disney lot is from Bruce Ornall, "At Walt Disney, Record Label Hits Sour Note," *Wall Street Journal*, May 14, 1997.

Danzig's information and quotations were taken from "Disney to Release Heavy Metal Album," *Las Vegas Review Journal*, October 10, 1996. Danzig's bio and interview were on the Hollywood Records website; "Disney to Release Album by Danzig, Known for Satanic Themes," *Los Angeles Times*, October 18, 1996; and *The New Rolling Stone Encyclopedia of Rock and Roll* (New York: Rolling Stone Press, 1995). Danzig's quotes are from the Hollywood Records website. Steven Batten's "Danzig days are here again [interview with Glenn Danzig]," is found in *Scene*, February 1997. Jon Young's "Danzig Knows the Power of the Dark Side," is found in *Musician Magazine*, April 1993. Information on the Danzig comics are taken from the Danzig homepage. Gil Kaufman's report appeared in *Addicted to Noise*, October 23, 1996. Lyrics are taken from the album Blackacidevil (Hollywood Records, 1996).

NY Loose information comes from Otto Luck's "NY Loose: Big Seeds from the Bad

Apple," *NY Rock,* March 1997. See also Brijitte West's interview with *RockNet,* September 1996, and Steve Flanagan's "NY Loose Backstage," *Backstage Pass,* October 1996. Lyrics are from their Hollywood Records album *Year of the Rat.* Information on the Human Waste Project was obtained from the Hollywood Records website.

All information concerning Flipp and Into Another is from Hollywood Records promotional material, which appears on the Hollywood Records website.

Disney's efforts to hire Whalley from Interscope Records is from Chuck Philips, "Whalley Decides to Return to Interscope," *Los Angeles Times,* May 6, 1997, and Chuck Philips, "Interscope President Quits; May be Headed for Hollywood Records," *Los Angeles Times,* May 3, 1997. The FBI's investigation of Interscope is discussed in Holman Jenkins, "Slumming in Rapland," *Wall Street Journal,* March 18, 1997. For more on the link between Interscope and Disney see Eric Schmuckler, "Ted Field's Green Light," *Forbes,* October 15, 1990.

Disney's purchase of Mammoth Records is detailed in Michael White's "Mammoth Records acquired by Disney," Associated Press, July 22, 1997. Mammoth Records's agreement with the Dust Brothers is based on the Dust Brothers' press release, "Mammoth Records Enters Joint Venture Agreement with Nickelbag Records," January 30, 1998, and was obtained from the PRNewswire. Examples of Mammoth's promotion of drug use are taken from the Mammoth Records website www.mammoth.com. Information concerning the Butthole Surfers was obtained from Kieran Grant, "Flushed with the success of toilet humor," Toronto Sun, October 17, 1996. Lyrics are taken from their album.

Chapter 3: Minnie Makes Room for Marilyn Chambers

The Harlan Ellison story comes from *Harlan Ellison's Stalking the Nightmare* (New York: Berkley Books, 1984). Details of the structure of Viewer's Choice comes from correspondence with Rebecca Kramer, Viewer's Choice, July 8, 1997. Disney's joining the Viewer's Choice partnership is described in "Disney buys into Viewer's Choice," *Broadcasting,* June 26, 1989. The creation of Hot Choice is described in Stuart Miller's "Now: Three-way Choice," Variety, February 15, 1993. Becky LeBeau's move from Playboy to Viewer's Choice is described in "Becky LeBeau, The Queen of Pay Per View," taken from her website. Becky LeBeau's comments are from "Centerfold Model Takes Her Place as 'Queen of Pay Per View,'" Soft Bodies Entertainment press release, May 1, 1997. All movie and program descriptions come from the Viewer's Choice's website: www.ppv.com.

Jim English's move from Viewer's Choice to Playboy TV is mentioned in Kim Mitchell's "Viewer's Choice–Request marriage waiting for Primestar restructuring,"

Cable World, June 6, 1997. Comments from Rebecca Kramer are based on her interview with the authors.

PART II: DISNEY'S SECRET WORLD

Chapter 4: "Safety Comes Last"

This chapter is based on interviews with former Disney employee Spencer Craig; current Disney employees Ben Keen, Sheila Randolph, Todd Eversen, Michael Overcash, Deborah Clark, Murray Cohen, and Frank Kubicki; and Orlando attorneys John Overchuck, John Morgan, and Eric Faddis.

The Disney safety report report is entitled *Walt Disney World Comprehensive Health and Safety Process: Performance Excellence in Action*, February 14, 1994.

Dorian Wright's case information is from John Overchuck, taken from his interview with the authors, as is the information on the Paul Santamaria case. The quote from Mike Potts is taken from Michelle Himmelberg's "Disney lays off workers in its facilities division," *Orange County Register*, July 22, 1997. The fire at Space Mountain is described in Bill Rams's "Disney fire keeps Space Mountain riders grounded," *Orange County Register*, August 7, 1997.

Details of Janet Wilder's death and comments by Mike Provost are from Sharon Bernstein, "Stuntwoman's Death is Ruled an Accident," *Los Angeles Times*, February 2, 1996. Information concerning the death of Matthew Gordy and statement by Dean Fryer of OSHA is from Phillip Brown, "State Fines Disney $5,000 In Death Of Thousand Oaks Man," *Ventura County Star*, April 30, 1998. OSHA inspections of Disneyland are discussed in Chris Woodyard, "New Disney Attraction Drives Up Attendance and Overtime Work," *Los Angeles Times*, April 14, 1995.

Chapter 5: Mickey Mouse Justice

Information concerning the Princess Maha El-Sudari case comes from Tony Pipitone's series on the case for WCPX-TV (CBS) Orlando; Christopher Quinn's "Deputies will be punished for not filing reports on Saudi Princess," *Orlando Sentinel*, November 21, 1995; and Detective Matt Irwin, who served on the Security detail for the 1997 visit. Excerpts from the Security manual are taken directly from the manual.

The structure of Disney World, Reedy Creek, and the two municipalities of Lake Buena Vista and Bay Lake are from an interview the authors conducted with Professor Richard Fogelsong and the testimony of Richard D. Keith, Assistant Fire Chief, Reedy Creek Improvement District, in *Sipkema* v. *Walt Disney World*, Case #CI95-5878. For general literature on the structure of Reedy Creek see Richard Foglesong, "When Disney Comes To Town," *Washington Post Magazine*, May 15, 1994, and Joshua Wolf Shenk,

"Hidden Kingdom: Disney's Political Blueprint," *American Prospect*, Spring 1995.

The 1989 internal Disney memo was an exhibit in that case. Perry Doran's quotes and the details of the Disney World Security Department are taken from his testimony in the Sipkema case. Eric Faddis's quote is taken from his interview with the authors. Terry Hoops's quote is taken from his testimony in the Sipkema case. Matt Irwin's comments were taken from his interview with the authors. Captain Robert Flemming's comments are taken from his testimony in the Sipkema case. Information from the drunk driving case on January 9, 1996, is taken from Tony Pipitone's report on WCPX-TV (CBS-Orlando), November 1997, and an interview with Eric Faddis. Sergeant Barbara Lewis's quotes are taken from her interview with the authors.

Comments concerning Disney's handling of crimes is based on interviews with Detective Matt Irwin and Commander Brad Margeson. Vicki Prusnofsky's and Terri Dorsett's cases are from Mark Fritz's "Walt Disney's other world," an Associated Press story that ran in *The Detroit News*, September 29, 1996.

Michael Gibbons's quotes are from his interview with the authors. The comments of Sheriff Kevin Beary, Ann Davis, and Sergeant Michael Cofield are taken from their testimony in the Sipkema case.

Information on the Shenck case is from an Orange County Sheriff's Office Investigative Report, October 9, 1989, Case #89-239847. Quotes from Detective Sam Bean are from his testimony during the Simpkema case.

Details of the Elena Boruchovas case came from Spencer Aronfeld in an interview with the authors, and the civil suit case file of *Boruchovas* v. *Disney*.

Chapter 6: Disney's Pedophile Problem

The Christopher Laber case information is from an interview with Matt Irwin by the authors, and from the arrest record (Orange County Sheriff's Office Investigative Report, Case #97-281247).

The Christopher Bradley case information is from an interview with Detective Matt Irwin by the authors, and from the arrest record, (Orange County Sheriff's Office Investigative Report, Case #97-138338); from the transcript of Corporal David Caldwell's interview with Bradley on April 7, 1997; and from the transcript of the Bradley-"Nikki" on-line chat provided by the Sheriff's Department.

Quotations are taken from interviews with Matt Irwin, Michael Gibbons, Bill Kelly, Todd Eversen, Spencer Craig, Eric Fortinberry, Sergeant Mark Thompson, Detective Matt Irwin, Professor Jack Enter, Doug Rehman, Rene Bray, Linda Drain, and Sergeant Barbara Lewis.

Details of John Mushacke's arrest came from his Florida Department of Law

Enforcement (FDLE) arrest record Obts. #0007856498 for agency case 242224, an interview with prosecutor Patty Duckworth, and the record of his plea before the court.

Information concerning the February 25, 1996, incident at Disney that was reported too late comes from an Orange County Sheriff's Office Incident Report, Case #96-070741, and the story by reporter Tony Pipitone on WCPX-TV (CBS-Orlando), November 1997.

The story concerning Jimmie Lee Dennis is based on an Orange County Warrant Arrest Affidavit, Case #96-379660, an interview with Linda Drain, and an interview with Rene Bray.

David Wayne Fisher's information comes from interviews with Eric Fortinberry's "Girl Scouts Say Leader Fondled Them," *Orlando Sentinel*, March 30, 1994, C3, and Matt Irwin's "Scouts parents sue schools," *Orlando Sentinel*, April 12, 1995, 1.

Chapter 7: Peeping Toms

Details concerning the Peeping Tom problem in Cinderella's Castle comes from the thirty-volume case file for *Denis K. Liberti, et. al.,* v. *Walt Disney World Company*, Case #94-533-CIV-ORL-19 at the U.S. District Court Middle District of Florida Court House. Terry Lee Neudecker's comments were taken from his testimony in the Liberti case. Rick Bradley's case information was taken from Disney's "Confidential" Incident Report #IS-06-118-91. The quote from Charles Sennewald comes from his report prepared for the Liberti case, dated November 14, 1994. The quotes from Jack Enter come from his interview with the authors and his report prepared for the case, dated November 14, 1994.

Quotes from John Giangrossi are taken from his deposition in the Liberti case and his statement to the Orange County Sheriff's Office, Case #92-007037. The statement by Harry Parsell concerning Peeping Toms in the 1970s is taken from his deposition in the Liberti case.

Comments by Tim Anderson are from his interview with the authors.

Details for the Harvey Cooper case come from Disney's "Confidential" Incident Report, Report #IS-14-08-92. Case information involving Vernon Donaldson comes from Disney's "Confidential" Incident Report, Report #IS-14-04-91. Essene Feliciano's arrest record was obtained from the Florida Department of Law Enforcement. Information for the Richard Seeley case came from Disney's "Confidential" Incident Report #1S 14-03-92; the Investigative Summary, Report #IS-14-08-92; and his statement to Disney Security, dated January 27, 1992.

Chapter 8: Mickey's Firehouse

This chapter is based on the sworn depositions filed in the civil suit *Ernest Jay Phillips and Belinda Phillips* v. *Reedy Creek Improvement District*, Case #96-560-CIV-

ORL-18. These include the depositions of John Conway, March 19, 1997; James Mix, May 21, 1997; Jay Phillips, November 22, 1996; Dante Battilla, June 23, 1997; J.R. Murphy, March 19, 1997; and sworn affidavits by Virgil Kendrick, July 29, 1997, and Lawrence Jessup, August 14, 1997. The authors also relied on Jay Philips's memo to Tom Moses, Reedy Creek Improvement District, September 1, 1995.

Details from the Dante Battilla case comes from his Charge of Discrimination filed with the Florida Commission on Human Relations, January 17, 1995, Charge #150951611. The comment by Dr. Edmund Bartlett comes from his Fitness for Duty Consult Occupational Medical Clinic report, February 15, 1996 on Jay Philipps.

Details of the sexual harassment case brought by Disney's female firefighters comes from their lawsuit, *Lang* v. *Disney* #94-693-CIV-ORL-3ABF-17.

The report by A.W. Coschignano comes in the form of a "Confidential: Attorney-Client and Work Product Privileged" memo dated January 23, 1996, sent by Coschignano to Disney.

PART III: THE CHILDREN'S IDEA FACTORY

Chapter 9: Animation

This chapter is based on interviews with animators Tom Sito, Phil LaZebnik, and Will Finn. The story of Thumbelina's screening and Disney's brand name comes from John Horn, "Can anyone dethrone Disney?" *Los Angeles Times*, June 1, 1997. General information concerning the profitability of Disney animation comes from Nina Munk's, "Disney's magic lamp," *Forbes*, November 22, 1993, and John Horn's "Disney lawsuit shows real power," Associated Press, June 24, 1997. Details of the changing shape of Disney's TV animation comes from Debra Kaufman's "Disney's New Breed of TV Animation," *Animation Magazine*, January/February 1997.

Michael Eisner's minimizing of animation is from Maggie Mahar, "Not-so-magic Kingdom," *Barron's*, June 20, 1994, and Joe Flower, *Prince Of the Magic Kingdom*, (New York: John Wiley and Sons, 1991).

Details of Walt's efforts to maintain the integrity of his animated works comes from Bob Thomas's *Walt Disney: An American Original*, (Hyperion: New York, 1994). Information concerning the possible hidden images in Disney films comes from "The Lion Kink," *The Economist*, September 9, 1995, and John Rex's "Aladdin Exposed," *Movieguide*, March 1995. Comments on Roger Rabbit were taken from "There's Dirt in Those Classics," *Variety*, October 1, 1996.

For a fascinating discussion of The Hunchback and Disney's heroines, see James Bowman, "Disney's Mickey-Mouse Religion," *The Weekly Standard*, July 1, 1996, and Susan Wloszczyna's "Sophisticated animation, story combine for a Quasi-adult film," *USA Today*, June 14, 1996.

Janet Maslin's comments on Mulan are taken from Janet Maslin's "A Warrior, She Takes on Huns and Stereotypes," *New York Times,* June 19, 1998. Comments on gay influence in animation were taken from Tom Provenzano, "The Lion in Summer," *The Advocate,* June 25, 1994. Comments from Deja concerning gay characterizations were taken from Steven Gaines's "Disney Comes Out of the Closet," *Buzz,* May 1995, 68. Comments from actors Ernie Sabella and Nathan Lane were taken from their *New York Times* interview, June 12, 1994. Tom Sito's comment about political correctness was made in an interview with the authors and was expanded on in Tom Sito's "Fight to the Death, But Don't Hurt Anybody! Memories of Political Correctness," *Animation World,* October 1996

Peter Schneider's comments concerning a "mission statement" were taken from "How Disney Keeps Ideas Coming," *Fortune,* April 1, 1996.

Chapter 10: The PC Princess

This chapter is based on interviews with Tom Sito, Will Finn, and Phil LaZebnik. Quotes from other Disney animators involved in Pocahontas are taken from Stephen Rebello, *The Art of Pocahontas* (New York: Hyperion, 1995). See also "Redesigning Pocahontas," *Journal of Film and Television.*

Information on how racial tensions in Los Angeles influenced the film is taken from Stephen Rebello's "Pocahontas: Bringing History to Life," *Animation Magazine,* July 1995.

Chapter 11: The Lyin' King

This chapter is based on interviews with Fred Patten, Fred Ladd, and Tom Sito; correspondence with Takayuki Matsutani, president Of Tezuka Productions; and Fred Schodt. The authors also greatly appreciate permission to use Fred Patten's paper *"Simba vs. Kimba: Parallels Between Kimba, the White Lion and The Lion King."*

Matthew Broderick's quote comes from Charles Burress's, "Uproar Over 'The Lion King,'" *San Francisco Chronicle,* July 11, 1994. The common elements in both projects are also described in "An open letter from Machiko Satonaka," released September 22, 1994. The Japanese animator sent the letter to Disney after *The Lion King* was released.

Biographical information on Osamu Tezuka comes from Frederick Schodt's *Dreamland Japan: Writings on modern manga* (Berkeley, California: Stone Bridge Press, 1996). The quote from *Time* magazine concerning Tezuka came from "A Nation In Search of Itself" *Time,* August 1, 1983 (Special Issue). Disney's claim that they never heard of Tezuka is from Charles Burress's "Disney—'Lion' Is Original," *San Francisco Chronicle,* July 14, 1994.

Michael Eisner's involvement in children's television programming at ABC in the early 1970s is described in Joe Flower, *Prince of the Magic Kingdom*, (New York: John Wiley And Sons, 1991). Disney's version on how it created *The Lion King* comes from Christopher Finch's "The Story of the Lion King," *Animation Magazine*, May/June 1994.

Information concerning Tezuka's awards at animation conferences come from an illustrated souvenir program book, The 18th Annual ANNIE Awards, 1990 (ASIFA-Hollywood). Comments by Takayuki Matsutani are from his letter to the authors, December 3, 1997. The quote by Sadao Miyamoto comes from an interview in a Japanese language magazine, "Japanimation, Bridge U.S.A.: Japanese Info-Tainment Magazine," October 15, 1997 (translation provided by Fred Schodt).

Chapter 12: Tinseltown Theft

Details and quotes from the Daryan Faeroe case come from Roger Roy's "Disney lawyers take dim view of glitter," *Orlando Sentinel*, February 23, 1991; Jeff Brazil's "Pixie Dust Case Takes Not-so-magical turn for Disney," *Orlando Sentinel*, May 16, 1992; and Alex Finkelstein's "Disney settles pixie dust claim," *Orlando Business Journal*, July 24, 1992.

Information and quotes on the SAK story come from Tom Brinkmoeller's "SAK celebrates its 20th year on skit row," *Orlando Business Journal*, September 22, 1997.

Information concerning the "Honey I Blew Up the Kids" case came from "Disney Settles in 'Honey, I Blew Up the Kids' Copyright Suit," Associated Press, January 12, 1994; "Disney settles 'Kid' lawsuit," *Daily Variety*, January 14, 1994; "Disney Settles Lawsuit," Associated Press, January 14, 1994; and "Disney settles copyright lawsuit," *Palm Beach Post*, January 13, 1994.

The Tom Girardi quote is from Robert Welkos's "Jury tells Disney to pay $300,000 in 'Honey' case," *Los Angeles Times*, November 13, 1993,

The Thomas McGlynn quote is from Diane Richard's "Freeze, kid. You need a license for that cake," *Minneapolis-St. Paul City Business: The Business Journal*, March 3, 1997. Details of the daycare center case came from Paul Richter, "Disney's Tough Tactics," *Los Angeles Times*, July 8, 1990, and "Cartoon Figures Run Afoul of Law," *Chicago Tribune*, April 27, 1989. Details of the Winnie the Pooh statue controversy are from Joe Flower's *Prince of the Magic Kingdom* (New York: John Wiley and Sons, 1991).

PART IV: MICKEY'S FLICKS

Chapter 13: Circus Miramax I

Bob Weinstein's quip about not wanting to be Walt Disney is from Lisa Gubernick's "We don't want to be Walt Disney," *Forbes*, October 16, 1989. Harvey Weinstein's confrontation with Scott Hicks is detailed in Peter Richmond, "Up From Down Under," *GQ*, December 1996. An excellent piece on the Weinsteins's early years is Lynn Hirschberg's "The Mad Passion of Harvey and Bob," *New York*, Volume 27, No. 40. The firing of an employee at a softball game and the comment about "Japanese management theory on acid" is from "The good cop/bad cop duo," *Fortune*, October 18, 1993.

Working Girls information is from the *Variety*, May 28, 1986, review and John Pierson's *Spike, Mike, Slackers, and Dykes: A Guided Tour Across a Decade of American Independent Cinema* (New York: Miramax Books, 1995).

The quote by Mark Gill concerning "sex sells" comes from Brendan Kelly, "Miramax News Flash: Sex Sells," *Daily Variety*, September 13, 1995. Miramax's financial difficulties prior to its purchase by Disney is from Judy Brenna's and Michael Fleming's "Shopping Miramax is a trying game," *Variety*, April 26, 1993. The purchase by Disney is discussed in "Maxed Out," *Premiere*, July 1993, and Claudia Eller's and John Evan Frook's "Mickey Munches on Miramax," *Variety*, May 3, 1993. Comments on the film *Fresh* are taken from review by *Variety*, February 7, 1994, and John Frook's "Call Harvey Mickey Mouth," *Variety*, November 29, 1993. The comment by Katzenberg concerning Walt "spinning in his grave" is from "Is Walt Spinning in His Grave?" *Newsweek*, May 31, 1993. Comments by Ralph Winter are from his interview with the authors. Quote by Joe Roth on the partnership comes from Claudia Eller, "On-Screen Chemistry," *Los Angeles Times*, December 1, 1995.

Comments from Patrick McDurrah were taken from his interview with the authors. Comments from John Pierson were taken from John Pierson's *Spike, Mike, Slackers, and Dykes: A Guided Tour Across a Decade of American Independent Cinema* (New York: Miramax Books, 1995).

The plot for *Heavenly Creatures* is from the September 12, 1994,*Variety* review. The struggle with the MPAA over *Clerks* is from Greg Evans's "Dershowitz outlines 'Clerks' rating appeal," *Daily Variety*, October 5, 1994, and John Brodie's "'Clerks' wins an R on appeal," *Daily Variety*, October 12, 1994. The struggle with the MPAA over *The Advocate* is from *Daily Variety*. The conflict over *Pret-A-Porter* appears in *Variety*, December 19, 1994.

Chapter 14: *KIDS*

The single best piece on Larry Clark and *KIDS* is Lynn Hirschberg's "What's the Matter With Kids Today?" *New York*, June 5, 1995. The details of Harvey Weinstein's interest in the picture and Larry Clark's past come from this piece. See also Charl Blignaut, "Sex, drugs and Larry Clark," *Mail and Guardian* (South Africa), February 27, 1997, and their interview with Clark. The comment about "most controversial film" is from John Brodie, "'Kids Causes Clamor," *Variety*, January 27, 1995. See also "Bold Before

Their Time," *Entertainment Weekly*, July 21, 1995, and "Controversy: 'Kids' for Adults," *Newsweek*, February 20, 1995. Comments from Patrick McDurrah come from his interview with the authors. The quotes from D.H. Mader were taken from D.H. Mader's "Lust and Death: The Photos of Larry Clark," *Gayme*, 1995. The comments by Richard Mohr are from his article "The Pedophilia of Everyday Life," *The Guide*, September 1996. The decision to release it unrated is from Thomas R. King's "Miramax Film Heightens Clash With Disney," *Wall Street Journal*, March 30, 1995.

Chapter 15: Circus Miramax II

Information concerning the controversy over *Priest* is taken from Richard Corliss's "God and man in Liverpool," *Time*, April 10, 1995; Marshall Fine's "Catholics upset over 'Priest' portrayal," *USA Today*, February 28, 1997; Anne Thompson's "A Holy War Over 'Priest,'" *Premiere*, March 31, 1995; and James Martin's "Celibacy and Sound Bites," *America*, May 6, 1995. The decision to postpone the release until after Good Friday is from "Release of movie delayed after protest," *Christian Century*, April 19, 1995.

The *Lie Down With Dogs* review quote is taken from *The Advocate*, August 22, 1995. Joe Roth's quote is from Claudia Eller, "On-Screen Chemistry," *Los Angeles Times*, December 1, 1995. Kevin Smith's comments about *Chasing Amy* and inspiration were taken from Allison Gaines's "Chasing Down the Rumors," *Entertainment Weekly* online. See also John Brodie's "'Amy' lands at Miramax," *Daily Variety*, November 3, 1995. Information on Quentin Tarantino is from Peter Biskind's "An auteur is born; director Quentin Tarantino," *Premiere*, November 1994. Joe Baltake's review of "From Dusk Till Dawn" appeared in *The Sacramento Bee*, January 19, 1996. Ralph Novak's comments were taken from Ralph Novak's "The Crow: City of Angels," *People* magazine's website. The *Washington Post*'s comments on *Curdled* are from Desson Howe's "Curdled: Blood Simple," *Washington Post*, October 4, 1996. Spike Lee's views on "Jackie Brown" are taken from Army Archerd's "Spike Lee Disses 'Nigger' Usage," *Variety*, December 17, 1997.

The seven-year Weinstein-Disney contract and Michael Eisner's comments are from Greg Evans's and John Brodie's "Miramax, Mouse Go for Seven More," *Variety*, May 13-19, 1996. Saul Zaentz's comments about the Weinsteins concerning *The English Patient* are from Mr. Showbiz interviews online, 1997.

Information concerning *The House of Yes* came from the review in *Daily Variety*, January 21, 1997, and John Brodie's "Sundance: Miramax Pays $2 million for Incest Movie," *Variety*, January 20, 1997.

Harvey Weinstein's appearance at Vernon Jordan's party is taken from "Stallone Shows Up at Clinton Vacation Party," *Reuters*, August 26, 1997.

Chapter 16: Victor Salva

Protest and comments by Gary Primavera are from John Horn's "Disney director has a pedophile past," an Associated Press story that appeared in the *Washington Times*, October 25, 1995.

Rebecca Winters's quotes were taken from Mike Bygrave's "The Shame of Disney," *Mail on Sunday* (London), January 7, 1996. Quotes by Winters and Birnbaum were taken from Bernard Weinraub's "A Director For Disney Once Jailed in Sex Case," *New York Times*, October 26, 1995. Birnbaum's comments about efforts to "keep an eye out" and the family's response in a press release are from Ted Johnson's "Disney hit with salvo on Salva," *Daily Variety*, November 1, 1995.

Tom Maurstad's review appeared in *The Dallas Morning News*, October 14, 1995. See also the review by Ken Tucker, "A Weirder Shade of Pale," *Entertainment Weekly*, November 10, 1995. Quotes by Lisa Hacker and Sandra Baker were taken from Jeffrey Wells's "A Question Disney Ducked," *Entertainment Weekly*, November 10, 1995.

Rumors of Roger Birnbaum's demise appeared in "A Powder Outrage?" Mr. Showbiz online, November 3, 1995.

PART V: DISNEY'S OTHER FACES

Chapter 17: Mr. Minnie Mouse

Information concerning Minnie Mouse comes from Spencer Craig's interview with the authors, and a current Disney employee's interview with the authors.

Details and quotes concerning gays at Disney comes from Steven Gaines's "Disney Comes Out of the Closet," *Buzz*, May 1995, and R.L. Pela's "Disney steps out," *The Advocate*, April 29, 1997. The *Orlando Weekly* quote is from Jeff Truesdell's "Kingdom come," *Orlando Weekly*, May 25 to 31, 1995. The quote by Elizabeth Birch and her conversation with Michael Eisner is from "Quote, unquote," *The Advocate*, March 4, 1997.

The sum of Gay Day money spent in 1995 comes from "Gay Day," *Orlando Sentinel*, May 29, 1995. Kelly McQuain's quote is from "The Magic Kingdom Invaded!" *Philadephia Gay News*, July 5-11, 1996. Details of Gay Day events come from the Official Web Site of Gay and Lesbian Day at Walt Disney World www.gayday.com. Details of the sights and sounds of Gay Day come from Brad Liston's "'Gay Days' Change Tone of Crowd at Magic Kingdom,'" Reuters, June 8, 1997; Jeff Truesdell's, "And a gay time was had by all," *Orlando Weekly*, June 6-12, 1996; Laura England's "Not thinking straight," *World*, June 17/24, 1995; and James Hannaham's "Deep Disney: Gay Day in the Magic Kingdom," *The Village Voice*, June 27, 1995, and "60,000 gays find it's a small world at Disney," *Detroit News*, June 9, 1997.

Information concerning health care benefits being reduced for employees came from a National Association of Broadcast Employees and Technicians news release "Disney Stockholders Get Strong Message: Don't Waste ABC Money and Workforce, Says NABET," from the PRNewsire, February 24, 1998. Comments by Rich Siwica are taken from Tom Brinkmoeller's "Arbitrator hears Disney, union arguments on partner benefits," *Orlando Business Journal*, July 22, 1996.

Information on Lauren Lloyd comes from "Lauren Lloyd: Disney's Crossover Achiever," *Out*, November 1994. Quotes from Craig Zadan, Neil Meron, and Mark Driscoll come from R.L. Pela's "Disney steps out," *The Advocate*, April 29, 1997.

Chapter 18: Heigh Ho, Heigh Ho...

Information on the Animation Consortium for Child Rights comes from Deborah Reber's "UNICEF draws on Talent to Advance Children's Rights," *Animation World Magazine*, March 1997.

Raids on factories making Disney clothes with child labor is reported in Patrick J. McDonnell's "Sweatshop Items Were for Big Firms, U.S. Says," *Los Angeles Times*, August 26, 1995. Disney was listed as "Greediest" in "The Neediest and the Greediest: Companies that continue to violate human and worker rights," National Labor Committee, November 28, 1997. For details of the Kathie Lee case and sweatshops in general, see William B. Falk's "Dirty Little Secrets," *Newsday*, June 16, 1996, and Barry Bearak's "Kathie Lee and the Sweatshop Crusade," *Los Angeles Times*, June 14, 1996. Information on Haiti comes from Nicole Volpe's "Haitian Labor Advocates Applaud Sweatshop Accord," Reuters News Service, April 14, 1997.

Conditions inside the Keyhinge Vietnam factory comes from *Working Conditions at Keyhinge Toys, Hoa Khanh Industrial Zone, Vietnam* (Hong Kong, April 1997: Asia Monitor Resource Center, Coalition for the Charter on Safe Production of Toys). See also "Disney/McDonald's Linked to Six Cent-an-Hour Sweatshop in Vietnam," National Labor Committee press release, May 6, 1997; Theo Emery's "Group hits Disney, McDonald's over toy factory conditions," *Boston Globe*, May 3, 1997; and "Hong Kong Toy Factory Commits Serious Health and Safety Violations and Unfair Labour Practices in Vietnam," The Coalition for the Safe Production of Toys (Hong Kong, March 4, 1997). Comments from Joe Allen come from his interview with the authors. Information concerning the conditions in the Chinese facilities came from the authors' correspondence with Mr. Chan Kai Wai, Hong Kong Christian Industrial Committee, January 17, 1998. Cases involving Xiao Wang, Xiao Xie, and Xiao Zhou are discussed in *Labour Rights Report on Hong Kong Invested Toy Factories in China No. 2*, Asia Monitor Resource Center, Hong Kong, April 1997. A Disney licensee's firing of Thai workers to replace them with child laborers comes from "Laid off staff rally to win better deal," *Bangkok Post*, September 27, 1996.

Background information on Burma comes from Robert S. Gelbard, Assistant Secretary of State for International Narcotics Enforcement Affairs, Remarks at the State Department Daily Press Briefing, February 28, 1997; Dennis Bernstein's and Leslie Kean's "People of the Opiate: Burma's dictatorship of drugs," *The Nation*, December 16, 1996; and "Doing Business in Burma," *New York Times*, December 16, 1996. See also Amnesty International Report 1997 under "Myanmar." Disney's links to Burma are discussed in Theo Emery's "Boycotting Burma," *Boston Globe*, December 8, 1996. For a detailed discussion of the Burma textile industry and Disney's involvement, *see Dirty Clothes, Dirty System: How Burma's military dictatorship uses profits from the garment industry to bankroll oppression*, (A Report by the Canadian Friends of Burma, Ottawa, 1996). Larry Dohrs's comments came from his correspondence via e-mail with the authors. See also comments of Joe Pang, a Disney licensee, in "Myanmar from the foreign businessman's point of view," *Asia Times*, June 26, 1996. Drug money involvement in the textiles sector comes from the U.S. Department of Commerce, National Trade Data Bank, April 1997. The quote from Chuck Mamiye comes from Theo Emery's "Made in Burma," *Boston Globe*, December 13, 1996. Roy Disney's interest in Burma is described in Yaroslav Trofimov's "Disney's image at risk over ties to Myanmar," *Asia Times*, January 28, 1997.

Concerning Disney's unwillingess to join in pledging to monitor child labor, see authors' interview with Linda Golodner, co-chairman, Apparel Industry Partnership. See also *Garment Enforcement Timeline*, U.S. Department of Labor, 1997, for recent list of companies that have taken the pledge.

Chapter 19: Mickey Mao

Disney's early forays into China in the 1980s, including a deal with Chinese Central Television, is from Julian Baum's "Making Donald a Peking Duck," *Christian Science Monitor*, November 6, 1986. Ovitz's comment about "nation-state" is from "The art of non-communication," *Variety*, December 16-22, 1996.

Nelson Ying's involvement with the China Pavilion and his description of "mainland investors" is from Linda Chong's "Orienting Orlando," *Asia, Inc.*, November 1993. Disney's involvement with the Chinese government media is from "Mickey Mao," *The Economist*, August 3, 1996.

Information on Splendid China comes from Linda Chonga, "Making Florida 'Splendid,'" *Asia, Inc.*, November 1993; and "New Order: China controls Central Florida theme park," *Orlando Sentinel*, January 15, 1994.

China's policy toward Western films is described in "China Cautiously Opens Door to Western Films," *China News Digest*, October 10, 1995, and David DeVoss's "Asia Goes to the Movies," *Asia, Inc.*, March 1995. The commercial expansion into China is described in "Why? Because We Won't Rip You Off," *Los Angeles Times*, June 3, 1993. Disney's invitation to Chinese dignitaries after Tianamen Square is described in Irene Chang's, "China Mayors tout Gains, Seek U.S. Understanding," *Los Angeles Times*, July 23, 1990, and the visit of Zhu Quizhan is outlined in "Mickey Mao?" *Los Angeles Times*, May 21, 1990.

Details of the structure of the Chinese media in the 1980s is from *Censorship Reports, #1: Censorship and Disinformation in the People's Republic of China, 1989* (London: International Centre on Censorship, 1989). Chinese Central Television's description of the 1989 massacre is from *Far Eastern Summary of World Broadcasts*, compiled by the British Broadcasting Corporation, SWB FE/0474, June 5, 1989.

Disney's problems with China over Kundun is described in Doug Tsuruoka's "Spotlight on China as Hollywood pressures Clinton," *Asia Times*, January 24, 1997; "China Threatens Disney over Dalai Lama Movie," *Los Angeles Times*, November 23, 1996; Bernard Weinraub's "Disney Will Defy China On Its Dalai Lama Film," *New York Times*, November 27, 1996; Conor O'Clery's "China open to Disney but not Dalai Lama," *Irish Times*, November 29, 1996; and Martin Walker's "Disney defiant on Dalai Lama film," *The Guardian*, November 27, 1996. The editorial praising Disney on Kundun is "The Mouse Makes a Stand," *New York Times*, November 27, 1996. Ovitz's departure as related to China policy is discussed in Paul Farhi's "Ovitz Departs Disney After 16 Months," *Washington Post*, December 13, 1996, and Anita Busch's and John Brodie's "Eisner's Home Alone," *Variety*, December 16-22, 1996. The editing of the China exhibit at Disney World is discussed in "Tibet disappears on the cutting room floor," *Asia Times*, May 1, 1997. The David Zucker quote is from Joe Mandese, "Is it Magic Kingdom or an Evil Empire?" *Advertising Age*, August 7, 1995.

Earnings from Disney animation in China is from "'Toy Story'; distributed to Chinese Audience," *Animation World*, June 21, 1996. Launching of the China Disney Club is described in "Has Disney Become the Forbidden Studio?" *Businessweek*, August 4, 1997.

Disney's agreement with Chinese National Radio is described in Helen Deal's "Tuning in to China's Wavelength," *Asian Advertising and Marketing*, February 7, 1997; Li Ning's "Disney Comes to China National Radio," *China Culture*, October 1996; and "Winnie Joins in Disney Legend," *Hong Kong Trader*, May 1996 (Information Technology Department of the Hong Kong Trade Development Council).

The visit by Yiu Yat Hung to Orlando is described in Cindy Barth's "Chinese visitor eyes City Hall space, Disney prospects," *Orlando Business Journal*, September 30, 1996. Visit by Eisner to Splendid China is from "Eisner's Splendid China visit sparks more splendid rumors," *Orlando Business Journal*, December 23, 1996.

Nelson Ying's announcing scholarships for Chinese diplomats at the University of Central Florida is from the University of Central Florida's website under "International Student Services hosts open house for new center."

Chapter 20: Don't Know Much About History

Information about Clinton's introduction into the Hall of Presidents and the reworking of the Hall of Presidents by Eric Foner comes from Jon Wiener's "Disney World Imagineers a President," *The Nation*, November 22, 1993, and Otis Graham's "Disney vs. History,"*Chronicle of Higher Education*, September 14, 1994. General information concerning Liberty Square and the Hall of Presidents is from Stephen Fjellman's *Vinyl Leaves: Walt Disney World and America* (Denver: Westview Press, 1992).

Quotes from Howard Zinn come from his book, *A People's History of the United States* (New York: Harper and Row, 1980). Eric Foner's quote concerning this book is taken from the dust jacket. Foner's comments concerning "new history" are drawn from the transcript "Who Owns History?" from the PBS program *Think Tank*, October 7, 1994, and his introduction to the book *The New American History* (Philadelphia: Temple University Press, 1991).*The Nation's* description of Foner is from Jon Wiener, op cit.

The details of the labor teach-ins and Foner's involvement come from Steven Greenhouse's "Labor Leaders and Intellectuals Are Forging New Alliance," *New York Times*, September 22, 1996.

Oliver Stone's quote concerning the origins of the film are from *An Oliver Stone Film: NIXON*, the press package released by Hollywood Pictures, 1995. Oliver Stone's quote about his desire to assassinate Nixon is taken from "Nixon, Disney daughters rip Stone film, call it 'distortion,'" *Associated Press*, December 21, 1995.

Early efforts to develop the film and Stone's "fact-finding trips"are detailed in John Taylor's "Nixon on the rocks," *American Spectator*, March 1996. David Hyde Pierce's quote is from "Pierce fearlessly signs on for Stone's take on 'Nixon,'" *Detroit News*, December 15, 1995. The efforts to ensure the accuracy of the White House setting are taken from *An Oliver Stone Film: NIXON*, the press package released by Hollywood Pictures, 1995.

The fear of litigation, forcing the rewriting of the script, comes from John Taylor, op cit. Stephen Ambrose's comments concerning Nixon's language, drinking, and the footnotes and research for Nixon comes from his review of the screenplay in *The Journal of American History*, March 1996.

Quotes from the film are taken from *Nixon: An Oliver Stone Film*. Includes the *Original Screenplay* by Stephen J. Rivele, Christopher Wilkinson, and Oliver Stone (New York: Hyperion, 1995). Daniel Schorr's quotation is taken from *ABC World News Tonight*, December 20, 1995.

Brett Dicker's quote comes from the Nixon study guide produced by Educational Resources, San Marcos, California, 1995.

Conclusion: The Mouse Betrayed

Michael Eisner's comments are from his 1994 annual report to shareholders and his speech before the American Society of Newspaper Editors, April 3, 1998. (Text was obtained from ASNE.) Quote from Janet Wasko is From Jill Jordan Spitz, "Why Are so many People Roaring Mad at the Mouse Now?" *The Orlando Sentinel*, August 31, 1997. Michael Eisner's comment about the "Appeal of Innocence" is from his speech published in *New Perspectives Quarterly*, Fall 1995.

Quote by Walt Disney concerning money is from Bob Thomas, *Walt Disney: An American Original*, (Hyperion: New York, 1994). *Brandweek* quote is from Rinker Buck, "Now's The Time To Come Along And Join The Lottery," *Brandweek*, April 15, 1991.

Story of cutting off refrigeration is from comments by a current employee. Story in which workers were reprimanded for changing toilet paper rolls too soon is from the authors' interview with Michael Duffy, president, Service Employees International Union, Local 362, Orlando, Florida.

Abraham Briloff's comment about Disney's accounting practices and profitability are taken from his articles in *Barron's*, published in the March 23, 1998, and May 11, 1998, issues.

Quote from Benjamin Barber is from Benjamin Barber, "From Disney World To Disney's World," *New York Times*, August 1, 1995.

INDEX